HANDEL'S MESSIAH

A RHETORICAL GUIDE

Judy Tarling

Punnett Press

2024

Punnett Press
3 North Street, Punnett's Town, Heathfield, East Sussex TN21 9DT, UK

© Judy Tarling 2024

All rights reserved

ISBN: 978 0 9932810 5 1

'MUSICK *is the principal* Entertainment *of* God,
and the Souls *of the* Blessed *hereafter.*'

William Tans'ur, Preface to *A New Musical Grammar and Dictionary* (1756)

Author's Preface

It is now ten years since the publication of *The Weapons of Rhetoric: a Guide for Musicians and Audiences* and the interest in exploring the connection between speaking and playing music in the rhetorical style has been growing in communities of historically-informed musicians all over the world. However, *Weapons* used musical examples from a wide range of repertoire that is likely to be unfamiliar to most non-specialist performers. Having established the rhetorical ground-rules for the use of the classical sources in performing a range of seventeenth- and eighteenth-century music, it now seems appropriate to apply these to a work familiar to every player or singer, revealing the way eighteenth-century music, composed using the rhetorical style, 'speaks' most effectively to an audience by using rhetorical techniques. By applying these to a well-known work it is hoped that these devices will be more easily recognised and used in performance.

This book is the first of a projected series of rhetorical guides which will include other well-known works by Handel, Bach and Purcell.

Judy Tarling
Punnetts Town, 2014

The Introduction

or 'The Mysterie of Rhetorique Unvail'd'

In his hand-book on *Messiah* Watkins Shaw implies that rhetoric is something negative, technical and dreary (1946, p. 23). He states that Handel's *Messiah* 'shows him at his best, not as a mere rhetorician'. By using the word 'mere' he passes censure on the idea of employing rhetorical techniques for musical composition, discounting them to suggest a level of competency only. This book hopes to show the opposite view, that Handel's rhetorical skills were used to raise the art of composition which combined words and music to a new height of expressiveness, judged to be 'sublime' by his contemporaries and continuously adored by audiences since the eighteenth century.

The aims of Classical rhetoric were to inform, move, and entertain or delight: *Messiah* fulfills these aims in various ways, proving its power to persuade through performances to millions of listeners since 1742, when it was first performed. In order to persuade us, *Messiah* uses the three types of Classical rhetoric: the deliberative mode is used for debate about what is to happen in the future, confirming the promise of the resurrection of the dead; the forensic, judicial type scrutinises evidence about past events such as Christ's betrayal and passion; the epideictic, used in rhetoric to praise or blame is here used for praise, of God, and of Christ, and to celebrate the company of believers. It is also used for commemoration. All these modes of speaking to persuade, borrowed from the Bible, are combined to form the thrust of *Messiah's* message.

How are we persuaded? What draws us in, captures our emotions and convinces and satisfies us in a performance? The answer lies in what makes a rhetorical performance, as opposed to merely a good one. In his *Mysterie of Rhetorique Unvail'd*, John Smith contends that the aim of rhetoric is 'to win belief in the hearer [...] The end of the discourse is, to wit, the affecting of the heart with the sense of the matter in hand' (1657, p.1). But how is this 'belief' and 'affect' to be brought about, as if for the first time, in a performance of a work so well known and so well loved as Handel's *Messiah*? Enough rhetorical questions. The answer lies in applying knowledge of the art of rhetoric itself.

In a poem published in Faulkner's *Dublin Journal*, 20 April 1742, Laurence Whyte describes his impressions of the first performance of *Messiah*, acknowledging the role of repetition, and describing the 'speaking' quality of the music:

> When various strains repeated and improv'd
> Express each different Circumstance and State
> As if each Sound became articulate (Deutsch, p. 547).

Eighteenth-century musical composition was based on the principles of rhetoric, assimilated into the composition process since the techniques of music and rhetoric were combined in the early sixteenth century. The resultant style was used either consciously or instinctively by all eighteenth-century composers. These were the same principles of rhetoric used in the compilation of the King James Bible (1611), which became the Authorised Version, written to be read aloud as if in a performance, to teach, and to reinforce belief in the Christian message. The early seventeenth-century literary style, recently refreshed by Shakespeare's use of language and invention of vocabulary, uses sounds and patterns of words which make it memorable, enjoyable and loved by audiences and readers of subsequent eras. Familiarity with some of these rhetorical forms and ideas will surely bring any performance to a new understanding of the musical language. Henry Peacham the elder (a contemporary of William Shakespeare) writes that 'to affect eloquence without the discretion of wisdom, is, as to handle a sweete instrument of musicke without skill' ('The Epistle Dedicatorie'). When approached through the application of rhetorical ideas, Handel's *Messiah* will reveal hidden delights to today's performers, enabling them to engage with their audiences afresh. We can become even more closely acquainted with this work which we thought we knew, but in a new way.

As rhetoric is only the rules of effective human communication analysed and written down, many accomplished performers will already be walking instinctively along the rhetorical road. Quintilian, the Classical rhetorician and our chief source for rhetorical ideas, considers that the ideal orator (i.e. performer) is a blend of natural talent and education (Quintilian, II xix). Having a more comprehensive and detailed knowledge of rhetorical ideas will give the already experienced musician skills to intensify their performance by using the rhetorical material that is embedded in the text and music, but has not previously been recognised as such. If a rhetorical point is passed over the performance is weakened and the whole purpose of 'the matter in hand' is undermined. It is likely that many of the audience will be unconscious of this lack of skill, because they will be replaying the familiar music in their heads, but if our task is to make each performance live as if for the first time of hearing, the 'new born offspring of the imagination' as Quintilian puts it, we need to replace the pre-digested sound in the heads of our listeners with something more immediate and convincing, which will astonish them with its freshness and vitality (Quintilian, X i 16).

The rhetorical concept of *enargeia*, derived from the Greek word *argos*, bright or shining, can be defined as making something more vivid. Contemporary reports of the first performance called *Messiah* 'sublime', and this heightening of emotional response is the aim of *enargeia*. Quintilian describes the process of bringing a topic to life: 'It consists firstly in forming a clear conception of what we wish to say, secondly in giving this adequate expression , and thirdly in lending additional brilliance, a process which may correctly be termed embellishment'. He calls this brilliant expression 'vivid illustration [...] more than mere clearness, since the latter merely lets itself be seen, whereas the former thrusts itself upon our notice'. It should not simply be narration but should be displayed 'to the eyes of the mind' (Quintilian, VIII iii 61-62). In other words, following instructions to the letter will not achieve the required affect, nor will it move the listeners. Delivering the rhetorical ideas using the techniques for which they were designed will help to project both the sense and the emotional affect without the necessity for gimmickry or exaggeration.

The three parts of this book follow the rhetorical agenda from the invention of an idea, through the composition process in Part One, followed in Part Two by a more detailed guide to delivery, and rounded off in Part Three with the audience's reception in the context of the sublime.

The sublime was a concept which would have been familiar to the Classically-educated eighteenth-century audience. The idea of the sublime and how it works in practice using the rhetorical figures described in Part One will be explored in Part Three using a well-known Greek literary text by Longinus in a translation from the eighteenth century.

Many passages in *Messiah* use figures of repetition or comparison, brought to life by harmony and dialogue, with solo voices interacting with the strings, at the same time painting the text in sound, and using other effects which employ silence or the rise and fall of the voices. It is the combination of some or all of these things which contribute to the sublime style so admired and sought after in the eighteenth century, and which has had such a profound affect on listeners, then and now. Handel's music reveals the masterly way that he combines all these rhetorical elements, which pile up, overlap and are difficult to separate into simple categories. For this reason, many of the musical examples will be used to illustrate more than one topic. Until the details of these rhetorical layers are recognised and are under the control and understanding of the performer, Handel's *Messiah* will remain, as the title of John Smith's book (1657) suggests, 'A Mysterie of Rhetorique' still veiled.

In Part One the story of the invention of *Messiah* is followed by a view of the complete text and its structure. Before going any further into Handel's contribution, the text is examined to show how rhetorical figures work in practice with some musical parallels. When the principles of how figures work are understood, it will become clearer how these can be applied to musical composition. Exclamations and questions receive their own treatment following the general section on figures of rhetoric. The art of setting a text to music involves representing the text in sound, and apart from the emotional affect needed to support the words, word-painting can be used to conjure up images of darkness, sheep or glory.

Part Two of the book opens by showing the approach to performance using the rhetorical principle of decorum, 'speaking appropriately'. The appropriate voice and tone for each number will be discovered here by recognising the affect, and the musical devices such as key, rhythm and intervals that Handel employed to express the text in music. After that, other factors such as dynamics, tempo, rhythm and silence will be seen in a rhetorical light. The choruses have a section to themselves which is led by an examination of the contrast between homophonic and polyphonic effects.

By the time the reader has arrived at the end of Part Two, way in which *Messiah's* power operates through the medium of rhetoric will have become clear. The contemporary descriptions by the listeners who described the work as sublime will sum up the reception of this great work in Part Three.

A Note on the Musical Examples

The musical examples in this book have been derived from a number of sources. There is no single definitive source for *Messiah*. Handel revised and added material as and when it was demanded by performing circumstances ('How beautiful are the Feet' has five versions with and without chorus). Many of these small alterations can be seen in the score copied by Handel's assistant J.C. Smith senior which was used in early performances, referred to misleadingly as 'the conducting score'. Handel would not have conducted, but rather directed performances from the keyboard. The examples presented here do not represent any final textual authority, but serve as convenient quotations which enable the reader to realise and apply the points made in the accompanying text. Punctuation and capitalisation of the text when quoted follows the 1743 word-book prepared for the first London performance (which can be found in Burrows, 1991 Appendix 1). This means that punctuation and some slurs have been added to the musical extracts which are not present in the manuscripts.

Slurs in the instrumental parts have been added following the slurs which are sometimes marked by Handel at the opening of a number, but not subsequently. Elsewhere, the author's suggested slurs are marked as dotted. Vocal slurring follows the beamed groups on syllables (without marked slurs), or a marked slur when the rhythm requires no beam. Notes on the bass stave marked 'org' double other vocal or instrumental parts at the same pitch following the convention of the time (e.g. Ex. 2.2.17 and 1.3.17).

A sans serif font has been used for text describing performance suggestions and descriptions that accompany the musical examples.

Rhetoric – the Sources

References to the Classical rhetoric texts are identified as follows:

- Q – Marcus Fabius Quintilian, *Institutio Oratoria*
- C – Marcus Tullius Cicero (followed by the title of the work)

The Introduction

- RH – The *Rhetorica ad Herennium*, a book much used in the classroom and thought (erroneously) by many to be by Cicero. It was often found bound with Cicero's *De Inventione*, and so both were referred to as 'Tully'.

Translations of the Classical sources are from the Loeb Classical Library Series (Harvard University Press) except for Longinus where William Smith's translation (Dublin, 1740) is used.

The rhetoric books by Henry Peacham (1593), George Puttenham (1589) and John Smith (1657) all contain indexes where the names of the figures can easily be found and references to these omit page numbers.

Editions and Previous Publications

Handel's autograph, available in facsimile edition (British Library RM 20.f.2, published 2009), has been consulted, as well as the score known as Handel's conducting score made by J.C. Smith senior (facsimile edition Scolar Press, Royal Musical Association, 1974) and the performing material bequeathed to the Foundling Hospital, now The Thomas Coram Foundation, copied in 1759.

Messiah was composed in three weeks during August and September of 1741, and in spite of the haste with which Handel must have been writing, using many short cut signs and omitting much detail in repeated passages, the manuscript is surprisingly clear and fluent. Some interesting changes made by Handel will be found in the text, reproduced here from the autograph manuscript in 1.7, as 'Second Thoughts'.

Samuel Arnold's printed edition, volume three of a complete Works of Handel (1787-97), would have been familiar to late eighteenth- and early nineteenth-century performers, and the examples in this book borrow his bass figuring which gives considerably more detail than Handel used in the autograph. Figures above or below the bass notes describe the intervals which rise from it and which combine to make a chord. A figured bass can often show the reader the musical point at a glance rather than forcing him to work out the harmony for himself. Dissonances are easy to spot if the figures 2, 7 or 9 are present. Cadenza points in arias occur over a 6-4 chord which moves to 5-3 before resolving onto the tonic. Arnold's edition contains a number of inaccuracies, particularly with regard to rhythm. He adds punctuation such as exclamation marks and yet omits many commas which are found in the word-book text (although not included by Handel in the speedily-written autograph, or found in the part books). There are also small differences in the text underlay and even the words themselves such as 'And lo' or 'But lo' in the arioso version; 'Who is this King of Glory?' or 'Who is the King of Glory?'; 'If God be for us' or 'If God is for us'.

There are many small differences between Handel's manuscript, the conducting score prepared by Smith, the 1743 word-book, and subsequent word-books printed for provincial performances. Words and word order are often confused and inconsistent. Both 'Burden' and 'Burthen' appear in the same source, and another favourite copier's mistake was 'and with his stripes are we healed' alternating with 'and with his stripes we are healed'.

The publisher John Walsh produced the first printed material from *Messiah*, which probably appeared in 1749 as part of a series presenting selections from Handel's oratorios. 'Songs in Messiah', published in parallel versions for voice, harpsichord and oboe or flute, or voice with instrumental parts, contains only the solos (recitatives and arias) and the overture but not the choruses. The first complete edition of *Messiah* was published by Randall and Abel in 1767 using material from Walsh's publications (Fuld, 1974, 1988). Subsequent printed editions appeared after Arnold's by Chrysander (complete works 1858-67), recently revised by Nicholas McGegan, Eleanor Selfridge-Field and John Roberts (2003); Prout (1904); Novello, edition and vocal score by Watkins

Shaw (1965) and more recently editions by John Tobin for Bärenreiter (1981), and Donald Burrows for Peters (1987). Clifford Bartlett's edition for OUP (1998) brings together in one place all the sources and the various versions of numbers Handel made in over fifteen years of revisions. Donald Burrows's excellent book *Handel: Messiah* in the Cambridge handbook series (1991) covers the circumstances of the first performances in Dublin and London, the context for the various versions of some arias, Handel's relationship with his librettist Charles Jennens, and the performance history. These topics will not be extensively re-visited in this book. Richard Luckett's book *Handel's Messiah. A Celebration* (1992) also gives much information about the performance history of *Messiah* from its first performance until modern times, as well as a short summary of the main variants. The various versions and the textual differences between the sources have been forensically examined by Watkins Shaw in *A Textual Companion to Handel's Messiah* (Novello, 1965) which also contains details of the solo singers who took part in the early performances.

The religious controversies of the day which might have inspired *Messiah's* creation will be briefly explored. A tribute on this topic should be paid to Ruth Smith's authoritative and ground-breaking book *Handel's Oratorios and Eighteenth-Century Thought* which has exposed the social, religious and political background to Handel's compositions through his oratorio texts, and has been an inspiration when researching the creation of *Messiah*.

Acknowledgements

Peter Lay laboured long and hard over Christmas and New Year 2013-14 setting the musical examples. He has created the book and dealt patiently with the author's sadly limited technological capabilities.

The illustrations are all from a family Bible printed in Amsterdam in 1728 and reproduced in facsimile by J.N. Voorhoeve (1978).

The reproductions from Handel's autograph MS are by kind permission of the British Library and those from the conducting score by kind permission of the Bodleian Library.

My colleagues, the readers, without doubt made this a better book, but I absolve them of any infelicities which remain: Annette Isserlis brought her extensive experience of the work to bear on certain points of performance. Peter Holman made many valuable suggestions which added an extra historical and musicological dimension to the text. Selene Mills, who sadly died the week after this book was published, did some wonderful work on the punctuation as well as pointing out details from a singer's perspective which the author (never having sung in *Messiah*) had overlooked. As a classical scholar and musician Selene was a keen advocate of rhetoric and its application to musical performance. Her encouragement and enthusiasm will be greatly missed.

I would like to thank Colin Coleman at the Thomas Coram Foundation who assisted in making the Foundling Hospital performing material available to view. I am also grateful to Simon Rees for drawing my attention to *Quarles' Emblems, Divine and Moral*, trumpeter Crispian Steele-Perkins for his comments about 'The Trumpet shall sound', and Brian Robins for providing the Largo references from John Marsh's journal.

Contents

Author's Preface v
The Introduction vii
    A Note on the Musical Examples ix
    Rhetoric – the Sources ix
    Editions and Previous Publications x
    Acknowledgements xi

PART ONE – INVENTION 1

1.1 The Invention of Handel's *Messiah* 1
    Jennens' Text Craft 2
    The Word-Book 3
    Performances of *Messiah* until Handel's Death 7

1.2 Structure and Performance 8
    Structural Silences 9
    The Text Part One 9
    The Text Part Two 12
    The Text Part Three 14
    Length 15

1.3 Figures of Rhetoric 17
    The Rhetoric Books 18
    Copia – How Many Ways? 19
    Comparison 26
    Catalogue of Figures 28

1.4 Exclamations and Questions 52
    Exclamations 52
    Questions 54

1.5 Word Painting 58
    Earth and Heaven 59
    Crowds 63
    The Pastoral 65
    Fire 69
    Darkness and Light 69
    Concord and Discord 71
    Soothing 71
    Anger 72

1.6 Decorum – Choice of Means 76
    Size and Decorum 79

1.7 Second Thoughts 82
    'Hallelujah' 82
    'And with His Stripes' – 'All we, like Sheep' 83
    'Why do the Nations' 84
    'If God be for us' 84
    'Ev'ry Valley' 85

PART TWO – DELIVERY 87

2.1 Decorum – Tone of Voice 87
- Tones of Voice 88
- The 'Speaking' Style 92

2.2 Emphasis 99
- The *Epizeuxis* 100
- Tessitura 100
- Length of Note 103
- Articulation Marks 103
- Slurs 107
- Variety 108
- Length of Phrase 110
- Harmony, Intervals 110

2.3 Dynamics 115
- Decorum 115
- Tessitura 115
- Choruses 119
- Harmony 120
- Affect 121
- Repeat piano? 123

2.4 Tempo 125
- Numbers and Words 126
- Adagio 126
- Andante 129
- Largo 129
- Tempo Relationships 131
- Pauses 135
- Recitative 136

2.5 Rhythm 139
- Affect of the Length of Notes 139
- Variety of Phrase Length 139
- Dotted Notes 140
- Syncopations 147
- Repeated Semiquavers 150
- Mixed Rhythms 151
- *Iamb* and *Trochee* 151
- *Anapaest* 153
- *Dactyl* 159

2.6 Silence 162
- *Aposiopesis* 162
- 'Sospiro' in Pathetic Affects 165
- Rhythmic Silence – the 'Loud Rest' 169
- Silences of Articulation 171

2.7 The Choruses 174

PART THREE – THE AUDIENCE 197
    The Audience 197
    The Sublime 200
A Peroration 205
Bibliography 207
    Messiah Editions and Performance Materials: 210
    Internet Sources 210
Index to Movements 211
General Index 213

PART ONE – INVENTION

1.1 The Invention of Handel's *Messiah* or *'A Scripture Collection'*

In Classical rhetoric, invention (*inventio*) begins the process of creation, so it is appropriate to discover how Handel's *Messiah* came about. Invention is not so much about waiting for inspiration as about how to treat an idea once it has presented itself, how to get the most out of it by exploring every possible avenue of expression, by looking at it from every point of view. Invention involves searching for the means by which to persuade the audience of the worthiness of your cause. The ideas to be transformed by Handel into a musical work had already been invented: the Bible is a text saturated with ideas in a rhetorical form, which has been drawn on by composers for centuries. Some of the music had been composed by Handel shortly before he started work on *Messiah*. During the summer of that year, he had written a set of Italian cantatas for two voices which were re-used in several numbers of *Messiah*.

On 10 July 1741 Handel's friend Charles Jennens wrote 'I hope I shall persuade him [Handel] to set another Scripture Collection I have made for him, & perform it for his own Benefit in Passion week' (R. Smith, 2012, p. 61). Handel and Jennens were life-long friends, close enough for Jennens to be able to suggest amendments to Handel's work and later criticise him for being too hasty with the composition of *Messiah*. Jennens had compiled the text from the Old and New Testaments, using many scriptural extracts which would have been familiar to Anglican worshippers through their daily use in the Book of Common Prayer. He chose extracts from the psalms and prophets, passages from the letters of the early Christians, and narrative passages from the Old Testament and the gospels. His choices would have been driven by two strongly-held beliefs: his position as a non-juror, refusing to swear loyalty to the king through his allegiance to the deposed Stuart dynasty, and his Protestant religious conviction as an anti-Deist. Deists held a belief in God based on religious truths discovered through a process of reasoning independent of any revelation in the form of miracles or prophecy, which they regarded with scepticism. The movement emerged during the seventeenth-century scientific revolution and came to prominence with The Age of Enlightenment. The choice of texts for *Messiah* could be seen as the fulfilment of the seventh Article of Religion, found in the Book of Common Prayer, which connects the Old and New Testaments through prophecy, and promises everlasting life through the mediation of Christ.

Jennens' choice of words is a tapestry of phrases taken from different sources, sometimes put together in the same aria, and only in a few cases is it a complete sequence of consecutive verses. This practice had precedent in the English verse-anthems of the previous century in which a selection of biblical texts was assembled to satisfy a particular agenda or purpose. It was often employed for special event anthems such as those written for coronations and funerals. A good example is Thomas Tomkins's 'Know you not' composed for the funeral of Prince Henry (1612), which uses passages drawn from II Samuel, Ezekiel, Lamentations, Psalms, Zechariah and Jeremiah all packed into a church anthem of modest length. The phrases are cherry-picked to convey lamentation and praise, mourning and glorification, adding for good measure the (non-biblical) loss for Great Britain of its greatest hope.

Jennens' Text Craft

Curiously, supporting the concept of the oblique which characterises *Messiah*, there are no representations of characters as are found in Handel's Old Testament oratorios, and no direct speech, only the reported speech of God and an angel. Christ's name is hardly mentioned until the resurrection in Part Three, but 'He' is referred to by the frequent replacement of the original biblical first person with the third, and the use of metaphorical imagery such as 'the Lamb of God'. This approach allows the listener space for private thoughts about the matter. As the work progresses and the allusion becomes clearer, listeners may feel pleased with themselves, as if a riddle has been solved, or they have found the answer to an obscure puzzle which chimes with their own way of thinking. Henry Peacham (1593) describes an *aenigma* as a figure from which 'the sense may hardly be gathered'. Although he says it is 'full of obscuritie, and darknesse, yet it is found in the sacred scriptures both in speech and in visions'. *Messiah* could be experienced as an *aenigma* on two levels: that of scripture itself with its parables and prophecies, and Jennens' particular selection of texts which have their own enigmatic agenda. The audience are left to draw their own conclusions from the story thus told.

In Jennens' choice of text for 'your Oratorio Messiah', as Handel referred to it in a letter to Jennens (29 December, 1741, reproduced in R. Smith, 2012, p. 23), the nativity story from Luke 2 is told nearly unchanged, from the angel bringing the news to the shepherds until the chorus 'Glory to God'. Luke's verse twelve, the laying in the manger, is the only verse omitted. The other unbroken sequence comes in Part Three, starting with 'For now is Christ risen', the final thought in the aria 'I know that my Redeemer liveth'. This sequence from I Corinthians 15. 20 continues through the mystery and the last trumpet until the end of 'But thanks be to God who giveth Us the Victory through our Lord Jesus Christ'.

Jennens crafts the Bible text to suit his purpose, sometimes changing or omitting words for a better flow, sound or rhythm, sometimes rearranging the words or the sequence of the texts. The text was described by a contemporary as 'the sacred Words as properly adapted for the occasion' (Burrows, 1991, p. 18). Another adaptation, as Ruth Smith has shown in her analysis of other oratorio texts, is to mould the text to the dramatic situation by altering the person or tense and omitting linking words and phrases (1995, p. 95). The original biblical 'For I know that my Redeemer liveth' (Job 19. 25) would be less assertive than the more direct 'I know that my Redeemer liveth'. Opening Part Three as it does, the connecting word 'For' would naturally seem to be dispensable, but this form of the text would have been familiar to users of the Book of Common Prayer where it opens the Order for The Burial of the Dead, being spoken (or sung) by 'The Priest and Clerks meeting the Corpse at the entrance of the Church-yard, and going before it, either into the Church, or towards the Grave'.

Connecting, but seemingly unimportant, words such as 'for', 'since' or simply 'and' can change the whole feeling of a statement and its affect. Handel's musical setting of 'For unto us' is derived from one of the recently-composed Italian duets and is commonly derided as incompetent, as it stresses what today is perceived to be an unimportant word, but it makes sense rhetorically. These pivot words which herald the other side of the argument, far from being superfluous, are important sign-posts for new ideas, action or other matter to be introduced. The biblical word 'for' *is* omitted by Jennens, however, between 'the twinkling of an Eye, the last Trumpet' and the opening text of the aria 'The Trumpet shall sound', making a more direct and commanding opening phrase.

Other changes to the text made by Jennens occur in 'I know that my Redeemer liveth', where the diversionary, and for his purposes irrelevant, words 'after my skin' are omitted between 'and though' and 'Worms destroy this Body'. The original text (also found in the Burial of the Dead) is 'And though after my Skin Worms destroy this Body, yet in my Flesh shall I see God' (Job 19. 26).

The double interrogative 'Why do the Nations so furiously rage together? Why do the People imagine a vain Thing?' was originally the shorter and less punchy 'Why do the Heathen rage and the People imagine a vain Thing?' 'The Company of the Preachers' was 'The Company of those that published it', a bit more of a mouthful than the rhythmic 'Preachers', which, as well as possibly being a faithful alternative reading of the word, also represents the Anglican choral presence more strongly in a chorus of believers.

Three sequences have the first person pronoun changed to the third, making the text more decorous for the context and assisting the allusion to Christ. Originally 'He gave His Back to the Smiters' was 'I gave my Back to the Smiters'. 'Come unto Him' was originally 'Come unto me ... and I will give you Rest'. 'Take my Yoke' and 'My Yoke is easy' become 'Take His Yoke' and 'His Yoke is easy'. The same process happens at 'Thy Rebuke hath broken His Heart', a powerful accusation which was originally the more intimate and pathetic 'Reproach hath broken my Heart; I am full of Heaviness'. 'All they that see me laugh me to Scorn' becomes 'All they that see Him laugh Him to Scorn'. This device, using the third person instead of the singular personal pronoun, turns a personal account from the Old Testament into a narrative which can be applied directly to Christ's experience in the imagination of the performers and audience, and by doing so, makes it more vivid.

Jennens certainly knew how to edit the text for decorous effect. Would we feel so exhilarated with the comparison of 'He is like fullers' soap', a less poetic agent of change following 'He is like a Refiner's Fire' but perhaps sensibly omitted? 'And He shall purify' omits yet another comparison: 'and purge them as gold and silver' starting at 'that they may offer unto the Lord an Offering in Righteousness'. Jennens also chooses to start the chorus directly with 'Worthy is the Lamb', although it was preceded by the words 'saying with a loud voice' which could easily have been incorporated into the end of the previous number (as in the 'and saying' which precedes 'Glory to God'). This clue, from Revelation 5. 12, and spoken by 'ten thousand times ten thousand' might have prompted Handel to choose such a grand opening, but he decides to avoid the oratorical cliché, giving us 'Worthy is the Lamb' directly, without introduction, following Jennens' text.

The Word-Book

Eighteenth-century audiences could buy a libretto or word-book of the oratorio or opera to be performed, which was sometimes on sale in advance. It was recommended that 'if People, before they went to hear it, would but retire a Moment, and read by themselves, the Words of the Sacred Drama, it would tend very much to raise their Delight when at the Representation' (letter to *The London Daily Post*, 18 April 1739, quoted in Deutsch, p. 481). Provoking and 'raising delight' is one of the three principles on which a rhetorical experience depends, and is sought by the listener. It was quite usual for members of the audience to attend rehearsals if they were privileged to know one of the performers or had other strings to pull and sometimes a ticket included admission to the rehearsals. This provided an additional opportunity to become familiar with a new work, and enjoy it all the more.

The Title Page

The title page of Jennens' word book for '*Messiah, an oratorio Set to Musick by Mr. Handel*' was adorned with two quotations:

MAJORA CANAMUS

The first, a Latin motto 'majora canamus' ('let us sing of greater things', or 'let us take a loftier tone'), is a quotation from the opening of Virgil's fourth *Eclogue*, known as 'the Messianic'. Derived from the prophecy of a Cumaean Sibyl, the poem describes the coming of a child who will usher in a golden age of peace. Contemporaries of Virgil thought it probably referred to the son of his friend Pollio, but, from the time of

1.1 The Invention of Handel's Messiah

Constantine the first Christian Roman emperor, it was believed with increasing persistence that the child was Christ, and that Virgil had somehow prophesied the virgin birth. In the Middle Ages, Virgil was looked upon as having been an unconscious prophet of Christianity whose natural virtue gave him power among the dead. St. Augustine saw a prophecy of Christ in Virgil's poem, as did Bishop Donatus of Fiesole in the ninth century (Bourne, 1916). The most famous poetic recreation of Virgil was by Dante in *The Divine Comedy* (first circulated in manuscript approximately 1314). Although Virgil was barred from heavenly paradise by being pre-Christian, he guides Dante through hell and purgatory, where they meet the Latin poet Statius (*Purgatorio*, Canto 21). When questioned about his Christian belief not confessed in his poems, Statius attributes his Christian conversion to Virgil's messianic poem.

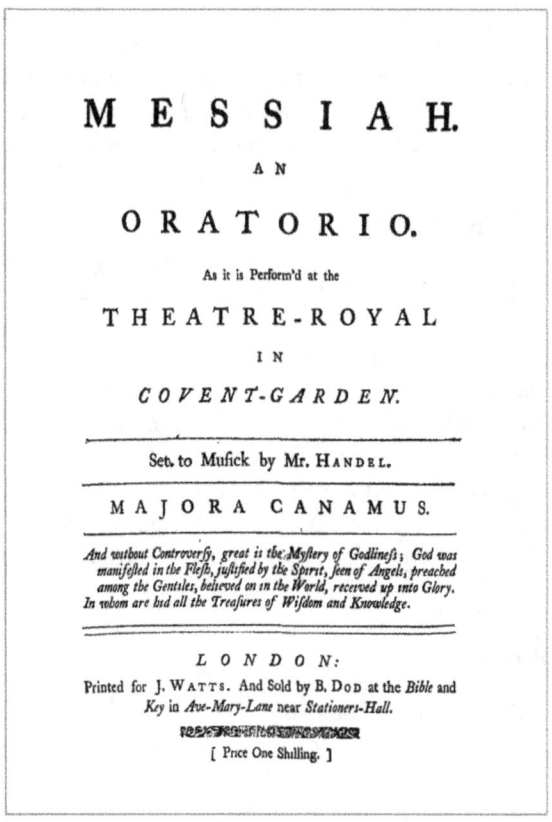

Title page of the Word-Book for the first London performance

In later centuries, this Latin motto was used by other authors to invoke heightened religious sensibilities through music. In Charles Quarles' *Emblems, Divine and Moral* (1630), the first illustration is of a figure crushing a pile of earthly treasures and exclaiming 'Majora Canamus' while gesturing towards heaven. A theorbo lies next to the figure. The Invocation opens with:

> Rouse thee, my soul, and drain thee from the dregs
> Of vulgar thoughts: screw up the heighten'd pegs
> Of thy sublime theorbo four notes higher,
> And higher yet, that so the shrill-mouth'd choir
> Of swift-wing'd seraphims may come and join,
> And make thy concert more than half divine.

The encouragement to tune 'thy sublime theorbo four notes higher' may be a reference to the *théorbe de pièces* (known in England as the lesser French theorbo) which was tuned a fourth higher than the instrument used for accompaniment (Diderot and d'Alembert 'Art du faiseur d'instrument de musique et lutherie' in *l'Encyclopédie métodique*, various editions

1782-1832 and Michael Prynne, 'James Talbot's Manuscript, IV Plucked Strings – The Lute Family, *Galpin Society Journal* 14, 1961).

René Rapin, a seventeenth-century poet, and Alexander Pope (early eighteenth) both re-invent and imitate Virgil's work. Pope's poem is called *Messiah. A sacred eclogue in imitation of Virgil's Pollio*. It is thrilling to read prophet's words so familiar to us in Pope's paraphrase (1709), published in 1712 in *The Spectator*:

> 'A Virgin shall conceive, a Virgin bear a Son!'
>
> 'Prepare the way! A God, a God appears'
>
> 'Sink down ye mountains, and ye valleys rise'
>
> 'The dumb shall sing, the lame his crutch forego
> And leap exulting like the bounding roe'.

Pope's poem ends: 'Thy realm for ever lasts, thy own MESSIAH reigns!' Pope, the epitome of all Classical scholars and a Catholic non-juror, has managed to combine Christian and 'pagan' thoughts convincingly. Thirty years later, the Protestant non-juror Jennens gathers up the same ideas to form the text for *Messiah*.

The two scriptural texts which follow MAJORA CANAMUS on the title page are taken from I Timothy 3. 16 and Colossians 2. 3. The few words which differ from the King James version are bracketed:

> And without Controversy, great is the Mystery of Godliness: God was manifested [manifest] in the Flesh, justify'd by [in] the Spirit, seen of Angels, preached among [unto] the Gentiles, believed on in the World, received up into Glory.
>
> In whom are hid all the Treasures of Wisdom and Knowledge.

This carefully chosen text is in fact a religious manifesto for *Messiah*. This and the whole of the 'scripture collection' for the work were chosen to argue the case for the truth and mystery of the Christian religion against the social backdrop of a sceptical faction in the eighteenth-century audience. The *Messiah* text could be read as a defence of established Anglican belief against the 'Controversy' provoked by the doubters of the 'Mystery of Godliness' known as Deists.

The Deists

The Deists were a disparate group of philosophically-minded intellectuals led by Enlightenment scepticism about the truth of miracles and prophecies. They sought to discredit the literal truth of the Bible, especially the Old Testament, and propagated the belief that the natural world itself was sufficient to reveal the existence and the will of God. This belief was encouraged by the new discoveries in science such as Sir Isaac Newton's study of optics and theory of magnetism.

Deism was accepted into the mainstream of Church of England thought by the publication of Bishop Butler's *Analogy of Natural and Revealed Religion* (1736), and supported by writers such as the Third Earl of Shaftesbury. There was also political pressure in the 1730s for its reconciliation with Anglican orthodoxy, and Caroline of Ansbach (who became Queen in 1727) was highly interested in Deism. Deism was refuted by David Hume in his *Dialogues Concerning Natural Religion*, written 1761-1771 but only published in 1779 after his death (Charlesworth, pp. 14-15).

Jennens studied at Oxford where his contemporary the young Duke of Beaufort had a drunken tutor who was condemned for 'so much Atheism, Deism, Debauchery and all kinds of immorality' (Midgley, p. 2).

One of the 'mysteries' which was challenged by the Deists was the Trinity. In the preface to a poem entitled *The Christian warrior properly armed: or the deist unmask'd. Being a faithful defence of the Holy Trinity. For the use of all Christian families* (1776) by William Tans'ur, the poem is addressed 'to GOD, and his READERS'. Tans'ur was a church musician known

1.1 The Invention of Handel's Messiah

as a psalmody composer and author of several musical tracts quoted elsewhere in this book.

> Of Christian *parents I was born*,
> Deistic Tenets *both did scorn*
> To CHURCH *of* England *well ally'd*,
> *And so continu'd till they dy'd.*

Later in the poem:

> To no vile *Deist* do thou yield,
> But still hold fast thy aiding *Shield*,
> By no means from thy *Colours* fly,
> Since CHRIST Himself is always nigh.

Several other references are made to 'vile Deists', and in other places in the poem the beliefs and traditions of the Church of England and scripture are defended.

Jennens' library was known to house a copy of the second edition of a religious tract by Richard Kidder, originally published in 1684. *A Demonstration of the Messias. In which the truth of the Christian religion is proved, especially against the Jews* contained the complete argument for the truth of Anglican belief. Many passages quote texts used by Jennens in *Messiah*, arguing the case for the outcome of the prophecies of the Old Testament, such as:

> To whom else can those words belong but to the *Messias*, and in whom were they ever fulfilled, but in our *Jesus* onely, where it is said: *He is despised and rejected of men, a man of sorrows and acquainted with griefs.*

> We have a remarkable Prophecy in the Prophet Zechariah, and the words are these: *Rejoice greatly O daughter of Zion; shout O daughter of Jerusalem: Behold thy King cometh unto thee.*

> The Psalmist predicted of the Messias in these words. All they that see me laugh me to scorn, they shoot out the lip, they shake the head, saying: *He trusted on the Lord that he would deliver him: let him deliver him, seeing that he delighted in him.*

Kidder sums up the argument 'In a word, the things foretold of the *Messias*, and fulfilled in *Jesus* were so *many*, and so *strangely fulfilled*, so much without any humane assistance, and so *contrary* to all *expectation*, and all the endeavours used to hinder the foretold event that he who considers these things with care must believe that *Jesus* is the *Christ* and that his religion is true' (p. 393). His last word is 'that our *Jesus* is that very *Christ* who was promised from the beginning, and was the hope and expectation of the faithfull in the Old Testament' (p. 479).

Jennens' text presents an oblique but convincing argument in support of Kidder, summed up and made explicit on his word-book title page, which justifies his choice of text for *Messiah*, which was:

- Part One: to tell of the prophetic visions of Christ's birth 'manifested in the flesh'. The shepherds are shown the birth.

- Part Two: to tell the mystery of his life and death 'believed on in the World'. It describes the passion, resurrection and ascension through prophecy. This is followed by depictions of the spread of the Gospel and the Kingdom of Christ.

- Part Three: to tell of his resurrection and ascension to be 'received up into Glory'. Immortality and the world to come.

Jennens follows the convention of writing an oratorio in three parts, but the extensive Part Two turns from the passion and ascension (the section ending 'Thou art gone up on high') into an examination of the spread of the gospel at the text 'The Lord gave the Word', and culminating in the 'Hallelujah' Chorus. Part Three is set in the afterlife promised to believers.

Performances of *Messiah* until Handel's Death

1741	22 August – 14 September	Handel composes *Messiah*
	18 November	Handel arrives in Dublin
1742	9 April	Public rehearsal in Dublin
	13 April	First performance
	1 June	Public rehearsal
	3 June	Second performance
1743	23 March	First London performance at Covent Garden
	25, 29 March	Repeat performances
1744	16 February	Performance in London by the Academy of Ancient Musick
1745	9, 11 April	Performances at the King's Theatre, London
1749	23 March	Performance at Covent Garden
	14 April	Performance at Oxford directed by Hayes
1750	12 April	Performance at Covent Garden
	1, 15 May	Performances at the Foundling Hospital
1751	18 April	Performance at the Foundling Hospital
1752	25, 26 March	Performances at Covent Garden
	9 April	Performance at the Foundling Hospital
1753-8		Every year performances at Covent Garden and the Foundling Hospital under the direction of Handel
1759	6 April	Last performance directed by Handel at Covent Garden
	14 April	Death of Handel

(derived from Watkins Shaw, *A Textual Companion*, p. 20 and Luckett, p. 161)

1.2 Structure and Performance

or 'Joining the Limbs'

Once the subject matter has been invented by the orator or composer (*inventio*) and he has decided what to say, the next stage in creating a rhetorical composition is the arrangement of the material (*dispositio*).

> Invention is the devising of matter, true or plausible, that would make the case convincing. Arrangement is the ordering and distribution of the matter, making clear the place to which each thing is to be assigned (RH, I ii 3).

> It is the embellishment of the argument once it has been discovered, and the arrangement of it in definite divisions, which makes the speech attractive to the audience (C, *De Inventione*, I xxx 50).

> For the fact that all the limbs of a statue have been cast does not make it a statue: they must be put together (Q, VII pref. 2).

> Artistic structure gives force and direction to our thoughts just as the throwing thong and the bowstring do to the spear and arrow (Q, IX iv 9).

> Artistic structure must be decorous, pleasing and varied. It consists of three parts, order, connection and rhythm (Q, IX iv 146, 147).

Surviving word-books for *Messiah*, printed for performances in various locations, show us how the work was set out in numbered scenes within the three parts. Some scenes use a group of consecutive verses, others are a mixture of complementary verses from the Old and New Testaments put together to make a point, alluding to and justifying the events of Christ's life as foretold.

It is important that the structure of the whole work is made plain by the performers, in order for the audience to be secure in the knowledge of where they are in the work and as a guide to what they are hearing. The sixteenth-century German schoolmaster Susenbrotus, in a rhetoric book that was used in English grammar schools, proposes that trying to deliver a work without understanding how it is put together is like trying to 'strike the mark with closed eyes'.

The Classical Greek writer and rhetorician Longinus writes in *On the Sublime* how

> an apt Connection of the Parts conduces as much to the aggrandizing Discourse as Symmetry in the Members of the Body to a majestic Mien. If they are taken apart each single Member will have no Beauty or Grandeur, but when skilfully knit together, they produce what is called a fine Person. So the constituent Parts of noble Periods, when rent asunder and divided, in the Act of Division fly off and lose their Sublimity, but when united into one Body, and associated together by the Bond of Harmony, they join to promote their own Elevation, and by their Union and Multiplicity bestow a more emphatical Turn upon every Period (p. 71).

Longinus also writes that 'Nothing so much debases Sublimity as broken and precipitate Measures' and in a similar vein Quintilian criticises those who construct an intricate tessellated pavement made of detached pieces which have no connections. The result is a cooling of the passions and waste of energy (Q, IX iv 113). To make the structure clear, the performers (or director) need to decide when to pause for a moment between movements, when to make a direct connection, and when to make a complete break, for example at the end of a scene (a process often sabotaged by inconvenient page turns). By reading the text alone, without the music, it can be seen that movements which start with the words 'and', 'for', 'then', 'since' or 'if' are more closely connected to the previous movement than those which start with a new statement, command, exclamation or fresh narrative. Accompanied recitatives and the few *secco* recitatives in *Messiah* introduce a topic which is developed in the following aria, and might flow further into a chorus. The fact

1.2 Structure and Performance

that an instrumental ritornello often finishes off a scene and opens the next with a new idea contributes to the natural separation of the ideas for the 'real time' listener. The closing ritornello acts as a mini-peroration, sums up the previous thought and gives the listener aural space for contemplation of the previous text. The next opening ritornello prepares him for the new idea.

Structural Silences

In order to show the structure of a lengthy grand choral work such as *Messiah*, the performers need to adopt a strategic view of the whole work (see tables below). Obviously the three principal parts are clearly defined, but the quasi-operatic scenes within these (specified in the 1743 word-book for the first London performance) need careful planning for either holding the tension between movements by continuing with a similar *tactus*, or separating one from the next. Occasionally, the connection between the scenes can be closed up for affect, for example in Part Two, if the gap between scenes I and II is minimised, the strong harmony for the opening of 'He was cut off' can be used to break the mood of 'His sorrow'. Scenes V and VI need to be closely connected, piling into the shock opening of 'Why do the nations'.

In the following tables, which provide the complete text from the 1743 word book:
- Close connections which should be made between movements are marked *
- Extended opening ritornello = Op rit
- Extended closing ritornello = Cl rit

The Text Part One

Source and form

	Sinfony (Overture) [Not in word book]*	
	Scene I [Prophecy of salvation]	
Isaiah 40. 1-3 Recit accomp	*Comfort ye, comfort ye my People, saith your God; speak ye comfortably to Jerusalem, and cry unto her, that her Warfare is accomplish'd, that her Iniquity is pardon'd. The Voice of him that crieth in the Wilderness; prepare ye the Way of the Lord, make straight in the Desert a Highway for our God. *	Op rit
Isaiah 40. 4 Air	*Ev'ry Valley shall be exalted, and ev'ry Mountain and Hill made low, the Crooked straight, and the rough Places plain.*	Op rit Cl rit
Isaiah 40. 5 Chorus	*And the Glory of the Lord shall be revealed. And all Flesh shall see it together, for the Mouth of the Lord hath spoken it.	Op rit
	Scene II [The coming judgement]	
Haggai 2. 6 Recit accomp	Thus saith the Lord of Hosts; Yet once a little while, and I will shake the Heav'ns and the Earth; the Sea and the dry Land: And I will shake all Nations; and the Desire of all Nations shall come.	
Malachi 3. 1	The Lord whom ye seek shall suddenly come to his Temple, ev'n the messenger of the Covenant, whom ye delight in: Behold he shall come, saith the Lord of Hosts.*	
Malachi 3. 2 Air	*But who may abide the Day of His coming? And who shall stand when He appeareth? For He is like a Refiner's Fire.*	Op rit Cl rit
Malachi 3. 3 Chorus	*And He shall purify the Sons of Levi, that they may offer unto the Lord an Offering in Righteousness.	
	Scene III [Prophecy of Christ's birth]	
Isaiah 7. 14 Recit	Behold! A Virgin shall conceive, and bear a Son, and shall call his Name Emmanuel, GOD WITH US.*	
Isaiah 40. 9 Air & chorus	*O thou that tellest good Tidings to Zion, get thee up into the high Mountain: O thou that tellest good Tidings to Jerusalem, lift up thy Voice with Strength; lift it up, be not afraid: Say unto the Cities of Judah, Behold your God.	Op rit
Isaiah 60. 1	O thou that tellest good Tidings to Zion, Arise, shine, for Thy	

1.2 Structure and Performance

	Light is come, and the Glory of the Lord is risen upon thee.	Cl rit
Isaiah 60. 2-3 Recit accomp	For behold, Darkness shall cover the Earth, and gross Darkness the People: but the Lord shall arise upon thee, and His Glory shall be seen upon thee. And the Gentiles shall come to thy Light, and Kings to the Brightness of thy Rising.*	Op rit
Isaiah 9. 2 Air	*The People that walked in Darkness have seen a great Light. And they that dwell in the Land of the Shadow of Death, upon them hath the Light shined.	Op rit Cl rit
Isaiah 9. 6 Chorus	For unto us a Child is born, unto us a Son is given; and the Government shall be upon his Shoulder, and His Name shall be called, Wonderful, Counsellor, The Mighty God, The Everlasting Father, The Prince of Peace.	Op rit Cl rit
Scene IV [Annunciation to the shepherds]		
Short version (11 bars) or D.C.	Pifa * [Not in word book]	
Luke 2. 8 Recit	*There were Shepherds, abiding in the Field, keeping Watch over their Flock by Night.*	
Luke 2. 9 Set both as Air and Recit accomp	*And lo, the Angel of the Lord came upon them, and the Glory of the Lord shone round about them, and they were sore afraid.*	
Luke 2. 10-11 Recit	*And the Angel said unto them, Fear not; for behold, I bring you good Tidings of great Joy, which shall be to all People. For unto you is born this Day, in the City of David, a Saviour, which is Christ the Lord.*	
Luke 2. 13 Recit accomp	*And suddenly there was with the Angel a Multitude of the heav'nly Host, praising God, and saying:*	
Luke 2. 14 Chorus	*Glory to God in the Highest, and Peace on Earth, Good Will towards Men.	Cl rit
Scene V [Christ's healing and redemption]		
Zechariah 9. 9-10 Air	Rejoice greatly, O Daughter of Sion, shout, O Daughter of Jerusalem; behold, thy King cometh unto thee: He is the righteous Saviour; and He shall speak Peace unto the Heathen.*	Op rit Cl rit
Isaiah 35. 5-6 Recit	*Then shall the Eyes of the Blind be open'd, and the Ears of the Deaf unstopped; then shall the lame Man leap as a Hart, and the Tongue of the Dumb shall sing.*	
Isaiah 40. 11 Air alto Matthew 11. 28-29 Air sop	*He shall feed his Flock like a shepherd: and He shall gather the Lambs with his Arm, and carry them in his Bosom, and gently lead those that are with young. Come unto Him, all ye that labour and are heavy laden, and He will give you Rest. Take his yoke upon you, and learn of Him, for He is meek and lowly of Heart: and ye shall find Rest unto your souls.	Op rit Cl rit Cl rit
Matthew 11. 30 Chorus	His Yoke is easy, His Burthen is light.	

Handel's use of the contrast between the severe overture in E minor which seems to deliberately avoid the major and the heavenly accompanied recitative in E major that follows can be more connected than might be usual for an opera or oratorio of this period, where normally they would have had no meaningful dramatic relationship. Handel invents a new dramatic connection between the overture and what follows, whereas in an Italian opera, a collection of dances might come after the overture before the action begins.

Burney writes that

> HANDEL's Overtures are generally analogous to the opening of the first scene of the Drama to which they belong, and may be called real prefaces or preliminary discourses to a book. In order therefore to suppress every idea of levity in so sacred a performance as the MESSIAH, he very judiciously finished the Overture without an Air ('Commemoration of Handel', p. 74).

1.2 Structure and Performance

If the Sinfony (overture) is the prelude, Scene I, derived from consecutive verses of Isaiah, an appeal for comfort for the people of Israel, seems to form the exordium of the work. The exordium's function, which is to set out the case, prepares the listeners' minds for what follows and gains admission to their thoughts. This is not the time for lingering. Quintilian describes the style of the exordium which 'should not resemble that of purple patches [...] it should seem simple and unpremeditated' (Q, IV i 60). The performer (in this case the tenor soloist) should not show excessive ingenuity but merely hint at emotion, not developing it too fully *yet*. The audience is at the start of a long journey.

> For the orator frequently prepares his audience for what is to come (Q, X i 21).

> Every introduction will have to contain either a statement of the whole of the matter that is to be put forward, or an approach to the case and preparation of the ground [...] but the opening passage put at the beginning of a case should be in due proportion to the importance of the facts, just as a forecourt or an entrance should be properly proportioned to the mansion or temple to which it belongs. [...] But the opening passage should be so closely connected with the speech as to appear to be not an appendage, like the prelude to a piece of music, but an integral part of the whole structure that follows (C, *De Oratore* II lxxix 320, 325).

Scene II commences with a rousing prophetical announcement from Haggai, 'Thus saith the Lord', which could be made to interrupt the mood of Scene I. If this were a staged work, one could imagine the singer rushing on from the wings to break the mood of the previous chorus. This dramatic gesture is followed by the conciliatory 'But who may abide'. This prophet is followed by consecutive verses from another, Malachi, connected by the opening words 'but' and 'and'. 'But who may abide' and 'And He shall purify' should follow on in a continuous flow. The grand choral conclusion of 'and He shall purify' rounds off the second scene.

A good break is needed before Scene III where a complete change of mood in the first recitative introduces the serene virgin birth prophecy from Isaiah. The gap between 'Arise, shine' and 'For, behold' should not be too close, as the contrast created between the finish of the bright 'light' which 'is come' and the magical opening of the 'Darkness' which 'shall cover the Earth' needs a moment of preparation to have its full effect. The air following, 'The People that walked in Darkness', which extends the darkness theme and emerges during its course into light, should be closely connected to 'the Brightness of Thy rising'. A short gap before the opening ritornello of the final chorus of this scene, 'For unto us a Child is born', prepares our return to the optimism of the prophecy. The conclusive ending to this scene needs recovery time before the next event, another complete change of scene.

The Pifa pastoral interlude changes the mood and introduces the shepherds (Scene IV). Only the first eleven bars appear in the Foundling Hospital performing materials (1760). This cut is part of the tightening-up process Handel undertook after the first performance, so there is a case for omitting the middle section and da capo if preferred. The Pifa can lead into the following recitative without a break in the continuo. From here, each stage of the story (consecutive verses from Luke) should be continuously connected by 'and lo', 'and the Angel', 'and suddenly', 'and saying....' running on without gaps, finally arriving at 'Glory to God'.

Scene V looks to the future of mankind and describes a joyful and optimistic prospect in a continuous sequence through to the end of Part One, listing all the marvellous things which will happen, with texts taken from both Old and New Testaments. It ends in a light but triumphant mood. In modern concert performances the main interval is usually taken at this point.

When he was directing a performance, Handel might have played one of his own organ concertos here. Later in the eighteenth century, a concerto (or sometimes three) might have been performed. At Drury Lane, in a performance of *Messiah* during Lent 1786,

1.2 Structure and Performance

concertos for cello (Mr. Crosdill), oboe (the elder Parke) and pianoforte (Miss Parke) were performed (Parke, p. 54).

In 1784, the Lent performances of oratorios at the Theatre Royal, Drury Lane included *Messiah*, but for some reason without the customary concertos on the first night of the season. The performance ended unexpectedly early, which had never happened before, and the coaches and carriages were not ready. His majesty had already risen from his seat when the Lord Chamberlain informed him of the circumstance, and His Majesty had to wait while the royal carriage was summoned (Parke, p. 32).

The Text Part Two

Source and form

	Scene I [Christ's Passion]	
John 1. 29 Chorus	Behold the Lamb of God that taketh away the Sin of the World.	Op rit Cl rit
Isaiah 53. 3 Air d.c. Isaiah 50. 6	He was despised and rejected of Men, a Man of Sorrows, and acquainted with Grief. He gave his Back to the Smiters, and His Cheeks to them that plucked off the Hair: He hid not His Face from Shame and Spitting.	Op rit Cl rit
Isaiah 53. 4-6 Chorus	Surely He hath borne our Griefs, and carried our Sorrows: He was wounded for our Transgressions, He was bruised for our Iniquities; the Chastisement of our Peace was upon Him.* *And with his Stripes we are healed.* *All we, like Sheep, have gone astray; we have turned ev'ry one to his own Way. And the Lord hath laid on Him the Iniquity of us all.	Op rit Cl rit
Psalm 22. 7 Recit accomp	All they that see Him, laugh Him to Scorn; they shoot out their Lips, and shake their Heads, saying*	Op rit
Psalm 22. 8 Chorus	*He trusted in God that He would deliver Him: let Him deliver Him, if He delight in Him.*	
Psalm 69. 21 Recit accomp	*Thy rebuke hath broken His Heart; he is full of Heaviness: He looked for some to have Pity on Him, but there was no Man; neither found He any to comfort Him.*	
Lamentations 1. 12 Air	*Behold, and see, if there be any Sorrow like unto His Sorrow!*	
	Scene II [Christ's death and resurrection]	
Isaiah 53. 8 Recit accomp	*He was cut off out of the Land of the Living: For the Transgression of thy People was He stricken.*	
Psalm16. 10 Air	*But Thou didst not leave His Soul in Hell, not didst Thou suffer thy Holy One to see Corruption.	Op rit Cl rit
	Scene III [Christ's ascension]	
Psalm 24. 7-10 Chorus	Lift up your Heads, O ye Gates, and be ye lift up, ye everlasting Doors, and the King of Glory shall come in. Who is this King of Glory? The Lord Strong and Mighty, the Lord Mighty in Battle. Lift up your Heads, O ye Gates, and be ye lift up, ye everlasting Doors, and the King of Glory shall come in. Who is this King of Glory? The Lord of Hosts: He is the King of Glory.	Op rit
	Scene IV [Christ received into heaven]	
Hebrews 1. 5 Recit	Unto which of the Angels said He at any time, Thou art my Son, this Day have I begotten Thee?*	
Hebrews 1. 6 Chorus	*Let all the Angels of God worship Him.	

1.2 Structure and Performance

	Scene V [The spread of the gospel]	
Psalm 68. 18 Air	Thou art gone up on High; Thou hast led Captivity captive, and received Gifts for Men, yea, even for thine Enemies, that the Lord God might dwell among them.	Op rit Cl rit
Psalm 68. 11 Chorus	The Lord gave the Word: Great was the Company of the Preachers.	
Romans 10. 15 Air (From a 1758 word-book) Duet/Chorus	How beautiful are the Feet of them that preach the Gospel of Peace, and bring glad Tidings of good Things! How beautiful are the Feet of them that bring good [glad] Tidings, Tidings of Salvation; that say unto Sion, Thy God reigneth, break forth into Joy, thy God reigneth!	Op rit Cl rit
Romans 10. 18 Chorus	Their Sound is gone out into all Lands, and their Words unto the Ends of the World.*	
	Scene VI [The world's rejection of the gospel]	
Psalm 2. 1-2 Air d.c.	*Why do the Nations so furiously rage together? and why do the People imagine a vain Thing? The Kings of the Earth rise up, and the Rulers take Counsel together against the Lord, and against his Anointed.*	Op rit Cl rit
Psalm 2. 3 Chorus	*Let us break their Bonds asunder, and cast away their Yokes from us.	Cl rit
	Scene VII [God's ultimate victory]	
Psalm 2. 4 Recit	He that dwelleth in Heaven shall laugh them to scorn; the Lord shall have them in Derision.*	
Psalm 2. 9 Air or recit.	*Thou shalt break them with a Rod of Iron; Thou shalt dash them in pieces like a Potter's Vessel.	Op rit Cl rit
	Scene VIII [Triumph of Christ's reign]	
Revelation 19. 6; 11. 15; 19. 16 Chorus	Hallelujah! For the Lord God Omnipotent reigneth. The Kingdom of this World is become the Kingdom of our Lord, and of his Christ; and He shall reign for ever and ever. King of Kings, and Lord of Lords, Hallelujah!	Op rit

Part Two of Handel's *Messiah* is without doubt the profound emotional core of the work, a *hypotyposis* which is in rhetoric a vivid representation in sound. Handel's music is fully operatic in style, dramatic and forward moving. It drives through scenes of flagellation and the depiction of the Man of Sorrows in the manner of a German passion play. All the rhetorical stops are pulled out to illustrate the agony, the lashing of whips, mocking and other pathetic affects. The first group of movements can be connected by a continuous pulse to enhance the dramatic effects, from the opening of 'Behold the Lamb of God' until the end of 'All We, like Sheep'. Through the whole patchwork of carefully chosen texts, Handel's music carries through the flow of ideas and emotions, the lows of corruption and highs of triumph to the conclusion: 'Hallelujah!'

As a prelude to the drama, Scene I presents a serious and dramatic overture in the French dotted style, 'Behold the Lamb of God', before launching into the highly emotional 'He was despised' leading us to the torturous 'Surely', a chorus composed of three contrasting sections. After 'And with his Stripes,' 'All we, like Sheep' a comic mocking of human frailty follows, ending darkly on the sad judgement of the Lord through our 'Iniquity'. The sorrows are heaped up in the next section, an eloquent appeal in a sequence for the tenor voice which flows through the vehement and the pathetic, with the sarcastic taunt of the chorus in 'He trusted in God'.

Scene II launches with an interruption to 'His Sorrow!' The following aria resolves the 'cutting off out of the Land of the Living' with a close 'but' connection.

Scene III is the isolated chorus 'Lift up your Heads' which is composed of questions and answers between semi-choruses, concluding firmly with the whole choir. The text of Scene IV follows on with a response in recitative and chorus with two adjacent verses from Hebrews, a tribute to the angels.

A short pause before Scene V will prepare for the serene air 'Thou art gone up on high', closely followed by the chorus, firm in its authority. Another small gap before 'How beautiful are the Feet' (included from 1745, not in the 1743 word-book), takes us straight into the next chorus. The transition from the mild 'ends of the World' to Scene VI, 'Why do the Nations', can be quick. The cadence of the short version facilitates this process. Too much gap here will destroy the surprise of the war-like opening ritornello. It makes sense to connect this closely with 'Let us break their Bonds asunder'. The momentum should be kept going through the next Scene VII 'laugh them to Scorn' into 'break them […] dash them in Pieces' (a short recitative in the Dublin version) pushing the vehement 'Derision' to its energetic limit. A space prepares the audience for the final Hallelujah chorus (Scene VIII) which will round off Part Two in triumph.

According to a letter written by James Beattie to the Rev. Dr. Laing thirty-seven years after the event, George II 'started up' at the words 'For the Lord God Omnipotent Reigneth' and remained standing until the end of the chorus. Audiences still expect to stand for the Hallelujah chorus (Deutsch, p. 854).

The Text Part Three

Source and form

	Scene I [The promise of eternal life]	
Job 19. 25-26 Air	I know that my Redeemer liveth, and that He shall stand at the latter Day upon the Earth. And tho' Worms destroy this Body, yet in my Flesh shall I see God.	Op rit
I Corinthians 15. 20	For now is Christ risen from the Dead, the First-Fruits of them that sleep.	Cl rit
I Corinthians 15. 21-22 Chorus	Since by Man came Death, by Man came also the Resurrection of the Dead. For as in Adam all die, even so in Christ shall all be made alive.	
	Scene II [The day of judgement]	
I Corinthians 15. 1-52 Recit acomp	Behold, I tell you a Mystery: We shall not all sleep, but we shall all be chang'd, in a Moment, in the Twinkling of an Eye, at the last Trumpet.*	
I Corinthians 15. 52-53 Air d.s.	*The Trumpet shall sound, and the Dead shall be rais'd incorruptible, and We shall be chang'd. For this corruptible must put on Incorruption, and this Mortal must put on Immortality.	Op rit Cl rit
	Scene III [Conquest of sin]	
I Corinthians 15. 54 Recit	Then shall be brought to pass the Saying that is written: Death is swallowed up in Victory.*	
I Corinthians 15. 55-56 Duet	*O Death! Where is thy Sting? O Grave, where is thy Victory? The Sting of Death is Sin, and the Strength of Sin is the Law.*	
I Corinthians 15. 57 Chorus	*But Thanks be to God, who giveth Us the Victory through our Lord Jesus Christ.	
Romans 8. 31, 33-34 Air	If God be for us, who can be against us? Who shall lay anything to the Charges of God's Elect? It is God that justifieth; Who is he that condemneth? It is Christ that died, yea, rather, that is risen again; who is at the Right Hand of God, who maketh intercession for us.	Op rit Cl rit
	Scene IV [Acclamation of Messiah]	
Revelation 5. 12-14 Chorus	Worthy is the Lamb that was slain, and hath redeemed us to God by His Blood, to receive Power, and Riches, and Wisdom, and Strength, and Honour, and Glory, and Blessing. Blessing and Honour, Glory and Pow'r, be unto Him that sitteth upon the Throne, and unto the Lamb, for ever and ever! Amen	

Audiences unfamiliar with Handel's *Messiah* could be forgiven for thinking that the 'Hallelujah' chorus was the end of the piece. It concludes nearly two hours of music with a rousing ending. Part Three is like the arrival in Dante's *Paradiso*, a prolonged resolution and home-coming in the new mood of resurrection. The first three scenes follow the text from Corinthians in a continuous sequence, taking us into a vision of the afterlife, opening with the sublime aria 'I know that my Redeemer liveth', and followed by the alternating choruses of death and resurrection.

A short gap before Scene II prepares the way for the 'mystery' (reminding us of the 'Mystery of Godliness' text on the title page of the word book), which should lead straight into the trumpet of the last judgement without a break. Scene III introduces a new tone in the recitative which connects death and victory, an idea taken up by the duet and which is linked musically to the following chorus. A short space before and after the air 'If God be for us' can frame this aria which could be considered the work's true peroration, the summing up and the final reflective appeal to the emotions. The epilogue is the rousing final chorus sequence and extended amen, which belong to Scene IV.

> The peroration is the most important part of forensic pleading, and in the main consists of appeals to the emotions [...] a task which forms the most powerful means of obtaining what we desire, and is also more difficult than any of those which we have previously considered, namely that of stirring the emotions of the judges, and of moulding and transforming them to the attitude which we desire (Q, VI ii).

> Conclusions are tripartite, consisting of the summing up, amplification, and appeal to pity. [...] The summing up gathers together and recalls the points we have made – briefly, that the speech may not be repeated in entirety, but that the memory of it may be refreshed (RH, II xxx 47).

> The peroration is the end and conclusion of the whole speech [...] The summing up is a passage in which matters that have been discussed in different places here and there throughout the speech are brought together in one place and arranged so as to be seen at a glance in order to refresh the memory of the audience (C, *De Inventione*, I lii 98).

> The peroration makes especial use of amplification; the effect of this should be to excite the spirits of the audience or calm them, and if they have already been so affected, to heighten their feelings or quiet them still more (C, *Topica*, xxvi 98).

Length

Although such drastic cuts as are shown below would be frowned upon today, performances which last over three hours are, thankfully, a thing of the past now that sprightlier tempos have generally been accepted. Part One is often performed alone near Christmas. In the eighteenth century, concerts consisting of favourite choruses and arias from *Messiah* were popular, often combined with extracts from other religious works of Handel such as *Samson*, *Jephtha* and *Judas Maccabeus*.

1.2 Structure and Performance

> As this ORATORIO has been found to exceed the usual length of the Concerts performed at Edinburgh, some Parts of it are to be omitted, which, in the following Copy, will be found printed in *Italics*.

Word-Book, Edinburgh 1772 warning of cuts

> PART II.
>
> CHORUS.
>
> BEHOLD the Lamb of God that taketh away the Sin of the World.
>
> SONG.
>
> He was despised and rejected of Men, a Man of sorrows and acquainted with grief. He gave his back to the smiters, and his cheeks to them that plucked off the hair; he hid not his face from shame and spitting.
> [Da Capo.
>
> CHORUS.
>
> *Surely he hath borne our griefs and carried our sorrows. He was wounded for our Transgressions, he was bruised for our iniquities, the chastisement of our peace was upon him. And with his stripes we are healed.*
>
> CHORUS.

Word-Book, Edinburgh 1772 showing cuts in italics

1.3 Figures of Rhetoric
or 'Garnishing the Manner of Utterance'

After inventing and arranging the material, the next stage in the rhetorical process is elaboration or decoration (*elocutio*). Decoration in rhetoric means using figures of speech to attract and hold the attention of the listeners, with tricks of sound and patterns of repetition which work on their emotions to persuade them of the argument. Quintilian considers that these are the chief ornaments of oratory (Q, X v 3).

> Figures serve to commend what we say to those who hear us [...] to relieve monotony by varying the language. For eloquence delights in variety, and just as the eye is more strongly attracted by the sight of a number of things, so oratory supplies a continuous series of novelties to rivet the attention of the mind. Figures relieve the tedium of everyday stereotyped speech and save us from commonplace language. They act as seasoning to style and increase its attractions (Q, IX i 21; IX ii 63; IX iii 3, 4).

The Greek rhetorician Longinus thinks figures indispensable for creating the sublime style, and that the combination of effects when two or three co-operate 'in a heap of figures' produces force, conviction and beauty (pp. 42, 53, 56). Some of these rhetorical devices have no exact parallel in music, only being available through the text. These include tropes such as metaphor or allegory (an extended metaphor), which draws parallels with other ideas or images. Word-painting could be considered a form of metaphor in music because it conjures up images in the mind of the listener. Another major category of figures uses the device of comparison to show similarities or contrast, which provoke thought and thereby enliven a topic.

John Smith's seventeenth-century biblical rhetoric book describes figures as 'garnishing the manner of utterance'. Smith follows the Classical sources in dividing figures into two purely technical categories: 'in the dimension or measuring of sounds or words [...] in the repetition of sounds or words' and figures of sentence which use longer constructions to 'move affections and passion' (J. Smith, pp. 5, 8). The figures in these two categories use word-play in repeating, adding or subtracting a word or syllable, altering parts of similar sounding words, or using constructions whose effect is based on repetition.

> To confer distinction upon style is to render it ornate embellishing it by variety. The divisions under distinction are figures of diction and figures of thought. It is a figure of diction if the adornment is comprised in the fine polish of the language itself. A figure of thought derives a certain distinction from the idea, not from the words (RH, IV xiii 18).

Rhetorical ornament may reside either in individual words, or groups of words. Words may be repeated, or reproduced with a slight change; sentences may repeatedly commence or end with the same word; the sentence may begin or end with the same phrase; the same word may be reiterated either at the beginning or at the conclusion, or may be repeated but in a different sense. Other effects may be had by the graduation or contrast of clauses, the elegant inversion of words, by arguments drawn from opposites, or the employment of different moods and tenses (Q, VIII iii 15; Q, IX i 34, 38, 39).

George Puttenham describes figures as giving speeches and sentences 'ornament or efficacie by many manner of alterations in shape, in sounde, and also in sence, sometime by way of surplusage, sometime by defect, sometime by disorder, or mutation' (p. 243). This method of composition, by small alterations of an idea or theme, was in common use by composers in the sixteenth century, especially in contrapuntal music, and supplements the rhetoric embedded in a text with musical versions of similar devices.

The word 'figure', although commonly used by musicians to refer to a theme, is in rhetoric a pattern or construction which usually needs two things to compare, contrast or repeat to form the figure. To distinguish the two, the word 'motif' is preferable to describe a theme or musical idea. Music brings other possibilities to the art of rhetoric which is normally applied to a single speaker, because it can draw on many voices in the service of variety and contrast: the choice of solo voice or choir, varied orchestral textures, intervals, harmony and counterpoint. If more than one voice speaks, an interchange of ideas is possible using argument or agreement. One speaker may also hold a discourse with himself, in music an effect created by dividing the line into high and low phrases, a device which can be made clear by using a change of tone for the two voices: the higher phrase loud and lower one soft, or vice versa, as clearly seen in 'Thou shalt break them' (Ex. 1.3.12).

The Bible is packed with rhetorical figures. Sometimes the same phrase may employ several figures simultaneously for different purposes. The piling up of figures in a text denotes a particularly high style of writing designed to persuade and move as well as to inform. Music or poetry in lower style, such as a folk song, nursery rhyme, simple chorale or hymn tune, is likely to use fewer figures. Figures make the text more memorable and can stimulate a strong emotional response at the same time, impressing the thought on the listener. Music rich in figures makes repeated listening more rewarding, as the listener becomes aware of different elements of the complex figural texture on each occasion.

Figures which use repetition, comparison and contrast can easily be transferred into musical language. In *The Temple Musick* (1706), the Anglican writer on church music Arthur Bedford wrote a defence of the style of composition used in cathedrals, including repetitions and melismas, which he describes as 'some of the *Graces* of our *present Musick*'. He is encouraged by the use of 'the utmost Strains which either Art or Fancy can invent ... to *please* their *Ears*, and *edify* their *Souls*' (R. Smith, 1995, p. 93). Repetition of the text, especially using counterpoint which was considered to obscure clarity, had been censored by sixteenth-century reformers, but it was welcomed back in the eighteenth century as a device for enhancing worship using rhetorical devices such as figures.

These devices had become an integral part of musical composition from the sixteenth century onwards, either with or without text. Handel's 'genius' did not emerge fully-formed, but relied on and developed from what came before. His musical palette became refined and superior, as Burney describes in his 'CHARACTER of HANDEL as a COMPOSER':

> All that the greatest and boldest musical inventor *can* do, is to avail himself of the best effusions, combinations, and effects, of his predecessors; to arrange and apply them in a new manner; and to add, from his own fource, whatever he can draw, that is grand, graceful, gay, pathetic, or, in any other way, pleasing. This HANDEL did, in a most ample and superior manner; being possessed, in his middle age and full of vigour, of every refinement and perfection of his time: uniting the depth and elaborate contrivance of his own country, with Italian elegance and facility ('Sketch of the Life of Handel' p. 39).

The Rhetoric Books

Henry Peacham's vivid descriptions from *The Garden of Eloquence* (1577), frequently quoted below, demonstrate the close analysis of figures and their best, most effective use. He follows these with examples of misuse, which he calls 'The Caution'. 'I have disposed into orders, described by their properties, distinguished by their differences, noted their singular uses, & added certain cautions to compass them for fear of abuse'. He writes that figures are 'as stars to give light, as cordials to comfort, as harmony to delight, as pitiful spectacles to move sorrowful passions, and as orient colours to beautifie reason' ('The Epistle Dedicatorie').

Peacham is often quoted in John Smith's later *Mysterie of Rhetorique Unvail'd* (1657). The title page of Smith's book describes it as 'conducing very much to the right understanding of the Sense of the Letter of the Scripture (the want whereof occasions many dangerous Errors this day)'. Smith's book is recommended as 'Flowers of Rhetorique out of the Garden of the holy Scripture, not only worthy of Commendation, but Publication; especially for their direction, who not being able to distinguish plain and proper from Figurative and Tropical Texts of Scripture [meaning tropes which use imagery to 'turn' the mind], are apt to run not only into gross absurdities, but dangerous and destructive Errors by such mistakes' ('To the Reader').

Both Peacham and Smith were writing in English for a general readership (other rhetoric exercise books in Latin were used in the school-room), principally as an aid to the understanding and reading of the scriptural texts.

Smith writes that his book is a

> Key to unlock and lay open those abstruse difficulties which the Tropes and Figures have hitherto, not only been mask'd with but locked up under; I mean from such at least, as are altogether unaquainted with the Greek tongue, and have not directed their studies to the subject [...]. For the bare reading of the Scripture, without searching into its heavenly mysteries and meaning, is like coming into a Treasury, wherein we see many costly things folded up, and some ends appearing out, but when they be all unfolded, then doth their glory more affect us for the present, yea, and leave in us a deep impression of their excellency ('To the Reader').

No apology need be made for applying the comments of these sixteenth- and seventeenth-century writers to an eighteenth-century situation. Their explanations and detailed analysis of the effects and uses of figures will be useful to a modern audience, which sadly lacks the knowledge of rhetoric that would have been common to any eighteenth-century gentleman with a Classical education. Smith's book continued to be read and reprinted well into the eighteenth century, the tenth edition being published in 1721, and in 1739 an abridged version was still available (Osborn, p. 219).

The Bible text with which most modern audiences will be familiar is the 1611 Authorised Version of King James, published when Peacham's 1593 edition would have still been current, and used by John Smith for his exclusively scriptural examples.

George Puttenham has also been quoted, as his quaint 'Englished' terminology derived directly from the Greek helps us to grasp the function and effect of the figures, and understand how and why they work, and also John Hoskyns's *Direccons For Speech and Style* (1599), which was drawn on by John Smith. Thus, the debt each generation of writers paid to the last records an unacknowledged tribute to their predecessors, and establishes a chain of knowledge and explanation for the reader which extends from the late sixteenth century well into the eighteenth. Smith describes this process as being like a child on a giant's shoulders who can see further than the giant (J. Smith, 'To the Reader').

All the sixteenth- and seventeenth-century rhetoric books, even those aimed at a deeper understanding of the Bible text, depend heavily on the Classical sources, principally Quintilian's *Institutio Oratoria* which is much quoted by authors such as John Smith and Peacham, and also encompass the Greek texts, many of which have been lost. Cicero's works (*Orator*, *De Inventione* and *De Oratore*) as well as the *Rhetorica ad Herennium* would have been well known and studied in the eighteenth-century school room and are frequently quoted by Quintilian and the later Classical sources.

Copia – How Many Ways?

One of the fundamental techniques of composition in the rhetorical style is the use of *copia*. What was known as 'the abundant style' encouraged writers and composers to express the same thought in as many different ways as was possible. Each way expressed its own rhetorical colour, according to the means employed.

1.3 Figures of Rhetoric

The school exercise book written by Erasmus for St. Paul's School in London at the beginning of the sixteenth century (*De Utraque Verborum ac Rerum Copia*, known as *De Copia*), became part of the standard curriculum in the following centuries all over Europe. Starting from a basic statement or idea, students were required to build a bank or treasure house of vocabulary (thesaurus) on which to call for their choice of words. The sound and rhythm of the words created diction. Quintilian calls diction 'a weapon for menace and attack' or merely used for the purpose of display (Q, IX i 33). After the choice of words, figures of speech were applied. Sometimes more than one figure at once, as will be seen in the examples which follow, to give a variety of emotional tones to the idea and by this means persuade the listener. Erasmus describes this process as dressing the body (the idea or motif) in a number of different costumes. The body remains the same, but it is dressed differently.

> Copiousness and facility in expression bear abundant fruit, if controlled by proper knowledge and a strict discipline of the mind' (RH, I i).

> Refining consists of dwelling on the same topic and yet seeming to say something ever new. It is accomplished in two ways: by merely repeating the same idea, or by descanting upon it. We shall not repeat the same thing precisely – for that, to be sure would weary the hearer and not refine the idea – but with changes (RH, IV xlii 54).

> Dwelling on the point occurs when one remains rather long upon, and often returns to, the strongest topic on which the whole cause rests [...] no opportunity is given the hearer to remove his attention from this strongest topic [...] this topic is not isolated from the whole cause like some limb, but like blood is spread through the whole body of the discourse (RH, IV xlv 58).

> Our ideal orator will speak in such a manner that he will cast the same thought into a number of different forms, will dwell on one point and linger over the same idea (Q, IX i 41).

In music, there are many additional possibilities of text-setting using repetition for variety. Handel demonstrates a natural ability to treat small musical motifs in the tradition of *copia*. Sixteenth- and seventeenth-century composers such as Schütz and Buxtehude had already been using a variety of emphases and rhythms to set the same text. Handel often changes the emphasis of the syllables in a reiterated phrase, to show all aspects of the text by varying the weighted syllables. For example, in the Hallelujah chorus, the first emphasis uses a long initial syllable for the dialogue between chorus and orchestra: HAL-lelujah, later changing to Hal-LE-lujah and then Halle-LU-jah for the short version, until the slow concluding statement Hal-LE-LU-JAH. The phrase 'The everlasting Father, The Prince of Peace' is set in several different ways (see 2.2 Emphasis pp. 108-9 and the passage in 'Glory to God' used below to illustrate Comparison: Exx. 1.3.9, 1.3.10).

Both poets and composers use other devices of *copia* such as amplification and contraction by adding or taking away length (see *Amplificatio* p. 37). They can shorten a phrase when repeated because it has already been understood or add extra material to develop the idea further. The same phrase can be set on long or short notes, varying the emphasis, note values or intervals each time.

1.3 Figures of Rhetoric

Ex. 1.3.1 'Behold, and see'

'Behold and see' illustrates typical employment of *copia*. The bass has different versions of the same rhythmic motif while the upper strings sigh in imitation of 'Behold', varying the intervals. The rising major sixth is a particularly pleading interval which is repeated in the violins after the vocal version, itself repeated higher without the rest, and decorated.

Ex. 1.3.2 'Behold, and see'

The violins pick up the vocal 'behold' and vary it. The size of the interval and its tessitura influence which of the repeated motifs should be more prominent and which less. Close lower intervals can be quieter and more relaxed than wider, higher or dissonant ones which are more forceful. The bass continues to find different harmonic ways to say the same thing. The various short repeated motifs support the voice while commenting upon it in various ways.

1.3 Figures of Rhetoric

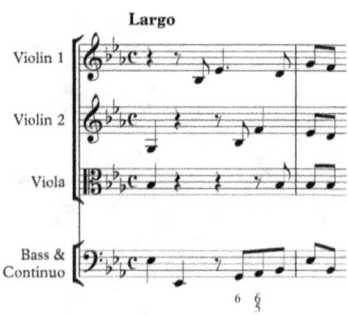

Ex. 1.3.3 'He was despised'

A similar rising rhythmic motif (or quaver up-beat to crotchet down-beat) is used at the opening of 'He was despised' but is continued to make part of a longer phrase. The second violins rise a fifth to F (starting from the same note, B♭) over the top of the firsts' rising fourth, creating a momentary dissonance. The firsts then rise up another step for the resolution of the phrase.

Ex. 1.3.4 'For unto us'

Patterns of semiquavers in the violin figuration show the eighteenth-century love of the serpentine curve in sound, where each repeated step can rise in dynamic.

William Hogarth, the eighteenth-century painter and contemporary of Handel, adopted the personal device of a flickering flame, chosen because it represented motion which he considered to be the spirit of a picture. Hogarth, although referring to forms, considers that 'the art of composing well is the art of varying well'.

> The waving line, or line of beauty, varying still more, being composed of two curves contrasted, becomes still more ornamental and pleasing [...] And that the serpentine line, by its waving and winding at the same time different ways, leads the eye in a pleasing manner along the continuity of its variety (pp. 55, 57).

In a musical context, it is the ear which is led by the 'waving and winding' of the phrase, but the serpentine curve can be seen on the page in the patterns of semi-quavers.

Ex. 1.3.5 'I know that my Redeemer liveth'

1.3 Figures of Rhetoric

The violins and bass exchange different versions of three descending notes which can be used to bring out the conversation between the dotted violins and the smooth bass line. Rhythmic alteration may be applied, as the first note of the violin phrase in the Foundling Hospital manuscript is sometimes quaver, sometimes semiquaver. In either case, the dotting should be gentle to match the serene affect.

Ex. 1.3.6 'Amen'

A good example of the 'piling up' of figures for a cumulative and grand effect. Count the number of ways. After rising in long waves, the word 'Amen' falls away from shorter, repeatedly rising peaks.

1.3 Figures of Rhetoric

Ex. 1.3.7 'Ev'ry Valley'

A firm, equally emphasised version of the text of 'Ev'ry Valley' is encouraged by the strings before the normal, less vehement, dotted version returns in the voice. The dotted quaver in the main version of the theme uses a semiquaver anticipation to the second syllable of 'VAL-ley' lightening the phrase and pushing the music forward. When this is omitted and the intervals are more strident, the theme becomes more severe and forthright.

Ex. 1.3.8 'Comfort ye'

'Iniquity' rises in a challenging gesture using an augmented fourth, which pulls up the movement (quasi pause on the E♯). The music then moves swiftly on to the 'pardon'd' cadence with 'Iniquity' now in more relaxed equal quavers instead of the dotted rhythm. The long dotted 'I-NI-quity' placed on a strong beat serves to emphasise the strong syllable making it slightly threatening.

1.3 Figures of Rhetoric

Ἀσπασμὸς Ἀγγέλου πρὸς τὴν Μαρίαν. | Luc. I, 28. | MARIA AB ANGELO SALUTATA.
The Annunciation of the Virgin Mary. | | Salutation de l'Ange à la S. Vierge.
Der Engel grüsset Maria. | | De Groetenis des Engels aen Maria.

1.3 Figures of Rhetoric

Comparison

> Comparison is a manner of speech that carries over an element of likeness from one thing to a different thing. This is used to embellish or prove or clarify or vivify (RH, IV xlv 59).

Rhetorical exercises in composition which aimed to develop the 'copious' style described above also used the two methods of comparison and contrast to highlight and vary ideas (see also *Antithesis* p. 39). As we have seen, Handel has endless capacity for small variation when a phrase or motif is repeated. Exact repetition, the *epizeuxis*, has another function (see p. 48). The following examples show further how he achieves this variety, but still maintaining the unity of ideas and structure. The audience might not be aware of the fine detail which makes this passage so attractive to listen to – it comes three times.

Ex. 1.3.9 'Glory to God'

1.3 Figures of Rhetoric

The first four bars of the chorus 'Glory to God in the highest' continues the high bass-line from the preceding phrase 'and suddenly there was with the Angel'. The heavenly trumpets are marked in the composition autograph '*da lontano e un poco piano*'. Heaven is, for the moment, far off. After the violins play a downwards vanishing motif where the voices stop, the lower (earthly) part of the chorus replies with 'and Peace on Earth' in unison. The next dynamic is a piano on the pulsing quavers after 'Peace on Earth' implying that the phrase 'Peace on Earth' should be sung and played loudly. The peaceful affect is most effective after a moderately loud unison for 'and Peace on Earth'. This idea is still part of the commanding, exclamatory text 'Glory to God in the highest, and Peace on Earth'.

In his orchestration of 'and Peace on Earth' Mozart not only marks it forte, but reinforces the phrase with horns, trombones and timpani. Tempting as it is to word-paint by singing 'Peace' softly, the effect of the piano comes magically out of the word 'Earth' at the point where the strings start pulsing. The semiquavers rise again in a natural crescendo to 'Glory to God in the highest' and descend in a shorter vanishing diminuendo to introduce the second 'And Peace on Earth' (Ex. 1.3.10).

Ex. 1.3.10 'Glory to God'

A comparison of these two similar extracts (Ex. 1.3.9 and Ex. 1.3.10) demonstrates Handel's use of rhetorical economy and variety. The first statement is the longest and extends the word 'Highest', which is decorated by the violins who vanish into a two-beat silence. 'And Peace on Earth' is then represented by a still unison in all parts. This happens again but now with note values halved on 'Highest'. The third time (Ex. 1.3.10) the silence is omitted and the violins continue straight into 'And Peace on Earth', which is now warmly harmonised and lower in tessitura, having meanwhile acquired 'Goodwill towards Men'. Again, the hushed piano dynamic in the strings comes out of 'And Peace on Earth'.

1.3 Figures of Rhetoric

'Glory to God' instruction for trumpets *da lontano e [o?] un poco piano*

Catalogue of Figures

The catalogue of figures with definitions and examples from the *Messiah* text which follows is drawn from the rhetoric sources of the sixteenth and seventeenth centuries. Some parallel musical applications for a similar figure used by Handel will appear after the text version. Sometimes, Handel's treatment of the text transforms the original word figure into a grander, more extended musical figure with a different affect, usually by using repetition or amplification of part of the text.

Quintilian writes helpfully that whether it is called a trope or a figure makes no difference as long as its stylistic value is apparent, since the meaning of a thing is not altered by a change of name: the value of a figure depends not on its name but on its effect (Q, IX i 7, 8).

The general definitions of the figures below, which are sometimes difficult to pin down and form a complex web of shifting relationships often spilling over into each other's territories, follow Richard A. Lanham, *A Handlist of Rhetorical Terms*.

If you enjoy this section, do get lost in the forest of rhetoric at http:/humanities/byu.edu/rhetoric/silva.htm. Here you will discover the endless overlapping of definitions and applications of figures.

To help the reader find their way around the following section, which probably includes many unfamiliar technical terms, the plan is as follows:

- Tropes: Simile, Metaphor, Allegory

- Ways of Speaking: *Accusatio, Aetiologia, Amamnesis, Antanagoge, Aphorism, Cataplexis, Characterismus, Chorographia, Confesso, Dialogismus, Hyperbole, Hypophora, Hypotyposis, Indignatio, Mempsis, Mycterismus, Oraculum, Pathopeia, Periphrasis, Prophecy, Prosopopeia* and *Anthypophora*

- Figures of Construction: *Amplificatio, Antithesis, Anastrophe, Asyndeton, Auxesis, Isocolon, Polysyndeton*

- Word-Play and Patterns of Repetition: *Adnominatio, Anadiplosis, Anaphora, Antistasis, Autonomasia, Antistrophe, Commoratio, Conduplicatio, Diacope, Epizeuxis, Homeoprophoron* (alliteration), *Homoioteleuton, Omission, Paronomasia, Ploce, Polyptonon*

1.3 Figures of Rhetoric

Joan. IX, 7.

Τυφλὸς ἀναβλέπων.
The eyes of the blind opened.
Ein Blind-gebohrner wird sehend.

OCULI CAECO APERTI.
Un aveugle recouvrant la vuë.
Een Blinde aan het gezicht geholpen.

Saur pinx.   Surugue sculp.

29

1.3 Figures of Rhetoric

Tropes: Simile, Metaphor, Allegory

> There will be metaphors of all sorts in great abundance, because these figures by virtue of the comparison involved transport the mind and bring it back, and move it hither and thither; and this rapid stimulation of thought produces pleasure (C, *Orator* 134).

Tropes (trope means literally a 'turn') are a large group of figures of speech which use comparison with images to heighten the meaning of the object or a thought. John Smith says 'there is no other trope more frequent, excellent and beautiful, than a metaphor'. An allegory is an extended metaphor which uses a story to draw parallels. Smith tells us 'a trope, is when words are used for elegancy in a changed signification; or when a word is drawn from its proper and genuine signification to another' and 'allegory is when the use of the same trope is continued in a long discourse'. The shepherd – flock – lamb metaphor is a thread that runs through the New Testament telling of Christ's life. Smith says Christ is also compared in the Bible to a vine, a rock, and a lion. Man is compared to a shadow, a flower, grass, a wolf, a bear, and a dog. Comparisons vivify by placing an image beside the things compared, provoking the listener to transfer the image or thought to another meaning.

There is no exact parallel in musical composition for a trope, but Handel manages to get around this problem by placing certain images in our minds using musical references, such as the pastoral drone style to refer to sheep or shepherds, or by using sound to paint subjects such as high hills or low valleys.

> 'Then shall the Eyes of the Blind be open'd, and the Ears of the Deaf unstopped; Then shall the lame Man leap as a Hart, and the Tongue of the Dumb shall sing'.

> 'He shall feed His Flock like a Shepherd: and He shall gather the Lambs with His Arm'.

> 'Worthy is the Lamb that was slain, and hath redeemed us to God by his Blood'.

> 'The Sting of Death is Sin'.

> 'Death is swallowed up in Victory'.

> 'Thou shalt dash them in pieces like a Potter's Vessel'.

> 'The First-Fruits of them that sleep'.

> 'Lift up your Heads, O ye Gates'.

'For He is like a Refiners Fire' is taken from the prophet Malachi by Jennens. John Smith gives us the example of the same metaphor used in St. Matthew's gospel:

> Christ is said to baptize with fire, whereby we may understand, that fire is there put for the power of the holy Ghost, which purifies and refines as fire (Matthew 3. 11).

Ways of Speaking

The Bible is rich in particular ways of speaking such as prophecy, commands, pleadings, threats, and hyperbole to support religious belief.

Accusatio, Categoria

A complaint, accusation or recrimination.

> 'Thy Rebuke hath broken his Heart'.

> 'For the Transgression of Thy People was He stricken'.

> Categoria is a forme of speech by which the speaker openeth and detecteth some secret wickednesse of his adversary, and laieth it open before his face (Peacham).

1.3 Figures of Rhetoric

Aetiologia

Giving a reason or cause.

'Since by Man came Death'

'He was cut off out of the Land of the Living: For the Transgression of thy People was He stricken'.

'Thou art gone up on High; Thou hast led Captivity captive, and received Gifts for Men, yea, even for thine Enemies, that the Lord God might dwell among them'.

> The tell cause, the reason rendrer [...] to fortifie our allegations by rendring reasons to every one (Puttenham).

> Aetiologia is a forme of speech by which the Orator joineth reason or cause to a proposition uttered [...] This figure is usuall in all good authors, and is of great strength in speech, for that the sentence said, hath always the reason joined unto it as an authenticke seale to an audience: and it serveth to confirmation and confutation. [...] The speaker in the use of this figure ought to be sure that the reason or cause which he joineth to the proposition be good & sufficient, lest he weaken that which he should confirme, and disgrace that which he should bewtifie (Peacham).

Note the use of the *isocolon* in the last phrase (see below, p. 43).

Anamnesis

Recalling ideas, events or persons of the past.

'The Lord gave the Word: great was the Company of the Preachers'.

'For the Mouth of the Lord hath spoken it'.

> It is a figure whereby the speaker calling to mind matters past, whether of joy, sorrow, &c. doth make recital of them for his own advantage, or for the benefit of those that hear him (J. Smith).

> The Caution: that evill matters bee not remembred, as to call into remembrance offences forgiven and long forgotten, or occasions which may renew unprofitable sorrow, or move anger, or actions of vanitie which were better to lye buried than to be revived (Peacham).

Antanagoge, concession

Ameliorating a fault or difficulty implicitly admitted by balancing an unfavourable aspect with a favourable one.

'But Thou didst not leave his Soul in Hell, nor didst Thou suffer thy Holy One to see Corruption'.

> The recompencer (Puttenham).

> A forme of speech by which the Orator joyneth to a precept, of virtue, a promise of reward, and to the contempt of as precept, he denounceth a punishment. [...] This forme of speaking doth always carry with it a mightie power and force to move men to the obedience of lawes and precepts: for by the promise it worketh a hope of that which men desire, and by threatning it moveth hate, and by them both an obedience of that which is commaunded: what forme of speech in this respect can do more, or what so much?' The Caution: This figure is then abused when promises of rewards or threatening of punishment, are used to move and further the obedience of unlawful precepts, or the performance of wicked counsel (Peacham).

1.3 Figures of Rhetoric

Aphorism

A short pithy statement of truth or doctrine popular in Biblical writing.

'God with us'.

'The Glory of the Lord shall be revealed'.

'His Yoke is easy'.

'The Lord gave the Word'.

'Thanks be to God'.

Cataplexis

Threatening punishment, misfortune or disaster.

'Thou shalt break them with a Rod of Iron; thou shalt dash them in Pieces like a Potter's Vessel'.

> A forme of speech, by which the orator denounceth a threatening against some person, people, citie, common wealth or country, conteining and declaring the certaintie or likelihood of plagues, or punishments to fall uppon them for their wickednesse, impietie, insolencie, and general iniquitie. The use pertaineth properly to deterre and drive men from sinne and wickednesse, and to force them to repentance [...] requires discretion and wisdome, to denounce (Peacham).

Characterismus

Description of the body or mind.

'A Man of Sorrows and acquainted with Grief'.

A type of *enargeia*, a vivid description which engages the mind. See also *pathopoeia*, *prosopopoeia*.

Chorographia

A description of a country.

'They that dwell in the Land of the Shadow of Death'.

Confessio, paromologia or paralogia

Conceding a point either from conviction of its truth or to use it to strengthen one's own argument.

'All we, like Sheep, have gone astray, we have turned ev'ry one to his own Way, and the Lord hath laid on Him the Iniquity of us all'.

> When the speaker granteth many things to his adversary worthie of commendation, and at the length bringeth in some notable crime, which oppresseth and quencheth all that was granted before [...] The utilitie of this figure, consisteth chiefly in confuting and removing the opinion of the hearer from some irking or error deeply rooted in his minde and affection, which the orator confuteth by a conclusion suddenly inferred for which respect it may be compared to the practice of undermining, which as it is hardly perceived till it hath wrought sudden subversion, so this figure maketh no shew of the purpose till it concludeth (Peacham).

Conquestio

Speaking in order to dominate the emotions of the listener.

> Used for lament or complaint and which seeks to arouse the pity of the audience (C, *De Inventione* I lx 106).

'Behold and see'.

1.3 Figures of Rhetoric

Dialogismus

A feigned speech between two or more voices.

> The right reasoner (Puttenham).

> When questioning and answering, when a sentence is made or fashioned in conference, which consists in question and answer (J. Smith).

Whenever the violins ruminate with the voice as in 'If God be for us' (Ex. 2.2.6), or when any upper voices are set against the bass, a dialogue is heard. The bass line is never an accompaniment to a tune. It holds the harmonic keys to the music and wields its power over the upper regions.

In rhetoric, an orator may have a conversation with himself, or answer his own questions. If more than one voice or part is available, the possibilities are endless for argument or agreement, either between solo voice and instruments, between choral voices, or choir and instrumental groups. A certain attitude needs to be adopted to bring the argument to the attention of the hearer. The debating parts should provoke each other.

Ex. 1.3.11 'Hallelujah'

In the opening of the Hallelujah chorus the instruments should enter into competition with the voices in the half-bar exchanges. The instruments win with the high D, which should be emphasised, while the voices stay on the same pitch (see p. 81).

Exuscitatio

An emotional utterance that seeks to move the hearers.

> 'Behold the Lamb of God that taketh away the Sin of the World'.

> 'Surely He hath born our Griefs, and carried our Sorrows'.

> 'Behold, and see, if there be any Sorrow like unto His Sorrow!'

1.3 Figures of Rhetoric

Hyperbole

Extravagant terms used for emphasis, not intended literally. A self-conscious exaggeration often used to support religious belief (Adamson *et al.*, p. 206).

> 'Then shall the Eyes of the Blind be open'd, and the Ears of the Deaf unstopped; then shall the lame Man leap as a Hart, and the Tongue of the Dumb shall sing'.

> 'Ev'ry Valley shall be exalted, and ev'ry Mountain and Hill made low, the Crooked straight, and the rough Places plain'.

> 'Their Sound is gone out into all Lands, and their Words unto the ends of the World'.

> 'He shall reign for ever and ever'.

> Hyperbole is, moreover, a virtue when the subject on which we have to speak is abnormal. For we are allowed to amplify, when the magnitude of the facts passes all words, and in such circumstances our language will be more effective if it goes beyond the truth than if it falls short of it (Q, VIII vi 76).

> A trope 'exceedingly enlarged' (J. Smith).

> The loud lier, otherwise called the overreacher [...] This manner of speech is used, when either we would greatly advaunce or greatly abase the reputation of any thing or person, and must be used very discreetly, or els it will seeme odious, for although a prayse or other report may be allowed beyond credit, it may not be beyond all measure (Puttenham).

> It is a sentence or saying surmounting the truth only for the cause of increasing or diminishing, not with purpose to deceive by speaking untruly, but with desire to amplifie the greatnesse or smalnesse of things by the exceeding similitude [...] for amplification especially when matters require either to be amplified in the greatest degree, or diminished in the least: by this figure the Orator either lifteth up high or casteth down low, either stretcheth things to the uttermost length, or presseyth them to the least quantitie: so high is the reach, & so wide is the compass of this figure, that it mounteth to the highest things, compasseth the widest, and comprehendeth the greatest. The Caution: two things especially are here to be noted and avoided, the one, that this figure be not used to amplifie trifles, or diminish the estimation of good things, by the one it becometh a vice of speech called Bomphiliogia, by the other it is turned into Tapinosis (Peacham).

Hypotyposis

The vivid representation of images, as is found in the opening sequence of Part Two of *Messiah*.

> Representation: a figure when a whole matter is expressed so particularly and in order, that it seems to be represented unto ocular inspection [...] a representing of a thing unto the eye of the understanding, so that it may seem rather to be felt or enjoyed then spoken of and expressed (J. Smith).

This calls to mind Quintilian's description of *enargeia* which is to express something so vividly as to display the matter to the eyes of the mind (Q VI ii 29; Q VIII iii 62; Q IX i 45). Vivid description is also recognised under the heading of *ekphrasis*.

Indignatio, sarcasmus

Arousing the audience's scorn or derision.

> 'Let him deliver him, if he delight in him'.

> The bitter taunt (Puttenham).

This example uses several elements of repetition for vehement affect: alliteration using h, d and l, the three-fold repetition of the word 'him' and the repeated syllable de-.

Mempsis, commiseratio

Complaining against injuries and pleading for help.

> 'He looked for some to have Pity on him, but there was no Man, neither found he any to comfort him'.

>> This forme of speech as it riseth from the griefe which is suffered for injuries, so doth it tend by complaint and praier to seeke succour and redresse, by this form billes of complaint are exhibited to the Courts of judgement, and supplications to Princes'. This form of speech of all others is most common and oftenest abused, for what is more common then complaints, and what speech oftener used without just cause then complaining one of another. Therefore in using this figure regard ought to be had that the complaint be not a false accusation [...] much ado about nothing, a hue and crie and no robbery (Peacham).

Mycterismus, tapinosis

Mockery of an opponent accompanied by gesture. Undignified language that debases a person.

> 'They shoot out their Lips, and shake their Heads'.

> The Fleering frumpe (Puttenham).

>> A disdainful gibe, or scoffe, near a sarcasm. Luke 16. 14. Thus the Pharisees derided Christ, they did not simply contemn him, but they shewed their contempt of him by their gestures (J. Smith).

>> A privie kind of mocke, or manner of jesting, yet not so privie but that it may well be perceived [...] the chiefe use of this figure serveth to represse pride, rebuke folly, and taunt vice: and may be likened to a blacke frost, which is wont to nip a man by the nose, before he can discerne it with his eye. The Caution: this figure must not be too obscure and darke, for by that it may loose the virtue and use, if it be not perceived, and therefore it is not to be used to simple and ignorant persons, which do want the capacitie & subtlety of wit to perceive it. Neither must it be rude or rusticall, which is the utter disgrace of it (Peacham).

Oraculum

The quoting of God's words or commandments.

> 'The Lord gave the Word: great was the Company of the Preachers'.

> 'Comfort ye, my People'.

> 'Then shall be brought to pass the Saying that is written: Death is swallow'd up in Victory'.

Pathopoeia

Sounds or words which excite emotion.

>> Expression of the affection of the mind derived from [*pathos*] which signifies every more vehement affection, or an exceeding stirring up of the affections of the mind. A form of speech whereby the Speaker moves the mind of his hearers to some vehemency of affection, as of love, hatred, gladness, sorrow, &c. It is when the speaker himself (being inwardly moved with any of those deep and vehement affections), doth by evident demonstration, passionate pronunciation and suitable gestures make a lively expression thereof (J. Smith).

Part Two of *Messiah* is particularly *pathopoaeic*. In music, strong dissonances, jagged intervals, rising phrases or sharp rhythms arouse strong emotions.

1.3 Figures of Rhetoric

Periphrasis

The use of many words to express one.

> 'He that dwelleth in Heaven'.

>> Circumlocution, or a speaking of one word by many: a figure when we shadow out a thing by some equivalent expressions (J. Smith).

Prophecy

A declaration of something to come.

> 'The Trumpet shall sound, and the Dead shall be rais'd incorruptible, and we shall be changed'.

> 'And the Glory of the Lord shall be revealed'.

Prosopopeia

A type of *enargeia* (vividness or distinctness) which describes the appearance of a person, imaginary or real, real or dead. It attributes a human quality to dumb things.

> 'Lift up your heads, O ye Gates, and be ye lift up ye everlasting Doors'.

> 'Speak ye comfortably to Jerusalem' (Jerusalem impersonated).

> 'O Daughter of Zion, O Daughter of Jerusalem' (also uses *anaphora*).

>> The false impersonation (Puttenham).

>> The faining of a person, that is, when to a thing senselesse and dumbe we faine a fit person, or attribute a person to a commonwelth or multitude ... Sometime to Cities, townes, beastes, birdes, trees, stones, weapons, fire, water, lights of the firmament, and such like things be attributed speech. The Caution: it is necessarie to provide that the person fained may speake to the purpose of the matter propounded, and give strength to the fainting cause, and also minister a pleasure to the hearer: for otherwise this figure shall be used without cause, speake without profit, and be applied without pleasure (Peacham).

>> The feigning of a person to speak, or the attributing of a person to the inanimate creatures; as, when we bring in persons that are dead, or the inanimate creatures speaking, or hearing &c (J. Smith).

Quintilian quotes Cicero who considers that impersonation of a real person demands a greater effort in speaking. Quintilian writes that it is a device which lends wonderful variety and animation to oratory. He says that by this means we can display the thoughts of our adversaries as though they were talking with themselves or we may introduce conversations between ourselves and others and put words of advice into the mouths of appropriate persons (Q, IX ii 29, 30).

Anthypophora is a similar device where the orator converses with himself. A common tactic in music is to divide one part into a high and low voice.

> *Anthypophora* signifies a contrary illation or inference, and is when an objection is refuted or disproved by the opposition of a contrary sentence (J. Smith).

Ex. 1.3.12 'Thou shalt break them'

1.3 Figures of Rhetoric

Ex. 1.3.13 'O Death! Where is thy Sting?'

The argument between these two voices has been going on for some time. When it nears resolution (notice the emphasised AND on anticipated down-beats), a different, less provocative stance is needed for the cadence which brings agreement.

Topothesia

A description of an imaginary, nonexistent place, as opposed to *topographia* which describes a real place.

'The Land of the Shadow of Death'.

Figures of Construction

Amplificatio

Amplification is an enlargement of a statement.

> To Amplifye and Illustrate, are two the chiefest ornaments of eloquence; and gaine of mens myndes two [of] the chiefest advantages, admyracon & beliefe, for how can yow commend a thing more acceptably to or attencon, then by tellinge us it is extraordinary, and by shewing us that it is evident (Hoskyns, p. 131).

'Darkness shall cover the Earth, and gross Darkness the People'.

Ex. 1.3.14 'For behold, Darkness shall cover the Earth'

The darkness which covers the earth is amplified by using bigger and more varied intervals for the repeated 'gross Darkness'. This leads us to the remote bright chord of F♯ major, which guides us out of the darkness for the next phrase 'but the Lord shall arise'. The word 'gross' enlarges the concept of 'darkness' (see also Ex. 2.2.3).

1.3 Figures of Rhetoric

Augmentation is most impressive when it lends grandeur to comparative insignificance (Q, VIII iv 3). A process of 'piling up' figures towards a climax employs the accumulation of words and sentences (Q, VIII iv 26). Other devices which amplify include *hyperbole* (self-conscious exaggeration), *incrementum* or *auxesis* (words or phrases placed in climactic order), and comparison (using two things of differing qualities).

> Amplification is the highest distinction of eloquence, which can increase the importance of a subject and raise it to a higher level, but also diminish or disparage it (C, *De Oratore* III xxvi 104).

In music, amplification can be achieved by doubling note values (Ex. 1.3.15), or by repeating a phrase in a higher tessitura and extending it with additional notes (Exx. 2.1.4, 2.5.16)

Ex. 1.3.15 'Let all the Angels'

'Let all the Angels' is sung at two levels of note value, quavers and crotchets, both simultaneously and consecutively. The amplification leads to the affect of grandeur (see Burney's comments, p. 189).

Ex. 1.3.16 'All we, like Sheep'

'Ev'ry one to his own Way' is aggrandised by ironic declamation in crotchets on the same pitch against diminished scurrying quavers.

Ex. 1.3.17 'Since by Man came Death'

The first two phrases amplify the phrase 'Since by Man...' by rising repetition and the addition of chromaticism before the reasoned outcome 'By Man came also...'

Antithesis

Conjoining contrasting ideas. Derived from *anti* (against) and *thesis* (state or question). The *Messiah* text is built on the contrasts of darkness and light, death and eternal life, and the frailty of mankind against the power of God.

> 'Ev'ry Valley shall be exalted, and ev'ry Mountain and Hill made low, the Crooked straight, and the rough Places plain'.

> 'The Heav'ns and the Earth; the Sea and the dry Land'.

> 'The People that walked in Darkness have seen a great Light; And they that dwell in the Land of the Shadow of Death, upon them hath the Light shined'.

> 'For as in Adam all die, even so in Christ shall all be made alive'.

> *Antithesis* is a style built on contraries which gives our speech impressiveness and distinction (RH, IV xv 21).

> The illustration of a thing by its opposite, or the placing of contraries one against another, as spokes in a wheel (J. Smith).

1.3 Figures of Rhetoric

> A quarrelling figure … for so be al such persons as delight in taking the contrary part of whatsoever shal be spoken (Puttenham).

Peacham quotes Quintilian who called this figure *contentio*.

> It is a proper coupling together of contraries, and that either in words that be contraries, or in contrarie sentences. A most excellent ornament of eloquence, serving most aptly to amplification, it graceth and bewtifieth the oration with pleasant varietie, and giveth singular perspicuity and light by the opposition, it is so generall that it may serve to amplifie and garnish any grave and weightie cause. The Caution: it behoveth to moderate the number of comparisons, lest they growe too great a multitude, which betrayeth affectation, a fault which ought to bee shunned. Secondly, to provide that we impaire not the beautie and strength of this figure by opposing things differing, instead of contraries (Peacham).

In music, opposing ideas can occur consecutively or simultaneously, using the device of a theme and countersubject. One idea is used to highlight the other. Contrasting intervals can be used, or sudden changes of rhythm, key, or harmony in consonance and dissonance. Johann Forkel (1788, quoted in Bartel, p. 200) describes *antithesis* as a form of proof, and the use of contrasting elements as a way of impressing ideas on the memory.

Ex. 1.3.18 'But who may abide the day of His coming?'

Antithesis shown in the contrasting sections of 'But who may abide'.

1.3 Figures of Rhetoric

Ex. 1.3.19 'For unto us a Child is born'

In simultaneous *antithesis* the violins decorate in their own style against the pillars of sound from the chorus: 'Wonderful, Counsellor, The Mighty God, The Everlasting Father, The Prince of Peace.'

Anastrophe

An unusual arrangement of words or clauses for poetic effect.

'All we, like Sheep, have gone astray'.

'For now is Christ risen'.

Asyndeton

Literally unconnected, the omission of conjunctions between words. *Asyndeton* is the removal of conjunctions which change the affect if added (add 'ands' or 'alsos' to the examples below). Longinus describes the disconnected phrases which give a feeling of agitation which both checks the flow of speech and drives it on.

1.3 Figures of Rhetoric

> 'Arise, shine, for thy Light is come'.
>
> 'Thy God reigneth, Break forth into Joy, glad Tidings, thy God reigneth'.
>
> 'Wonderful, Counsellor, the Mighty God, The Everlasting Father, The Prince of Peace'.

Handel repeats this last phrase several times, once omitting 'the' in 'The Prince of Peace' making it even more of an *asyndeton*.

The *Rhetorica ad Herennium* says this figure has animation and great force but needs to be concise (RH, IV xxx). Puttenham calls it defective and 'loose language' because it lacks 'good band or coupling', that is connective elements.

Contrast the effect of saying 'Arise, shine' with 'Rise and shine'.

> Asyndeton keepeth the parts of speech together without the helpe of any conjunction [...] chiefly to avoid the tedious repeating of a conjunction, partly for the better sound of the speech, and partly for expedition and brevitie, and it serveth most aptly to utter things of like nature. [...] The greatest fault that may be committed in this figure is, when it uttereth contraries, as if one should say, pleasure, paine, peace warre, life death, it were very unapt in sense, and ill sounding in the eare (Peacham).
>
> Disjoynted, or without copulative [...] A figure when in a heap or pile of words, a conjunction copulative it [sic] not only for speed and vehemency, but for pathetical Emphasis sake left out. [...] *Veni, vidi, vici*. Here if the words were copulated with conjunctions, the quick vertue, vehemency and earnest affection of the speech would languish and decay (J. Smith).
>
> You will find that by smoothing the Roughness, and filling up the Breaks by such additions, which was before forcibly, surprisingly, irresistibly pathetical, will lose all its Energy and Spirit, will have all its Fire immediately extinguished. To bind the Limbs of Racers is to deprive them of active Motion and the Power of Stretching. In like manner the Pathetic, when embarrassed and entangled in the Bonds of Copulatives, cannot subsist without Difficulty. It is quite deprived of Liberty in its Race, and divested of that Impetuosity by which it strikes the very Instant it is discharged (Longinus, p. 43).

See *polysyndeton*, the opposite effect, where many conjunctions are used (p. 44).

Auxesis

A figure of amplification, the units of which should build towards a climax (Q, VIII iv 27).

> 'Yet once a little while, and I will shake the Heavens and the Earth; the Sea and the dry Land; And I will shake all Nations; and the Desire of all Nations shall come'.
>
> 'His name shall be called Wonderful, Counsellor, The Mighty God, The Everlasting Father, The Prince of Peace'.

> The advancer [...] to urge and enforce the matter we speake of, we go still mounting by degrees and encreasing our speech with wordes or with sentences of more waight one then another, and is a figure of great both efficacie and ornament (Puttenham).
>
> This figure is chiefly set forth by tropes of words, forasmuch as they paint out things by similitudes, and make them more evident by setting images before the eies. [...] The use hereof helpeth mightily to express a matter which requireth either great praise, or dispraise, and it is often-times in great and grievous complaints, signifying the greatnesse and excesse of suffering. The Caution [...] required in great causes, and not to amplifie everie small matter and foolish trifle, which is a vanity to be shunned, for that common custome to amplifie small things is more fit for a common lier, than meete for a grave and modest orator (Peacham).

1.3 Figures of Rhetoric

Susenbrotus, a sixteenth-century German schoolmaster wrote that *auxesis* occurs when something is advanced by step, not only to its highest degree, but at times in a way even beyond that (1566 trans. Brennan, p. 68).

Auxesis, also called *incrementum* or *gradatio*, lends itself easily to musical composition where successive (usually short) phrases can rise to a (longer) climax (see Exx. 1.3.19, 1.5.17, 2.1.8, 2.1.10, 2.2.25, 2.7.5).

> The *marching figure*, for after the first steppe all the rest proceede by double the space, and so in our speach one word proceedes double to the first that was spoken, and goeth as it were by strides or paces; it may as well be called the *clyming* figure, for *Clymax* is as much to say as a ladder (Puttenham).

The 'doubling of the space' (does he mean 'pace'?) is known in music as stretto, as the same music becomes compressed in time. *Auxesis* in music usually rises in pitch, conforming to the idea of a ladder.

Burmeister describes how all musical pieces are replete with the simple version of this ornament (pp. 173-4).

Ex. 1.3.20 'For unto us a Child is born'

The phrase 'and the Government shall be upon his Shoulder' rises in repeated steps encouraging a crescendo towards the top of the ladder by each voice in turn.

Isocolon, Compar, Parison

Phrases of approximately equal length and corresponding structure.

> 'Then shall the Eyes of the Blind be open'd, and the Ears of the Deaf unstopped. Then shall the lame Man leap as a Hart, and the Tongue of the Dumb shall sing'.

> 'His Yoke is easy
> His Burthen is light'.

> 'He was cut off out of the Land of the Living: for the Transgression of thy People was He stricken'.

> 'As in Adam all die, so in Christ shall all be made alive'.

> 'For this Corruptible must put on Incorruption, and this Mortal must put on Immortality'.

> 'O Death, where is thy Sting? O Grave, where is thy Victory?
> The Sting of Death is Sin, and the Strength of Sin is the Law'.

> 'Blessing and Honour, Glory and Pow'r'.

By removing the central connecting 'and', in the Biblical text 'Blessing, and honour, and glory, and power' this figure is changed by Jennens from a *polysyndeton* into an *isocolon*.

> The figure of even, because it goeth by clauses of egall quantitie, and not very long, but yet not so short as the cutted comma: and they geve good grace to a dittie (Puttenham).

> An even gate of sentences, answearing each other in measures interchangeably (Hoskyns, p. 151).

1.3 Figures of Rhetoric

The *Rhetorica ad Herennium* says we should not count the syllables for that would be childish (RH, IV xx). It is the general impression which makes the effect. The 'O Death' example contains two *isocolons* placed consecutively. The *isocolon* often uses figures of repetition to connect and make a relationship between the two parts. To set this text using two voices facilitates a doubling of the 2 x 2 elements which can interlink endlessly, first posing two questions, then making two firm answers.

Polysyndeton

The use of a conjunction between each pair of clauses.

> 'And the Government shall be upon his Shoulder; and His Name shall be called Wonderful, Counsellor, The Mighty God, The Everlasting Father, The Prince of Peace'.

> 'And lo …' (or 'But lo'!)
> 'And the Angel …'
> 'And suddenly …'

> 'To receive Power, and Riches, and Wisdom, and Strength, and Honour, and Glory, and Blessing'.

> We may call it the coople clause for that every clause is knitted and coupled together with a coniunctive (Puttenham).

> A figure which knitteth together the parts of an oration with many continuations, contrary to that above [asyndeton]. This figure hath the most speciall respect to knit many things of like nature together, and to distinguish and separate contrary matters asunder, and for this cause it may be called the chaine of speech, forasmuch as every chaine hath a conjunction of matter, and a distinction of links. [...] The caution: too long a continuance in adding conjunctions bringeth a deformitie to this figure, and therefore ought to be avoyded (Peacham).

> Diversity and many wayes joyned or coupled together […] a figure signifying superfluity of conjunctions, and it is when divers words are for their weightinesse, (and not without an Emphasis) knit together with many copulatives (J. Smith).

Word-Play – Patterns of Repetition

The human ear seeks patterns in sound, generating expectation which can then be surprised by a change. The ear stores what it has heard and uses this information to compare what has already been heard with the following sounds, either for confirmation of the same thought, or to notice a change. This variety holds the listener's attention.

> The frequent recourse to the same word is not dictated by verbal poetry; rather there inheres in the repetition an elegance which the ear can distinguish more easily than words can explain (RH, IV xiv 20).

> What pleasure can an orator hope to produce [...] unless he knows how to fix one point in the minds of the audience by repetition, and another by dwelling on it [...] It is qualities like this which give life and vigour to oratory; without them it lies torpid like a body lacking the breath to stir its limbs. But more than the mere possession of these qualities is required; they must be deployed, each in their proper place and with such variety that every sound may bewitch the hearer with all the charm of music (Q, IX ii 4, 5).

> Repetition can produce the effect of force or of grace. Cumulative repetitions make our utterances more vigorous and emphatic, and produce an effect of vehemence such as might spring from repeated outbursts of emotion (Q, IX i 33; IX iii 54).

The possibilities of word play using repetition are many and varied. Repetition can be exact, in which case it is usually for emphasis (the *epizeuxis*) or use small differences (in music, changes of interval or rhythm) to highlight various forms of the same thought. Peacham describes repetition in a general sense, *synonimia*, when 'by variation and change of words that be of like signification, we iterate one thing diverse times'. The ability to

1.3 Figures of Rhetoric

express the same thought in as many as two hundred different ways, the *copia* of Erasmus's school text *De Copia ac verborum*, formed the basis of the abundant rhetorical style taught in the classroom and used in everyday life. The 'garnishing' of speech, far from being criticised as over-elaborate, was encouraged and admired.

The repetition of longer passages in a slightly altered form also reinforces the idea. Apart from the obvious da capo aria, Handel finds other possibilities. In his revised version of 'He shall feed his Flock like a Shepherd' (first part of the text from Isaiah), he repeats the whole alto aria using the soprano voice, creating a surprising and refreshing moment as, instead of the alto voice staying on the same pitch level, the soprano takes over a fourth higher with the second part of the text from the gospel of St. Matthew: 'Come unto Him all ye that labour and are heavy laden', but set to the same music.

Adnominatio

Two words of different meaning but the same sound brought together. Alliteration is another use of similar sounds.

'King of Kings and Lord of Lords'.

'The Sting of Death is Sin and the Strength of Sin is the Law'.

Anadiplosis

The repetition of the last word in a line in the first clause of the next. The first example repeats several words from the previous list, creating a rich pile of words without a definite pattern:

'... to receive Power, and Riches, and Wisdom, and Strength and Honour and Glory and Blessing. Blessing and Honour, Glory and Pow'r, be unto Him'.

'How beautiful are the Feet of him that bringeth glad Tidings, Tidings of Salvation'.

> The redouble (Puttenham).

> This exornation [embellishment] doth not onely serve to the pleasantnesse of sound, but also to adde a certain increase in the second member. Of some this figure is called the Rhetoricall Eccho, for that it carrieth the resemblance of a rebounded voyce, or iterated sound. The Caution. In this figure we ought to take heede, that the word repeated be not put in the weaker clause, or without new matter, or vainly as in wanton songs (Peacham).

Mattheson considers that this figure, with other similar figures of repetition, might have been invented for musical use, being so naturally suited to musical composition (II.14.46).

Ex. 1.3.21 'But who may abide'

> The first violins finish the cadence and start again on the same note (A). This provides a link which offers an opportunity to change both the sound quality and attack. The cadence should be short and quite forthright, and the following up-beat gentle for the opening ritornello of 'But who may abide'.

1.3 Figures of Rhetoric

Anaphora

Literally, carrying back, using the repetition of the same word or words at the beginning of successive clauses or verses.

'That her Warfare is accomplish'd; that her Iniquity is pardon'd'.

'He was wounded for our Transgressions,
He was bruised for our Iniquities'.

'O thou that tellest good Tidings to Zion
O thou that tellest good Tidings to Jerusalem'.

'Then shall the Eyes of the Blind be open'd, and the Ears of the Deaf unstopped;
Then shall the lame Man leap as a Hart, and the Tongue of the Dumb shall sing'.

'Come unto Him all ye that labour,
Come unto Him all ye that are heavy laden'.

'Thou shalt break them with a Rod of Iron;
Thou shalt dash them in pieces like a Potter's Vessel'.

> Repetition in the first degree we call the figure of report. [...] and is when we make one word begin, and as they are wont to say, lead the daunce to many verses in sute (Puttenham).

> Relation, or a bringing of the same again; derived from [anaphero] refero, to bring again, or rehearse. It is the repetition of a word of importance and effectual signification: or, it is a figure when several clauses of a sentence are begun with the same word or sound (J. Smith).

Ex. 1.3.22 'His Yoke is easy, His Burthen is light'

Handel adds an emphatic 'AND' to emphasise the final statement of the text which finishes Part One.

Handel often creates an opportunity for repetition in setting the text. By repeating the beginning of a phrase he can hold the listener's attention until the whole phrase emerges. For example 'Glory to God, Glory to God in the Highest' and 'Thus saith the Lord of Hosts' which becomes 'Thus saith the Lord, the Lord of Hosts', thereby adding weight and emphasis to the title. The text can also be pruned and then filled out: 'Why do the

Nations rage, why do the Nations so furiously rage together?' In 'But Thanks' he multiplies the thanks: 'But Thanks, but Thanks, Thanks, Thanks be to God'. This is developed in all the voices creating a shower of thanks.

Burmeister describes *anaphora* as the repetition of similar pitch patterns in several but not all voices of the harmony, in the manner of a fugue, although not actually a fugue (p. 187). Kircher (1650 quoted in Bartel, p. 188) says it is a passage frequently repeated for the sake of emphasis. It is often used in vehement affections such as ferocity or scorn.

Antistasis

Opposition, counterplea. Repetition of a word in an opposite or contrary sense.

> 'Captivity captive'

> 'The Kingdom of this World is become the Kingdom of our Lord and of his Christ'.

> 'As in Adam all die, so in Christ shall all be made alive'.

Antonomasia

Use of an epithet instead of a proper name, which some rhetoricians liken to the figure *synecdoche*.

> 'Him that crieth in the Wilderness'

> 'The Lamb of God'

> 'The Lord of Hosts'

>> The surnamer (Puttenham).

>> It is a form of speech by which the orator for a proper name putteth another, as some name of dignity, office, profession, science or trade. [...] It helpeth much in praising or dispraising, by the equall comparison, it serveth readily for copie [richness of utterance] and varietie. The Caution. The faultes that may be committed in this figure are these, to give a lesse name then the dignitie requireth, as speaking to a king to say, Your worship [...] and to use any name which is unfit for the person to whom it is attributed (Peacham).

Antistrophe

Repetition of the closing word or words of consecutive clauses or sentences.

> 'But the Lord shall arise upon thee
> And his Glory shall be seen upon thee'.

>> The counterturne (Puttenham).

Commoratio

A figure which literally 'lingers', emphasising a strong point and repeating it several times.

> 'The Kingdom of this World is become the Kingdom of our Lord and of His Christ'.

>> The figure of aboade ... the perswader finding a substantial point in his matter to serve his purpose, should dwell upon that point longer than upon any other lesse assured, and use all endeavour to maintaine that one, and as it were to make his chief aboad thereupon (Puttenham).

>> A form of speech by which the orator knowing whereon the whole weight of his cause doth depend, maketh often recourse thither (Peacham).

Conduplicatio

Repetition of a word in succeeding clauses.

> 'If there be any Sorrow like unto his Sorrow!'

> 'Together against the Lord and against his Annointed'.

> 'Take his Yoke upon you' ... 'his Yoke is easy'.

1.3 Figures of Rhetoric

Diacope

Repetition of a word with one or a few words in between.

'If there be any Sorrow like unto his Sorrow!'

'Darkness shall cover the Earth, and gross Darkness the People'.

'King of Kings and Lord of Lords'.

'For ever and ever'.

> This figure may be used to express any affection, but it is most fit for a sharpe invective or exprobation. The repetition of a wanton or idle word is a vice to be shunned in this figure (Peacham).

Epizeuxis

Emphatic repetition of a word with no other words in between.

'Comfort ye, comfort ye my People'.

'Glad Tidings, Tidings of Salvation'.

> The cuckowspel. Ye iterate one word without any intermission (Puttenham).

> This figure serves to the Emphatical setting forth of the vehemency of the affections and passions of the mind (J. Smith).

> A figure whereby a word is repeated, for the greater vehemencie, and nothing put betweene: and it is used commonly with a swift pronunciation. [...] This figure may serve aptly to express the vehemencie of any affection, whether it be of joy, sorrow, love, hatred, admiration, or any such like, in respect of pleasant affections it may be compared to the quaver in Musicke, in respect of sorrow, to a double sigh of the heart, & in respect of anger, to a double stabbe with a weapons point. [...] Words of many syllables are unfit for this repetition, for if one should repeate abhomination, it would both sound ilfavouredly, and also be long a doing: for the difference is great betweene saying, O my sonne, my sonne, and O abhomination, abhomination, the one hath brevitie and beautie, the other prolixity and deformitie (Peacham).

Ex. 1.2.23 'But thanks'

In music, the *epizeuxis* is frequently used to extend the setting of a text. Handel uses it in the opening of the chorus 'But thanks be to God' by adding extra 'Thanks' for emphasis, with commas. The excessively polite effect of all these 'Thanks' could be exploited in performance, possibly with gesture, but certainly with facial expressions. Use the comma to bring out the figure.

Handel creates many examples of this figure wherever a word is repeated, for example, in the first voice 'O Death, O Death, where, where is thy Sting?' and in the second voice 'O Grave, O Grave, where, where is thy Victory?'

Ex. 1.3.24 'O Death, where is thy Sting?'

The duet 'O Death, where is thy Sting?' is an extended *epizeuxis* between two voices which is built around the double phrased *isocolonic* text (both phrases using similar numbers of syllables, see above p. 43). The voices chase each other round the four points: 'Death' and 'Sting', 'Grave' and 'Victory', before agreeing at cadences.

Ex. 1.3.25 'Since by Man came Death'

Another *epizeuxis* 'shall all, SHALL ALL be made alive'. The second 'shall all' is more emphatic because the quaver-crotchet rhythm is changed to two equal crotchets and, although some of the voices keep the same pitches on the equal crotchets, the violins repeat their arpeggio which rises to the highest point for the emphatic second 'shall all'. Again, the comma is useful in bringing out the figure.

1.3 Figures of Rhetoric

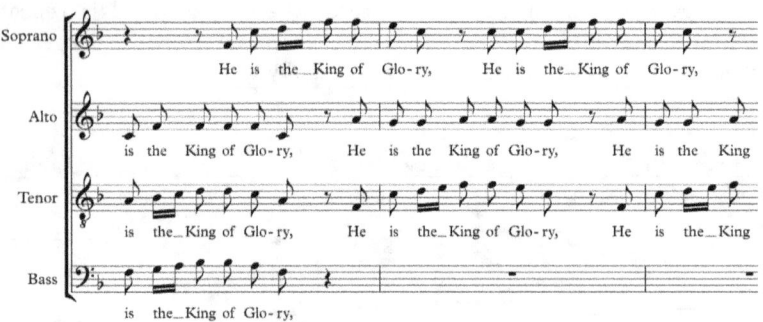

Ex. 1.3.26 'Lift up your Heads'

Static multiple repetitions of the same phrase on very similar pitches impress the idea upon the listener.

Homoeoprophoron (alliteration)

Recurrence of an initial consonant or sound.

'He was cut off out of the Land of the Living'.

'The rough Places plain'.

'The Prince of Peace'.

'Their Words unto the ends of the World'.

'The Sting of Death is Sin and the Strength of Sin is the Law'.

'He trusted in God that he would deliver him if he delight in him'.

Homoioteleuton

The use of similar endings to words, phrases or sentences.

'He was despised and rejected of Men.'

'Let Him deliver Him, if He delight in Him.'

'If God be for us, who can be against us?'

The *Rhetorica ad Herennium* describes the figure as using word endings which are similar although indeclinable: 'You dare to act dishonourably, you strive to talk despicably; you live hatefully, you sin zealously, you speak offensively'. 'Blusteringly you threaten; cringingly you appease' (RH, IV xx).

Omission

Almost *anaphora*, but a word is omitted on repetition.

'For unto us a Child is born, unto us a Son is given'.

'Since by Man came Death, by Man came also the Resurrection of the Dead'.

Also used to assume an omitted word or syllable: oft (often), turtle (dove), massy (massive), grot(to).

Syncope

Omission of letters or syllables from the middle of a word: 'Heav'ns', 'ev'ry'.

Paronomasia

Using words which resemble one another.

'Comfort ye [...] speak ye comfortably'

The nicknamer ... ye play with a couple of words (Puttenham).

A figure which declineth into a contrarie by a likelihood of letters, either added, changed, or taken away. [...] This figure ought to be sparingly used and especially in grave and weightie causes, both in respect of the light and illuding forme, and also forasmuch as it seemeth not to be found without meditation and affected labour (Peacham).

Likeness of words: derived from [*para*] which in composition, signifies amiss, or with some alteration and [*onoma*] *nomen*, a name. A figure when by the change of one letter, or syllable of a word, the signification thereof is also changed (J. Smith).

Ploce

An emphatic repetition.

'King of Kings and Lord of Lords'.

The doubler, otherwise called the swift repeat (Puttenham).

A forme of speech by which a proper name being repeated signifieth another thing. [...] It containeth in it also a repetition pleasant for the brevitie [...] and likewise for the Emphaticall signification in the repeated name (Peacham).

A binding together, or a continuation without interruption: a figure when a word by way of emphasis is so repeated, that it denotes not only the thing signified, but the quality of the thing. Hereby the proper name of any man well known, being repeated, signifies the nature and permanent quality of the man, whose name it is (J. Smith).

Polyptonon

Repetition of the same words with different endings and beginnings.

'Captivity Captive'.

'King of Kings and Lord of Lords'.

'Since by Man came Death, by Man came also the Resurrection of the Dead'.

'For this Corruptible must put on Incorruption, and this Mortal must put on Immortality'.

A variation of cases, or a change of the termination [similar to *paronomasia* above]. A figure when several cases of the same noune, and tenses of the same verb, are used in conjoyned clauses (J. Smith).

Questions and exclamations are also figures of speech and their importance has gained them a separate chapter which follows.

1.4 Exclamations and Questions
or 'Behold', 'How' and 'What'

> Through the figure, reasoning by question and answer, we ask ourselves the reason for every statement we make, and seek the meaning of every affirmation [...] This figure is exceedingly adapted to the conversational style, and both by its stylistic grace and the anticipation of the reasons, holds the hearer's attention (RH, IV xvi 23).

The text of *Messiah* is rich in exclamations, questions, and exclamations in the form of questions. Key words for indicating exclamations include 'O', 'How', 'What', and in the specific case of *Messiah* also 'Surely', 'Behold', 'Let' and, most famously, 'Hallelujah!'

Exclamations

The exclamation is, according to many rhetoric books, to be reserved for 'vehement' affections. The exclamation is defined as a strong statement expressing a particular emotion, and should be delivered with the appropriate spirit. The emotion could be anger, joy, frustration, surprise, or celebration. Peacham gives twenty-four different types, which include questions used as exclamations. The rhetorical exclamation can easily be translated into music, and Handel treats his exclamations with a variety as diverse as the sentiments expressed by the text. The Latin figure *exclamatio*, in Greek *ecphonis*, is easily identified and is described by all the major theorists. Quintilian distinguishes between the spontaneous type and the artful, calculated type. The exclamation is a recognised figure of musical rhetoric and appears in various forms in the musical theory books (by Mattheson, 1739 and Scheibe, 1730). The figure carries the emotion; it is not the emotion itself; and so we find exclamations expressing a wide range of 'passions' including joy, sorrow, vengeance, fear, despair and defiance.

Michael Praetorius thinks that the exclamation should always use a raised voice in order to move the affections (*Syntagma Musica* III, 1619, p. 231 quoted in Bartel, p. 267) and Walther considers that because it is agitated it should use an upward leaping minor sixth (*Musicalisches Lexicon*, Leipzig, 1732, quoted in Bartel, p. 268). Peacham's extensive list includes more gentle exclamations such as 'marvelling' which surely should be delivered *sotto voce*. His examples of biblical exclamations include:

- Of love: O how amiable are thy tabernacles thou Lord of hosts? (Psalm 84)
- Of sorrow: Alas my daughter, thou hast brought me low (Jephtha)
- Of anger: O cursed tyrannie, O most detestable cruelty (no source)
- Of joy: O Death where is thy sting? (I Corinthians 15)
- Of feare: O thou man of God, flee such things (I Tim. 6)

The last example (Paul to Timothy) is dissected by Peacham to show how many affections may be contained in one thought: love, fear, hatred and care (pp. 62-3).

The vehemency of the voice should express 'the greatness of our affections and passions', and thereby 'move the like affections in our hearers'. The 'Caution': this figure should not be used without a great cause 'for it is a manifestation of follie to use an exclamation upon small occasions, and for light causes'. Secondly, 'that it be not often used lest it becomes odious'; and thirdly, 'that it be not applied unaptly in the partes of a treatise or public oration: it were ridiculous to begin a publicke speech with this figure, crying O, or Alasse: it might sooner move laughter than lamentation' (Peacham, p. 63). This last point

1.4 Exclamations and Questions

might apply to public speeches, but musical forms often open with an exclamation, for example 'Kyrie eleison'.

In contrast to Peacham's extensive list for using in speech, Mattheson divides exclamations into only three categories for musical use:

- Astonishment, such as a joyous shout or an encouraging command. He says this should be ruled by the affection of joy using lively brisk music and large, leaping intervals.

- Secondly, the outburst which expresses longing, desire, beseeching which can also be frightening or fearful. He says this should use uncommon intervals and tenderness.

- The third type is the scream resulting from dismay or astonishment because of atrocious events. The dominant affection is desperation represented by unruly intervals, and a raging turmoil of fiddling and piping (II 9.65-67).

The first true exclamation we encounter in *Messiah* is one of many exclamatory 'Beholds': 'Behold, a Virgin shall conceive', not just a story-line but an exclamation of wonder or 'marvelling' (*thaumasmus*) set in a simple *secco* recitative, which is both the first entrance of the soprano voice and the opening of a new narrative scene. Far from being vehement, it is none the less a powerful moment of wonder at a miracle. Mystery and wonder should be conveyed in the voice, and the continuo should not be too forthright, but explore the chords gently.

The word 'Behold' next appears as a command in 'O! thou that tellest', the command being to 'Behold your God' and 'Behold, the Glory of the Lord is risen upon thee'. These multiple uses of the word 'Behold' illustrate the varied emotions which may be provoked in the listener by a single word.

The next exclamation is another 'Behold' and occurs at the opening of Part Two with 'Behold the Lamb of God', a command to observe the Son of God performing the miracle of taking away sin. It is set in a declamatory dotted overture style, which Mattheson says is unsuitable for voices. The instrumental dotted style which opens the scene later dissolves into a style more compatible with voices when the exclamation moves into the text 'that taketh away'.

Another exclamation follows in 'Surely' (meaning certainly), 'he hath borne our Griefs and carried our Sorrows' following the aria 'He was despised'. The first word is reiterated by the whole chorus together in an *epizeuxis*, for extra emphasis, and never breaks into parts, which would weaken its power to affirm. 'Surely' is set on a dotted three-note rhythm, implying that every syllable should be pronounced, each on a different pitch, to the occasional incredulity of the modern performer who has 'surely' been tempted to suppress the middle syllable out of timidity. Perhaps this is a case of Handel's Germanic style of word-setting, but it is none the less powerful for being that. In rhetoric, there is always the possibility that a particular word or syllable may be emphasised for effect: *diastole* is a figure where a syllable that is usually short is made longer or more emphatic, and *epenthesis* is the addition of a letter, sound or syllable to the middle of a word. If you want a label for this example, take your pick.

The next exclamation: 'Behold, and see, if there be any Sorrow like unto his Sorrow!' comes after the desolation of 'but there was no Man, neither found He any to comfort Him' (Ex. 2.6.7). An appeal to pity of the most vehement order, with the initial rising fifth for the appeal moving in the next bar to a rising minor sixth, repeated later in the re-iteration of the text transposed one step higher. The word 'Sorrow' is like a sob, set by two short notes followed by a rest, a gasp (Ex. 2.1.5).

A completely different exclamation is found in the aria 'How beautiful are the Feet of them that preach the Gospel of Peace'. The exclamation 'How beautiful?' implies the

1.4 Exclamations and Questions

answer: 'very beautiful'. Again, a sense of wonder and Peacham's 'marvelling' should give this aria a mysterious but reassuring atmosphere.

Handel's best known exclamation, 'Hallelujah!' rounds off Part Two of *Messiah* in a triumphant climax, following the equally but differently vehement breaking of the potter's vessel. The Hallelujah shout is passed back and forth from chorus to orchestra in an exultant exclamation. Again, as in 'Surely', the key exclamation word is sung homophonically by all voices in the same rhythm, before being used a foil for the next contrapuntal section of the text 'for the Lord God omnipotent reigneth'.

Questions

> There is the practice of putting the question and answering it oneself, which may have quite a pleasing effect (Q, IX ii 14).

Jennens' choice of text uses questions both to provoke and to exclaim. In *Messiah* we find many questions which demand answers from the listener, who usually assumes the character of the believer. In speech, a question rises to provoke a falling answer, an easy device to transfer to music. An imperfect cadence can provoke a musical response which answers by returning to the starting point. Silences and pauses can also provoke answers. The rhetoric books give various ways of using questions, and all of the following are employed in various ways by the text of *Messiah*:

- *Pysma* (asking many questions that require diverse answers)
- *Hypophora* (asking questions and immediately answering them)
- *Erotesis* (a 'rhetorical' question that does not require an answer)
- *Subjectio* (the questioner suggests the answer to his own question)
- *Erotema* (using a question to affirm or deny something strongly)

Our first question is a doubling up:

> 'But who may abide the Day of His coming? And who shall stand when He appeareth?'

Handel's gentle musical setting belies the strength of the questions, and the last few words of each question are reiterated not only by the singer but (wordlessly) by the strings who should 'play' the words:

> 'But who may abide the day of his coming (strings imitate 'the day of his coming'), the day of his coming, But who may abide the day of his coming (strings repeat 'the day of his coming'), the day of his coming?'
>
> And who shall stand when he appeareth, when he appeareth (strings repeat 'when he appeareth') when he appeareth, and who shall stand when he appeareth?'

The beginning of the question is then repeated for variety and the double question is now, finally presented complete:

> 'But who may abide, but who may abide the day of his coming, but who may abide the day of his coming, and who shall stand when he appeareth, and WHO SHALL STAND (emphasised in longer equal notes) when he appeareth?'

The next part of the text (marked Prestissimo) borrows the question from the pastoral first part (Larghetto) and incorporates it into the fiery music:

> For he is like a refiner's fire.
> ['and' is omitted here] Who shall stand when he appeareth?
> For he is like a refiner's fire. For he is like a refiner's fire.
> And who shall stand when he appeareth?

The result is that the same question is set with contrasting music which alternates between the gentle larghetto and the fierce prestissimo, with a demanding *aposiopesis* before the return of the pastoral mood (Ex. 2.6.2).

Puttenham describes *erotesis* as 'when we aske many questions and looke for none answere, speaking indeed by interrogation, which we might as well say by affirmation', a sort of persuasion by inquiry. The music portrays calm reassurance, or as Puttenham describes it, affirmation. John Smith says that *erotesis* is an interrogation or questioning which demands a strong affirmative or vehement denying. He describes this interrogation as forbidding, challenging the expected answer. In answer to the question 'who?' the assumed answer is '*everyone* [of the faithful chosen] is waiting for His coming, *everyone* [of the faithful chosen] shall stand when He appeareth'.

Peacham describes *erotema* as 'a forme of speech by which the orator doth affirm or deny something strongly'. He says 'this figure giveth to speech not onely life and motion, but also great strength and a coragious countenance, which is much commended in the supporting of good causes, and also very necessary to countenance truth and verity: and it may aptly be compared to the point or edge of a weapon, wherewith the Champion defendeth himself, and wounded his enemie'. Handel uses a very subtle weapon in a good cause.

More questions appear in Part Two, used to reinforce the coming of the King of Glory:

'Lift up your heads, O ye Gates, and be ye lift up, ye everlasting doors, and the King of Glory shall come in. Who is this King of Glory?'

The high voices of the semi-chorus questioners appear not to know who 'this' King is, thus creating an opening for an answer from the low authoritative voices of the others: 'The Lord strong and Mighty; the Lord Mighty in battle' and after the question is repeated, we hear a different answer: 'The Lord of Hosts: He is the King of Glory', and we realise it is the same Lord, strong and mighty in battle as well as being the King of Glory. Smith describes a person who speaks to himself and answers the questions as *dialogismus* 'as if talking to another, doth move the question, and make the answer'. One problem with Handel's setting in this case is that he always sets the word 'He' on a weak part of the beat, without ever emphasising it, as he logically should have done: If read aloud, the answer to the question 'Who is the King of Glory?' would be 'HE is the king of Glory', not 'he IS the king of glory' which only makes sense without the question. A solution to this awkwardness might be to emphasise HE and IS, both positioned on short notes of equal value.

This chorus is followed by another, rather weak and enigmatic question set in a short recitative which rises at the end: 'Unto which of the Angels said He at any time, Thou art my Son, this Day have I begotten thee?' *Aporia* is another form of questioning where the orator deliberates about an issue with himself, in this case concerning the comparative roles of the angels and Christ made flesh.

The next questions are arranged in another pair and are truly vehement demands:

'Why do the Nations so furiously rage together? And why do the People imagine a vain Thing?'

Peacham describes the questioning figure, *pysma*, whereby 'the orator doth demand many times together, and use many questions in one place, whereby he maketh his speech very sharp and vehement'. He says the figure 'serveth fitly for pitiful complaints, provocations, insultations, confirmations, and such like … it is mighty to confirme, to confute, to provoke, to cause attention, to move affections, and it is well and aptly represented in the conflict of battaile, as in the manifold strokes of the sword, thicke volies of arrows, and in the thundering peales of cannon shot'. He describes the very act of the repeated question as like making an attack on the listener: *Why* do the nations rage? *Why* do the people imagine?

1.4 Exclamations and Questions

Peacham's examples of the figure *ecphonis* (exclamation) include this exclamation of joy or gladnesse: 'O Death where is thy Sting? O Grave where is thy Victorie?' This might seem contradictory if we think only of word-painting, but, as always, it is the emotion behind the thought which gives us our joy: death holds no terrors because God gives us victory.

Our final question, set in a long and moving aria, could be considered the peroration of *Messiah*, preparing us for the culmination in 'Worthy is the Lamb'. Using reasoning described in the figure *hypophora*, where questions are asked and immediately answered, the text challenges us to answer the questions:

> 'If God be for us, who can be against us? Who shall lay anything to the charge of God's Elect? It is God that justifieth; Who is he that condemneth? It is Christ that died, yea, rather that is risen again; who is at the Right Hand of God, who maketh intercession for us.'

Hoskins (1599) describes the figure *paronomasia* as 'a pleasant touch of the same letter, Sillable, or word, with a different meaning'. The word 'who' is used here repeatedly in two senses: first as a question, and then to relate the question to Christ's presence in heaven and his 'intercession for us'. All our questions are unequivocally answered, any doubts finally laid to rest.

1.4 Exclamations and Questions

1.5 Word Painting
or Valleys, Wings and Worms

The text leads the way to the invention of the music. Certain images will offer obvious solutions (hills, valleys, arise, angel's wings fluttering). Other ideas or concepts are more abstract (darkness, light, iniquity, glory). Representations of objects, movement or people in sound would be impossible without an additional emotional context, and this is what music is able to express. Is darkness terrifying, or just shady? Does water rush in a torrent or meander gently? Emotions can be represented without concrete images, so in general rising music is hopeful and descending music represents sadness or despair. Harmony can be warm when full, harsh if dissonant, or calm and soothing. In contrast a unison, where all parts play the same lines without harmony, is lonely and cold; similarly a chord without a third in it. Rhythmic motifs can energise with rising dotted rhythms in arpeggios, or calm with equal ones descending in smooth intervals. Notes sound confident if the intervals between them are large, consonant and spaced out. Wavering close intervals sound vague and hesitant. Any unusual chromatic movement will be disturbing and provoke strong emotions.

Certain natural ideas such as the bass representing the earth (as in Purcell's ground bass 'laid in earth'), going up to heaven or down to hell were commonplaces, but when used excessively were thought by some to be childish. A palette of colours and textures provides an infinite variety of tools: tessitura, harmony, choice of voice or orchestral texture, any of which can be combined with a variety of rhythmic choices, all governed by tempo. Johann Mattheson described the possible effects as being like the bottomless sea, in other words infinitely variable, only limited by the imagination of the composer, and not to be used like a lexicon (I 3.83). Certain combinations of rhythms or intervals were used in a natural way to express various emotions. The German composer and theorist Johann Philipp Kirnberger (1721-1783) provided a table of intervals and their affects which could be used as a guide to expressing emotion, pointing out the difference between small and large intervals and their direction, up or down (pp. 103-4).

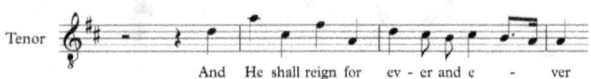

Ex. 1.5.1 'Hallelujah'

The large, striding, consonant intervals express glory, power and confidence in the future. This theme may be derived from the well-known hymn tune *Wachet auf, ruft uns die Stimme*, which uses descending fourths instead of the major sixths (Larsen, p. 170). Kirnberger describes descending major sixths as being a bit terrifying.

1.5 Word Painting

Ex. 1.5.2 'Ev'ry Valley'

Some literal word painting. The strings make giant detached steps for 'Mountain and Hill' then, in an *antithesis*, **the voice illustrates 'made low'. The violins introduce the closely oscillating 'crooked' which is then made 'straight' on a plain note.**

Another obvious device is to illustrate the person or persons speaking (angels or preachers). All these elements make up a natural, unforced, vivid method of expression in sound, easily understood by the listener on first hearing. The performer can exercise decorum by enhancing the written effect, matching the delivery to the musical ideas. In Handel's music there are no hidden theological messages or obscure number symbolism as in the music of Bach. Handel's music is open and transparent, instantly accessible to audiences then and now, and this immediacy must play an important part in his immense and lasting popularity.

Earth and Heaven

Ex. 1.5.3 'I know that my Redeemer liveth'

Downward movement and low notes represent worms and earth. The worms wiggle stubbornly for five bars in E major over an intermittent rising bass line, but the harmony takes a more hopeful turn with the word 'yet' which leads us via the D♮ into optimistic A major with a continuous bass-line replacing the hesitant intermittent one, to the comfort of the cadence for 'shall I see God'. Later, the same rhythm lulls us to sleep (Ex. 2.5.11).

1.5 Word Painting

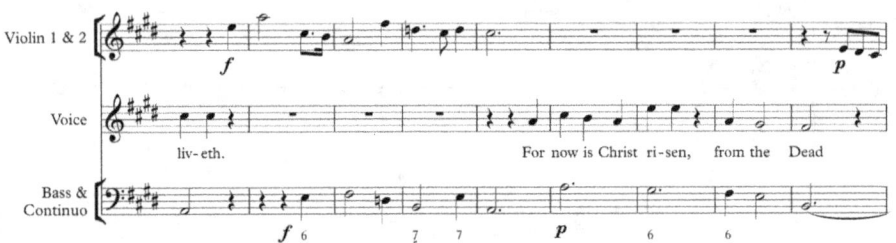

Ex.1.5.4 'I know that my Redeemer liveth'

'Risen' goes up to heaven. 'Dead' falls away downwards.

Ex. 1.5.5 'Hallelujah'

'The Kingdom of this World' is relatively low in tessitura, and falls down further as trumpets and timpani drop out, returning for 'the Kingdom of our Lord' which is sung and played in the higher registers.

Ex. 1.5.6 'Why do the Nations'

'The Kings of the Earth' really do 'rise up' in the violins (see p. 84).

1.5 Word Painting

Ex. 1.5.7 'Thou art gone up on high'

The voice goes 'up on high' and in Ex. 1.5.8 the dead are 'raised'.

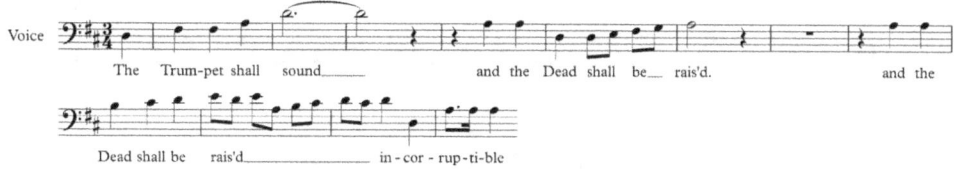

Ex. 1.5.8 'The Trumpet shall sound'

Ex. 1.5.9 'O thou that tellest'

Naturally, 'Arise' and 'lift up' do just that. 'Voice' is more positive than 'lift up' because it is higher, and because of the harmonic shift upwards in the bass.

Ex. 1.5.10 'O thou that tellest'

The second 'arise' is higher, so could be a little louder than the first.

Ex. 1.5.11 'And lo'

The angel's gently fluttering wings lack the earthly bass register. Upper strings accompany the voice (high cellos double the violas), and this feature continues through 'and suddenly', still in heaven for the start of the next chorus, 'Glory to God' (Ex. 1.3.9).

1.5 Word Painting

Ex. 1.5.12 'And suddenly'

The mood should be excited 'suddenly' by the bright, shimmering semiquavers, now Allegro and therefore faster than the Andante tempo instruction for the angel's wings.

Ex. 1.5.13 'Glory to God'

At the end of chorus 'Glory to God', the instruments rise to heaven (the bass again doubles the violas). The dynamic is piano and silences appear, contributing to the *pp* disappearing affect illustrating 'God in the highest'. We have been on earth and are now returning to the *lontano* heaven.

Ex. 1.5.14 'Thus saith the Lord of Hosts'

'I will shake the Heav'ns and the Earth, the Sea and the dry Land'. Words illustrated are: shake, Heav'ns (high), Earth (low).

'Highest' heaven and low peace on earth are illustrated in the chorus 'Glory to God' (see Exx. 1.3.9, 1.3.10).

Crowds

Ex. 1.5.15 'The Lord gave the Word'

The text 'Company of the Preachers' asks for a crowd singing together.

1.5 Word Painting

Ex. 1.5.16 'Lift up your Heads'

'The Lord of Hosts' rises with each repetition using call and response (one voice calls and the rest of the 'Hosts' answer) in a rhetorical *auxesis*, leading to the culmination 'He is the King of Glory' which is set in syllabic music against longer note values for richness of affect.

Ex. 1.5.17 'Let all the Angels'

In 'Let all the angels', simultaneous slow and fast versions multiply the idea of 'all' the angels.

The Pastoral

Running through the whole of *Messiah* is the pastoral theme: lamb, sheep, shepherds, flock. The Pifa theme, derived from Italian traditional music, opens the nativity story and conjures up the aural image of shepherds on a hillside. The piffaro is a small shawm which was used by peasants in Italy, often accompanied by bagpipes which are represented by the droning bass. During Handel's stay in Rome (1706-10) it is most likely that he would have heard some of the nativity cantatas performed at feasts customarily held on Christmas Eve for the pope, cardinals and any important visitors. The general topic was often the shepherds' discovery of the baby Jesus and their joy at his birth. Sometimes the character of Mary or an angel was included.

Ex. 1.5.18 Pifa

Handel's interlude recreates the effect of a rustic drone over which is played a tune in lilting compound time derived from the Italian hills. The extra part for the third violins doubles the first violin to create two parallel octave melodies moving in thirds (violin two/viola and violins one/three). This rich effect should be light, joyful and lively, not heavy and dirge-like. The written-out ornament (fourth beat of bar two) should not be too snapped or violent.

1.5 Word Painting

Ex. 1.5.19 'He shall feed His Flock'

The pastoral effect is used next in 'He shall feed his Flock like a Shepherd'. Again, Handel uses the compound time signature and intermittent drones.

Burney judges this movement which 'has ever been in great favour with performers and hearers' to be in Handel's 'best *Siciliana* style'. He compares it to the 'lulling pastoral at the end of Corelli's Eighth Concerto, *'Fatto per la notte di natale'* ('Commemoration of Handel', p. 78).

The chorus opening Part Two starts with the dramatic 'Behold the Lamb of God', composed in the style of a French overture as the Lamb of God is to be sacrificed for the sins of the world. Handel refrains from a trite pastoral musical reference, saving the drone for comic effect to illustrate 'All we, like Sheep' where the opening motif in the bass can be persistently emphasised on every beat.

Ex. 1.5.20 'All we, like Sheep'

The perky quaver rhythm in the bass at the opening could be slurred in pairs from the second beat for extra monotonous comic effect.

1.5 Word Painting

Luc. II: 16.
Ποιμένες εὑρίσκουσι τὸν Ἰησοῦν κείμενον ἐν τῇ φάτνῃ. | PASTORES INVENIUNT JESUM INFANTEM.
The Shepherds find the Child Jesus lying in a manger. | Les Bergers trouvent Jesus couché dans la créche.
Die Hirten finden Jesus in der Krippe. | De Herders vinden het Kindeken in de Kribbe.

1.5 Word Painting

Ex. 1.5.21 'All we, like Sheep'

The sheep are also found wandering. They have 'gone astray' and have 'turned' ev'ry one to his own Way'. They go astray and disappear in contrary motion.

Ex. 1.5.22 'All we, like Sheep'

The vacillating sheep are illustrated in a rhetorical *antimetabole* on the word 'turning' which keeps going back on itself for no purpose.

The final pastoral reference in the text occurs in the final chorus 'Worthy is the Lamb that was slain' but again, Handel refrains from word-painting 'Lamb' or 'slain', preferring to illustrate the grandeur of the text. Some performances attempt to word-paint in sound by the over-emphasis or the unsuitably heavy and detached 'that – was – slain'. It is the nobility of the worthiness we need here. The imagery of slaying is in the past and has already been fully illustrated in Part Two.

Fire

Ex. 1.5.23 'But who may abide?'

The 'Refiner's Fire' is illustrated by sudden stabs of flares or sparks.

Darkness and Light

A true rhetorical trope, depicting darkness and light in musical terms offers various possibilities. Tessitura, dynamic and harmony or lack of it are used to depict both effects.

Ex. 1.5.24 'For behold'

In the opening of the 'Darkness' passage, the assumed dynamic is piano, but this is not specified until the voice enters. Close intervals in contrary motion from the pivot key note B portray uncertainty and hesitancy in a murmuring pattern, staying low until the text 'but the Lord shall arise' allows the music to ascend and open out in a sunrise effect. The strings should avoid an accent on every pair, but feel four, or even two, large beats in a bar.

1.5 Word Painting

Burney describes this music as 'a very curious expression of the words [...] where the chromatic and indeterminate modulation, seems to delineate the uncertain footsteps of persons exploring their way in obscurity' ('Commemoration of Handel', p. 75).

Handel's powers of invention are exercised in various ways to represent darkness. Avoiding a single solution he tailors the effects to the particular situation. The depiction of darkness here is very different from that found in *Israel in Egypt* where the chorus of the children of Israel wander in 'thick darkness'. There he uses dissonant, pulsating harmonies. The 'Darkness deep' in *Theodora* is expressed in yet another way: the shades of night are depicted by heavy steps and silence.

Ex. 1.5.25 'For behold'

The movement ends with 'the Brightness of thy Rising' leading to the very bright chord of F♯ major. If using unequal temperament, the keyboard player should be persuaded to omit the A♯ so that the second violins can tune their third sweetly.

Ex. 1.5.26 'The People that walked in Darkness'

The following aria starts in stark unison 'T.S.' i.e. tasto solo, meaning that the basso continuo should be unharmonised. The dynamic is naturally piano. The cold, lonely feeling lasts until the people 'have seen a great Light' where the harmony returns. The whole movement retains the wandering, lost atmosphere. The people are feeling their desolate way in the darkness.

Ex. 1.5.27 'The People that walked in Darkness'

'Death' arrives with a disturbing lurch onto a low pedal in a Phrygian progression, with chromatic movement over.

1.5 Word Painting

Concord and Discord

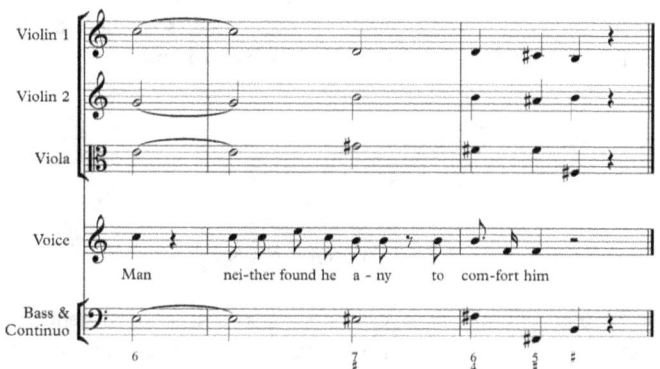

Ex. 1.5.28 'Thy Rebuke'

The end of 'thy Rebuke' ends in the major 'to comfort him'.

Ex. 1.5.29 'Behold the Lamb of God'

The ending of the first chorus of Part Two ends with an 'empty' chord with no warm third in it, representing the desolate 'Sin of the World'.

Soothing

Ex. 1.5.30 'Comfort ye'

'Comfort ye' is accompanied by a pulsing rich harmony in the bright, hopeful, optimistic key of E major, a foil to the dark E minor which ends the overture.

The slurs with dots under imply groups of smooth pulsed notes using bow vibrato, not to be separated or accented. The middle of the bar is arguably stronger than the first

1.5 Word Painting

beat as it is a long note. The bass imitates but has a short note and a rest. The first syllable of the voice interrupts the arrival note of the cadence with a good consonant, and should enter promptly. This number is too often dragged out by a self-serving soloist, but as it is the first vocal event of the work, shouldn't be too slow (see description of the Exordium p. 11). There's a long way to go.

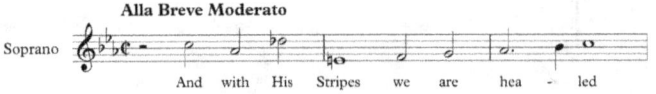

Ex. 1.5.31 'And with His Stripes'

'And with His Stripes' offers an image of healing rather than violence, using smooth rising and falling scales. The opening jagged intervals do suggest past wounds, but could be viewed as conciliatory rather than presently painful. Making too much contrast between the 'stripes' and the smooth healing could result in an exaggerated parody.

Anger

The vehement emotions of anger and conflict are expressed with violent strokes, loud repeated notes, and violent dotted rhythms. Monteverdi claims to have invented the idea of using the Pyrric measure to represent anger (*Madrigali guerrieri et amorosi*. Venice, 1638).

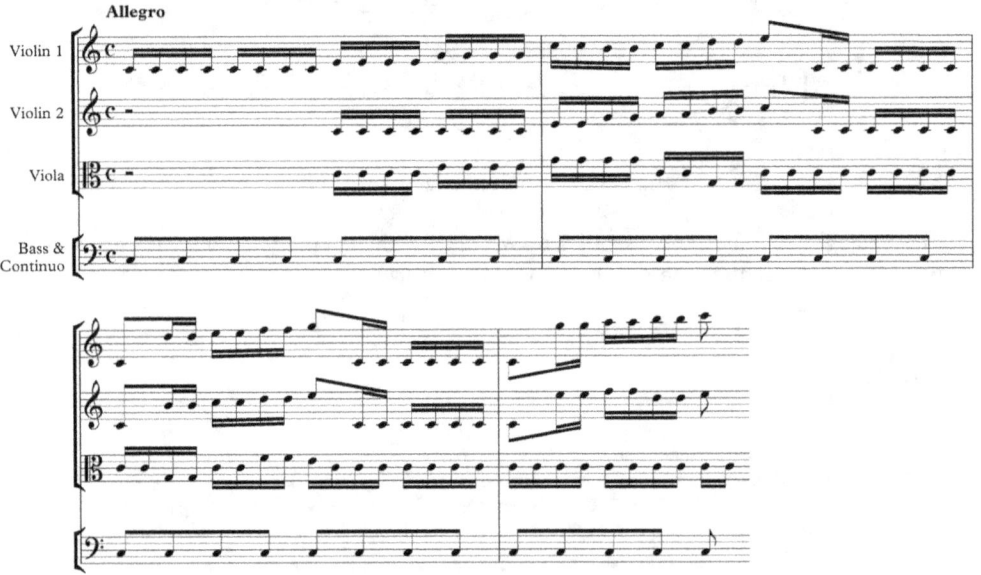

Ex. 1.5.32 'Why do the Nations?'

The upper strings make upward thrusts, returning each time to the unison. Random lengths of phrase, unisons and harmonised passages show the chaos of the raging.

1.5 Word Painting

Ex. 1.5.33 'Why do the Nations?'

The voice rages in triplets against the persistent D semiquavers to convince us further.

Ex. 1.5.34 'All they that see Him'

'Laugh him to scorn' is represented by shrieking violins, lashing dotted notes, lurching pairs of slurred notes and staccato pulses in the bass. 'They shoot out their Lips and shake their Heads' is illustrated by pairs of crude undulating semiquavers in the strings leading to a harsh diminished seventh chord (G♭ in the first violin part) which should be sustained onto the first beat of the next bar to achieve a rhythmic (silent) first beat.

1.5 Word Painting

Here every pair of semiquavers should be accented to enhance the violent lashing effect. The pairs lead to the long held note on 'Saying', then finish with a sharply dotted cadence which shouldn't be underplayed.

Ex. 1.5.35 'Thou shalt break Them'

The two-voiced violin writing with all the violins in unison is a high forceful complaint, doubled in its punctuated lower voice by the bass line.

Ex. 1.5.36 'Thou shalt break them'

The violins join the bass in unison on the chromatic second beats (F to F♯, G to G♯). The voice uses strong rhythmic rising fourths on 'Potter's' to propel the line forward.

Ex. 1.5.37 'He was cut off out of the Land of the Living'

'He was cut off out of the Land of the Living' should crescendo to the strong dissonance (7-4-2) making an antithesis with the cadence at the end of the previous 'Sorrow'.

1.5 Word Painting

Χριϲὸς ἐμπαίζεται ὑπὸ τῶν ϲρατιωτῶν. Matth. XXVII, 29. CHRISTUS ILLUSUS.
Christ mocked. Les Soldats se moquent de Jesus-Christ.
Christus wird verspottet. Christus bespot.

Picart delin. Folkema sculps.

1.6 Decorum – Choice of Means
or 'Suiting the Matter'

> Such being the variety entailed by the different portions of our pleading, it is sufficiently clear that our delivery must be adapted to our matter (Q, XI iii 174).
>
> For though we may speak of a word as appropriate, distinguished or sublime [...] when we praise words, we do so because they suit the matter (Q, I v 3).
>
> We shall achieve lucidity and clearness [...] by setting forth our story in words which are appropriate (Q, IV ii 36).
>
> It is of the first importance that we should know the requirements of time, place and character on each occasion of speaking (Q, IX iii 102).

For a composer, choosing how to express a text will depend on the occasion, the means available and the time involved in both composition and performance. For a performance of an already composed and published work, similar choices will have to be made: where, who, how many and how long? There will be no single correct answer to these questions.

If limited choice is available, the composer has to make the best of whatever is at hand according to the situation. Handel had no particular group of players and singers in mind when he composed *Messiah*, but his choice of orchestration, although standard in eighteenth-century terms seems today to provide a very limited palette of instrumental colour. However, his powers of invention drew on every possible rhetorical device to express the text in the most appropriate way using the means available.

For the first performance in Dublin he used strings, trumpets and timpani, a harpsichord and an organ which he had transported to Ireland, with a choir comprised of the solo voices combined with a group of cathedral choristers, some of whom sang solos. The chorus was probably no more than three or four to a part. This resulted in less differentiation between the solo vocal sound and the choral, as is mostly heard and expected today.
(John Butt, www.dunedin-consort.org.uk/files/media/file/messiah_extended_notes.pdf, accessed 30/3/2014)

Messiah requires a minimum of four solo voice roles, although all the solos were frequently shared out in Handel's time with the soprano numbers often being performed by a woman and a boy. The tenor, as was customary, takes the role of narrator, and is used for the extended sequence which starts with 'All they that see Him laugh Him to scorn' through 'Thy rebuke' to 'He was cut off out of the Land of the Living'. The bass voice is used for darkness and anger. The contralto is awarded the deep pathos of 'He was despised'. The soprano is saved for the angel's words in the Christmas scene, and carries us into the afterlife with 'I know that my Redeemer liveth'. Apart from the soprano music and the bass voice rage, much of the text is gender neutral, affording Handel the opportunity to re-assign arias according to circumstances.

The 'principale' part-books for the vocal soloists also contained all the choruses. It can be deduced from the Foundling Hospital parts (missing the first soprano part-book) that the second soprano sang 'But who may abide', 'Thou art gone up on high' and 'If God be for us'. That leaves for the first soprano 'There were Shepherds', 'And lo', 'And the Angel said unto them', 'And suddenly', 'Rejoice greatly', 'Then shall the Eyes of the Blind', 'He shall feed His Flock – Come unto Him', 'He was cut off', 'But Thou didst not leave', 'How beautiful are the Feet', and 'I know that my Redeemer liveth' (Watkins Shaw, 1965, pp. 93-94).

The trumpets are reserved for 'Glory to God', 'Hallelujah', 'Worthy is the Lamb' and the final part of 'Amen' (all of these have two) and 'The Trumpet shall sound' (one solo).

1.6 Decorum – Choice of Means

The solo voices are often used in dialogue with unison violins and the continuo bass section ('Rejoice', 'O thou that tellest'). When the violas are included, as in 'He shall feed His flock like a Shepherd' or 'He was despised', we can enjoy the richer harmonic texture which contrasts with the unison violin numbers. There are no arias which feature divided violins without the violas being present. The texture thus alternates between the unison treble/bass plus voice, and four-part harmony plus voice. Apart from the short *secco* recitatives, only the duet 'O Death, where is thy Sting?' and the *a capella* 'Since by man came Death' and 'For as in Adam all die' use basso continuo alone without upper strings.

Burney writes

> After this [...], the short Semi-chorus: "*Since by man came death,*" in plain counterpoint, by the principal soprano, counter-tenor, tenor, and base, without instruments, had a sweet and solemn effect, which heightened the beauty of the following chorus: "*By man came also the resurrection of the dead.*" And the Semi-chorus, "*for as in Adam all die,*" sung in the same unaccompanied manner, by three of the best singers in each of the four species of voice, contrasted admirably with the full Chorus – "*Even so in Christ shall all be made alive.*"
>
> The effect of contrast in these movements, alternately sung with, and without instruments, was so agreeable and striking, that it were to be wished more frequent use was made of such an easy expedient ('Commemoration of Handel', p. 86).

In the choruses, the instruments double the vocal parts much of the time, but are given their own moments of glory, adding figuration to enrich the homophonic texture of the voices, for example as in 'For unto us a Child is born' at the words 'Wonderful, Counsellor, The Mighty God, The Everlasting Father, The Prince of Peace'.

Ex. 1.6.1 'For unto us'

The violins have independent decorative material while the violas and bass double the voices.

1.6 Decorum – Choice of Means

Ex. 1.6.2 'And He shall purify'

The full chorus are doubled by the string section in a mixture of long lines set against fast moving parts. Here three levels of rhythm combine to give a sublime moment.

If the text is read through without the music, it is immediately obvious that there are very few opportunities for *secco* recitative, but Handel chooses accompanied recitative with a rhythmic string accompaniment for many different dramatic effects, quasi arioso. Accompanied recitative also provides a change of style which is used for variety, and sometimes forms a bridge between numbers, connecting two consequent events or facts. For example 'the Voice of Him that crieth in the Wilderness' leads into 'Ev'ry Valley', and 'For behold, Darkness shall cover the Earth' leads directly into 'The People that walked in Darkness'.

Woodwind (oboes and bassoon) were added after the first London performance. 'A fair copy of the score and all parts of my oratorio called the Messiah' were bequeathed by Handel to the Foundling Hospital. Two performances were given there in 1750 and then one every year until 1777 (see table p. 7). The payment list for performers who took part in the 1758 performance names twelve violins, three violas, three cellos, four oboes, four bassoons, two contrabasses, two trumpets, two horns and one drum (Deutsch, p. 800). Horns probably doubled trumpets at the lower octave except when the trumpets had solo roles as in 'Glory to God' and 'The Trumpet shall sound'. The oboes are tacet for all the accompanied recitative and arias and are mostly employed doubling the chorus parts, with only a few notes of their own in 'Their Sound is gone out'. Oboes act as a useful reinforcement for situations where the violins have their own material. The wood-wind doubling is not only for volume, but adds definition to the contrapuntal lines. It is likely that the oboe parts in the Foundling Hospital set were copied from those used in the 1754 performances for which J.C. Smith, rather than Handel himself, was responsible (Bartlett, p. vii). The bassoon part in 'For behold' carries instructions to play or remain silent which coincide with the piano and forte markings defining the presence of the solo singer. The double bass should generally drop out for any passages which use the tenor clef. 'Con ripieno' and 'senza ripieno' markings are found in the conducting score and were probably added for a performance in 1749 when a greater number of players was available, but this does not reflect general practice. Watkins Shaw provides a detailed examination of the various versions, cast of singers and early performances (Shaw, 1965, pp. 95-102, 109-126).

Size and Decorum

The balance between choir and orchestra will be relative to the circumstances and the means employed. Smaller instrumental forces will have to make more effort to distinguish between piano and forte than a large orchestra. The sound of very large amateur choirs tends to be weaker and more diffuse than smaller more accomplished ones. The acoustic of the building may be dry if carpeted, which reduces the dynamic differences, or very resonant if stone.

The twentieth-century tradition of repeating the first part of the *Messiah* overture piano may have originated in performances which used big wind sections. The word-book for the performance at the Handel commemoration festival (1784) lists 12 first oboes, 14 second oboes, 7 flutes, 25 bassoons, 1 double bassoon, 3 trombones, 12 horns and 5 drum players, these set against a string section which has 50 first violins. The total number of performers is 513.

Mozart's scoring also added flutes, clarinets, horns and trombones to the original line-up of strings with modest numbers of wood-wind (horns had already been used to double the trumpet parts in the choruses). The only dynamic marked by Mozart in the overture is forte in bar one (no other instruction for the repeat). A performance which took place in York Minster on the 25 September 1828 was described by the editor of the *Yorkshire Gazette*:

> In the performance of the Messiah, this morning, Mozart's wind instrument accompaniments contributed greatly to the general effect; [...] In the commencing overture, the first movement was played full with the wind instruments; and afterwards repeated piano with the violins, &c., unaccompanied by the former.

In this performance, the orchestra list published in the *Gazette* includes 6 flutes, 6 'clarionets', 12 oboes, 12 bassoons, 14 horns, 6 trumpets, 12 trombones (alto, tenor and bass), 4 bass horns and 4 serpents. The effect of all these instruments dropping out on the repeat would have been quite dramatic even taking into consideration the massive string section: 100 violin players, led by Cramer, 32 violas, 24 cellos, led by Robert Lindley, and 16 double basses, led by Dragonetti. It would be a short step from this situation to the assumption of the piano repeat in later performances, even without the large wind band. It had obviously become expected by the audience and performers alike and remained the standard interpretation until rhetorical ideas began to undermine the weight of tradition in late twentieth-century performances.

Watkins Shaw criticises Mozart's arrangement of *Messiah* (made in 1789) as 'alien' to Handel's style because the effect of silences are destroyed by being filled, and trumpets are used profligately so that their powers, reserved by Handel for special moments, are weakened. Subsequent editions, for example by Prout and Henry Wood, which Watkins Shaw describes as 'monstrous', incorporate many of the wind additions which were originally composed to replace the earlier obligatory keyboard. The bass singer James Bartleman, a significant figure in reviving Purcell's songs, no doubt feeling that Handel's economical scoring had been undermined by an attempt to up-date it, refused to take part in the first English performance of Mozart's version in 1805 (Shaw, 1946, p.17). However, from our more distant historical perspective, Mozart's version can be judged on its own terms and is generally regarded as a masterpiece.

Relatively large forces had already been assembled for the St. Cecilia Festivals held in London at the end of the seventeenth century. The choirs of St. Paul's Cathedral, Westminster Abbey and the Chapel Royal together with some theatre singers had combined to form a choir of about sixty voices with an instrumental band of twenty to twenty-five. At that time provincial centres such as Bristol had choral performances with a total of about thirty performers with instrumentalists travelling between local centres to take part, and principal players coming from London (Pritchard, pp. 98-9).

1.6 Decorum – Choice of Means

After 1760, performances of oratorios and especially *Messiah* were the mainstay of fundraising for charitable causes and became a manifestation of civic pride and a demonstration of piety in society. Handel's music loosened the purse strings like no other, and could be used as a vehicle to demonstrate publically the Christian virtue of charity (Pritchard, pp. 1, 29). Having started in secular locations such as assembly rooms and theatres, as the festival movement developed in the 1750s and 60s the chorus and orchestra became enlarged by combining various collegiate and cathedral choirs, and the performances moved into large religious buildings which were obviously more suitable. The first cathedral performance of *Messiah* took place in Bristol in 1758. The following year it was performed in Hereford for the Three Choirs Festival, but not in the cathedral. Religious music was normally part of morning service in the festival period, with oratorio performances held in the evening. When the oratorio performance was moved to the morning, it replaced the festival service leaving the evening free for balls, dinner, etc. The oratorio thus assumed a more religious aspect than previously, when it had been a concert event (Pritchard, pp. 44, 52, 31).

In the north of England, choral singing was centred round the chapel with its psalm singing tradition (Pritchard, p. 118-186). Manchester, and Lancashire as a whole became the hub of a northern choral tradition of singing oratorio which lasts to this day, with the twentieth-century performances of *Messiah* by the Huddersfield Choral Society becoming legendary in their own time. In the 1770s, a small group of leading female singers from the north were so highly regarded that they were engaged by southern festivals to lead the choral sections (Pritchard, p. 143).

The eighteenth-century Charles Dibdin remarked

> Halifax [...] is said to be the most musical spot for its size in the kingdom: [...] children lisp 'For unto us a child is born', and cloth-makers, as they sweat under their loads in the cloth-hall, roar out 'For his yoke is easy and his burden is light.' I have been assured, for a fact, that more than one man in Halifax can take any part in the choruses of the Messiah, and go regularly through the whole oratorio by heart; and, indeed, the facility with which the common people join together throughout the greatest part of Yorkshire and Lancashire, in every species of choral music, is truly astonishing (quoted in Pritchard, p. 186).

In the north, local professional musicians tended to organise one-off, small-scale performances in their towns and village. This was in contrast to the growing festival movement in the south where large groups of musicians were assembled for several days' worth of oratorio performances, balls, dinners and concerts. The players were predominantly gentlemen amateurs led by imported professionals, with an amalgamated choir of cathedral and collegiate singers.

The Handel Commemoration of 1784 was, according to Burney, exceptional for three reasons: the size of its chorus, the ability of the performers, and the precision of the massed forces who all were able to see the director and the leader, without the services of what Burney called the *Manu-ductor* ('The Commemoration of Handel', p. 15).

Large cathedrals were not designed with concert audiences in mind, and musical details may not carry well beyond the first few rows. Further back, all the audience may hear is a general impression of the performance. An exception, Charles Burney tells us, is the 'happy construction of Westminster-Abbey for cherishing and preserving musical tones, by a gentle augmentation without echo or repetition', where every detail and nuance of the singer could be heard ('The Commemoration of Handel', p. 80). But the experience of hearing this great music performed in an awe-inspiring building, even with imperfect acoustics, will usually compensate for the lack of musical detail.

For the Handel Commemoration performance of *Messiah* the orchestra was arranged in tiers rising up to the windows. Burney invokes the image of Dante's nine circles of paradise, filled with cherubim and seraphim who 'continually do cry &c.'

1.6 Decorum – Choice of Means

> Now, as the orchestra in Westminster Abbey seemed to ascend to the clouds, and unite with the saints and martyrs represented on the painted glass in the west window, which had all the appearance of a continuation of the orchestra, I could hardly refrain from imagining that this orchestra was a point or segment of the celestial circles: and perhaps no band of mortal musicians ever exhibited a more imposing appearance to the eye or afforded more ecstatic and affecting sounds to the ear than this ('The Commemoration of Handel', p. 84).

The continuing gargantuan *Messiah* tradition offended George Bernard Shaw writing in 1891:

> Why, instead of wasting huge sums on the multitudinous dullness of a Handel Festival does not somebody set up a thoroughly rehearsed and exhaustively studied performance of the Messiah in St. James Hall with a chorus of twenty capable artists? Most of us would be glad to hear the work seriously performed once before we die (quoted in Luckett, 1992, pp. 223-4).

Whatever the circumstances, an effort to realise the subtle dynamic effects derived from the speaking style should be made at all costs. As has been noted, the very first performances of *Messiah* were not in churches at all, but concert halls and theatres, or crowded assembly rooms, venues where the acoustics would have been relatively dry, the audience quite close to the performers, and without stained glass saints to supplement the orchestra. At the Foundling Hospital, performances took place in the chapel, and after Handel's death were directed by the younger Smith who held the position of organist there. After the 1760s churches began to be used to accommodate the larger forces employed after Handel's death.

It should be clear from this that there is no 'correct' size of choir for a performance of *Messiah*. The most important rhetorical aspect to consider (as well as the economics) is that of balance, between choir and orchestra and between the sections of the choir, taking into account the acoustics of the building and the seating arrangements for the audience's enjoyment. If the choir is able to provide soloists who can take part in the whole performance, that is, sing in the choruses as well as the solos, this will add an eighteenth-century dimension to the performance.

Having chosen the means with which to express the text, the composer has to relinquish control into the hands of the performers. Handel supervised the first performances himself, so was able to bring his influence to bear on the outcome. For us, his part in the task of 'speaking appropriately' is over. It is now up to the performers to convert these ideas into sounds which faithfully represent his work for today's audience.

1.7 Second Thoughts

It cannot be known exactly when Handel made the alterations to his first thoughts. He could have made alterations moments after putting pen to paper, but there was a 'run-through' in Chester on his way to Dublin and alterations could also have been made at that point. Watkins Shaw argues that some changes were made to the MS even after the conducting score had been copied by Smith. He surmises that Smith's score was copied between 14 September 1741 and November, before Handel set off for Dublin (Shaw, 1965, p. 31). Whenever they were made, the revised ideas show how the change of a note or extension of a moment can intensify the music at a certain point. In the other cases he deletes an idea which detracts from the immediacy of a phrase or the effect of a transition.

In the case of 'Ev'ry Valley' it is possible that the extra bars were performed in Dublin, even though they are lightly crossed out in the MS, before being obliterated by patches of paper fixed with wax in the conducting score.

'Hallelujah'

After starting with a high D in the first violins, Handel realised that it could be put to better use in the second bar where it would emphasise the repetition of the phrase with a high note using the same rhythm but different intervals (rising fifth and tone, then falling sixth and semitone).

1.7 Second Thoughts

'And with His Stripes' – 'All we, like Sheep'

'And with His Stripes'

'All we, like Sheep'

The connection between 'And with His Stripes' and 'All we, like Sheep' originally had a transitional cadence which was then crossed out.

'Why do the Nations'

Handel decided that the flourish, instead of rising directly from the A semiquavers, should start from a lower point (E) in order to 'rise up' even further.

'If God be for us'

Amplification is added to a decorative connection in a similar manner to the previous extract. Avoiding the obvious rising arpeggio, Handel's second thought (bar inserted) is to take the arpeggio downwards so that it can rise further in a graceful serpentine curve, suspending the moment of arrival at the top of the phrase.

1.7 Second Thoughts

'Ev'ry Valley'

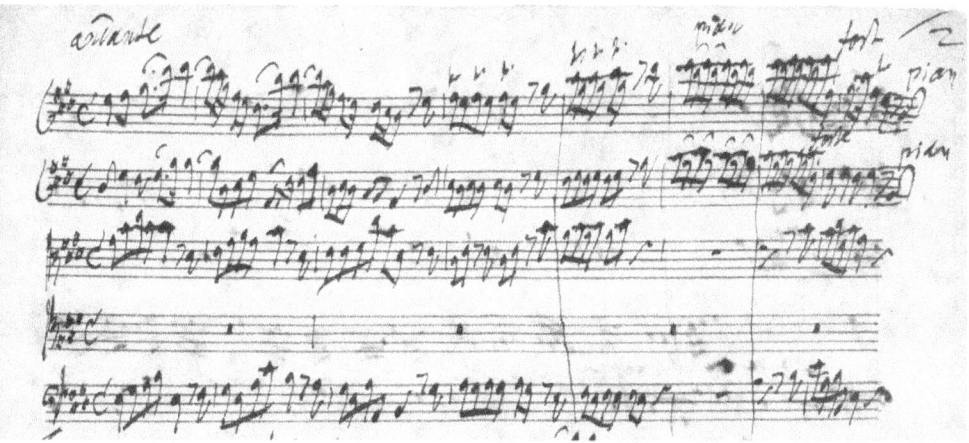

The sixth bar in 'ev'ry Valley' is lightly crossed out in Handel's MS. The trilled pairs are extended in the third phrase but then considered to be too much static repetition. The conducting score shows patches pasted over the offending bars.

'Ev'ry Valley' Handel's conducting score.

1.7 Second Thoughts

PART TWO – DELIVERY

2.1 Decorum – Tone of Voice
or Speaking Appropriately

The composer has invented the matter, arranged it and decorated it, and the work is now ready for delivery (*pronunciatio*) by the orator or performer. The other divisions of rhetorical performance, memory (*memoria*) and gesture (*actio*), which includes the visual aspects of performance, will now come in to play to transfer the ideas to an audience.

Decorum is defined in the Classical rhetoric books as 'speaking appropriately' or 'speaking to a purpose', and will govern every choice a performer makes, not only in the performance of the music, but in choosing an appropriate venue or the style of dress. The term 'gesture' covers the complete visual effect a performer has on the audience. This might include dress, deportment, entering and leaving the stage, facial expression, connection with other performers on the platform, and acknowledging applause. Delivery does not just mean playing or singing the notes correctly and accurately, but encompasses the whole task of communicating the ideas and emotions represented in the music to the audience.

Quintilian emphasises that the most important part of delivery is 'the necessity of adapting the voice to suit the nature of the various subjects on which we are speaking and the moods that they demand: otherwise our voice will be at variance with our language' (Q, XI iii 45).

Using the appropriate voice tone is crucial for communicating the message. The term 'speaking appropriately' describes the performer's choice of tone of voice, and will already have influenced the composer's choice of key, dynamic, articulation, rhythm, harmony and tempo which all support and contribute to the effect of the text. These elements of compositional choice will help the performer decide on the appropriate mode of delivery and tone of voice. Using an inappropriate tone will be confusing to the listener and may have a quite different affect from the intended one. A merely neutral tone in the tradition of performance which 'allows the music to speak for itself' will make the message harder for the audience to grasp. The music might sound well, but the emotional connections will be missed. Every detail embedded in the composition should be matched by delivery if the communication is to be successful.

> Give me the knowledge of the principles of music, which have power to excite or assuage the emotions of mankind (Q, I x 31).
>
> Many have said that the faculty of greatest use to the speaker and the most valuable for persuasion is delivery (RH, III xi 19).
>
> It is not enough to discern what is to be said unless you have the ability to say it fluently and with some charm (C, *Brutus* 110).
>
> The same speech with a change of speaker would be a different thing (C, *De Oratore* III lvi 213).
>
> For many poor speakers have often reaped the rewards of eloquence because of a dignified delivery, and many eloquent men have been considered poor speakers because of an awkward delivery. [...] Therefore the one who seeks supremacy in eloquence will strive to speak intensely with a vehement tone, and gently with

2.1 Decorum – Tone of Voice

> lowered voice, and to show dignity in a deep voice, and wretchedness by a plaintive tone (C, *Orator*, 56).
>
> Then, corresponding to the content of the words, we shall modify the delivery in all kinds of tone, now to sharpness, now to kindness, or now to sadness, now to gaiety (RH, III xiv).
>
> Variety of tones is an aid to eloquence [...] the excitement which should mark the rise of anger, and the change of tone that is characteristic of pathos (Q, I xi 12).
>
> Good delivery ensures that what the orator is saying seems to come from his heart (RH, III xv 27).
>
> Everything must seem to spring from the case itself rather than the art of the orator (Q, IV ii 126).
>
> Fire alone can kindle, and moisture alone can wet [...] accordingly, the first essential is that those feelings should prevail with us that we wish to prevail with the judge [i.e. audience], and that we should be moved ourselves before we attempt to move others (Q, VI ii 28).
>
> For when our audience find it a pleasure to listen, their attention and their readiness to believe what they hear are both alike increased, while they are generally filled with delight, and sometimes even transported by admiration (Q, VIII iii 5).

But what is the correct tone of voice to use for an oratorio? Is it a musical sermon? Or is it a sacred opera? An eighteenth-century writer described oratorio as 'a musical Drama, whose subject must be scriptural, and in which the Solemnity of Church-Musick is agreeably united with the most pleasing Airs of the Stage' (R. Smith 1995, p. 22). In other words, pleasing and entertaining, without indecorous humour, but to be enjoyed and used as a stimulus to religious devotion. The first London performance of *Messiah* (which took place in a theatre) was advertised in the *Daily Post* as 'A New Sacred Oratorio'.

To discover the appropriate tone the solo singer or chorus member should ask 'who am I?' and 'what is my purpose?' Even a narrator may have different personas according to the context. Prophecy, warning, denial, appeal, argument, questioning, affirmation and accusation all have their own tones of voice and modes of speaking, which are characterised in musical terms by tessitura, rhythm, tempo and general affect. These characteristics support the text and the dramatic situation and are derived from the natural way a human being expresses emotion: appeals to pity rise in pitch; shouts are short, high and loud; agitation moves continuously; sobbing or hesitation uses short rests and intermittent notes for affect; intoning or commanding is monotonous and steady.

Certain keys acquire specific associations: F major pastoral, D major glorious and triumphant (the key suits trumpets), D minor serious, and for Handel the key of E major was especially heavenly.

Tones of Voice

In the following section the mode of speech and the means employed to portray it are described. Who is speaking, in what manner and for what purpose?

Tuning in the eighteenth century was unequal, and the choice of key had a real effect on the tone, and consequently on the emotional colour. Keys with more sharps and flats, remote from the tonal centres, gave the possibility of cloudy or uncertain tonality. 'Home' keys with no sharps or flats were clearer and brighter.

Sources: J. Rousseau (1691), Charpentier (1692), Mattheson (1713-19), Rameau (1722), contained in Rita Steblin, *A History of Key Characteristics in the Eighteenth and the Early Nineteenth Centuries*, and Ross Duffin, *How Equal Temperament Ruined Harmony (and Why You Should Care)*.

2.1 Decorum – Tone of Voice

		Key affect and mode of expression	The speaker and tone of voice
PART ONE			
Sinfony		E minor: dark, pensive, grieved (Mattheson).	
Comfort ye	T	E major: fatally sad (Mattheson). Handel's favourite key for evoking heaven. Soothing, reassuring in soft pulsing quavers. Falling motifs.	God through the Prophet.
Saith your God		God speaks in rising crotchets.	Voice of God.
The Voice of him		Punctuated command.	Command to prepare.
Ev'ry Valley	T	E major. Bright, positive. Hyperbolic optimism. Firm rising dotted motif.	Statement of belief, prophecy.
And the Glory	Ch	A major: Joyful (Charpentier). Smooth transition from previous key. Rising to 'Lord'.	Wondrous prediction by chorus of believers.
For the Mouth of the Lord		Intoned in long notes.	Statement of fact.
Thus saith the Lord	B	D minor. Serious (Charpentier). Dramatic threat interrupts (no down-beat). Rising dotted motif leads to first word. Shaking illustrated.	Words of God.
The Lord whom ye seek		Change of tone.	Prophet.
But who may abide?	B	D minor. Same key but more gentle. Statement of belief. Calm, assured.	Rhetorical question, invitation by believer.
For He is like a Refiner's Fire		Supernatural comparison, agitated, leaping flames. Dramatic ending.	3rd person narrative.
And He shall purify	Ch	G minor. Sweet and tender (Rameau). Light short quavers.	Quietly confident prediction by believers.
Behold a Virgin	S Secco recit	Magical transition into D major. New voice and feeling.	Prophecy spoken by angel. Exclamation. Prediction.
O thou that tellest	S	D major. Joyful mood continues from previous. Lively running notes.	Exclamation by prophet.
Behold your God		Calm, still, reverend.	Command.
Behold your God	Ch	Shout, declamation.	Exclamation of joy.
For behold, Darkness	B	B minor. Lonely, melancholic (Charpentier). Sudden change to bleak unison in dark bass voice. Creeping intervals. Pulsing beat. Ends in the remote bright F# major leading to…	Narrative prophecy and warning ending in hope.
The People that walked	B	B minor, key of darkness. Passes through A major for light, F# major and back to B minor for death. Lonely stark unisons. Wandering melody line.	Statement of miracle. Dark narrative.
For unto us a Child is born	Ch	New feeling. G major hopeful, sweetly joyful. Glittering fast notes decorate choral shouts of wonder.	Prophetic announcement.
Pifa		Pastoral rustic. Joyful, with drones resonating in C major and introducing	
There were Shepherds	S Secco recit	the long held note in the bass which anticipates the contrast with the next accompanied recit.	Narrative statement.
And lo (set both as accompanied recit and aria)	S	F major pastoral. Most beautiful and virtuous (Mattheson). Flutter of wings piano, lacks earthly bass.	Narrative exclamation.
And the Angel said	S	Ends in the very distant key of F# major.	Continuation of the story.

2.1 Decorum – Tone of Voice

		Key affect and mode of expression	**The speaker and tone of voice**
And suddenly	S	D major chosen for trumpet which follows. Bright semiquavers shimmer for praise of God, still no earthly bass.	Surprise in narrative.
Glory to God	Ch	Exclamation in D major. Glorious trumpets in heaven *da lontano*. Choral exclamations unified.	Chorus of heavenly host praising.
Goodwill		Resolute counterpoint for 'goodwill towards men'.	Hopeful affirmation.
Rejoice	S	B♭ major gives new shocking feeling after D major. Bouncy lively rhythm, rising motifs. Set in both simple and compound time signatures.	Command in the form of exclamation.
Then shall the Eyes	S Secco recit	Transitional passage.	Prophecy.
He shall feed	A-S	B♭ major calm, pastoral. Soothing falling motifs. Lilting rhythms.	Hopeful calm promise.
His Yoke is easy	Ch	Still B♭. Joyful (Charpentier). Light easy short quavers.	Encouraging, persuasive.

PART TWO

Behold the Lamb of God	Ch	G minor. Serious, magnificent (Charpentier). Dramatic, portentous, grave. Dotted rhythms in serious overture style.	Command.
He was despised	A	E♭ major tragic. Pathetic and serious (Mattheson). Emotional appeal. Falling appoggiaturas pathos. Rich dissonant harmony.	Narrative description.
He gave his Back		C minor. Agitated dotted accompaniment soft with stabbing dissonances.	
Surely	Ch	F minor. Deep despair (Mattheson). Unified expression. Dotted accompaniment. Dissonances.	Appeal and exclamation of grief.
And with His Stripes	Ch	Still F minor. Jagged chromatic intervals then smooth lines.	Expression of consolation.
All we, like Sheep	Ch	F major, pastoral again. Short crotchets comic with 'folk' bass. Broken lines to 'go astray'.	Cheeky confession.
And the Lord		Slower serious ending appeals to guilt in longer note values in F minor.	Change of tone for final appeal.
All they that see him	Ch	B♭ minor. Gloomy, terrible (Charpentier). Ends in E♭ major.	Cruel mocking narrative.
He trusted in God	Ch	C minor. For complaints (Rousseau). Firm rising line for fugal discussion.	Derision of trust.
Let him deliver him		Many voice entries multiply the challenges.	Sarcastic taunt.
Thy Rebuke	T	Starts in the remote A♭ major, ends in B minor. Chromatic opening.	Accusation, lament.
Behold, and see	T	E minor. Pensive, grieved (Mattheson). Rising intervals for emotional appeals. Ends in B major.	Exclamation of disbelief using hyperbolic comparison.
He was cut off	T	Opens on strong dissonance. Jagged lines. Ends optimistically in E major.	Narrative of harsh fact.
But Thou didst	T	A major hopeful, devotional (Rousseau).	Mitigating argument.

2.1 Decorum – Tone of Voice

		Key affect and mode of expression	**The speaker and tone of voice**
not leave		Purposeful andante bass line.	
Lift up your heads	Ch	Another shock to F major: virtuous (Mattheson). Low and high cohorts ask questions and answer them.	Command, rhetorical demands which are answered.
Unto which of the Angels	T Secco recit	Transitional function leading to A major.	Prophecy seeking reassurance.
Let all the Angels	Ch	D major bright, joyful. Slow and fast versions of short text reinforce message.	Request for encouragement.
Thou art gone up	S	D minor serious, pious (Charpentier). Rising phrase. Soothing falling motifs.	Tribute.
The Lord gave the Word	Ch	B♭ major magnificent (Charpentier). Company of faithful sing together busily in reply. Call and response.	Simple intonement of the word of the Lord.
How beautiful are the Feet	S-A	G minor/C minor gloomy, sad (Charpentier). Lilting rhythm. Dialogue with violins.	Exclamation of beauty and admiration for deeds done.
Break forth (only in Dublin version)	Ch	Broken quaver octaves, semiquavers joyous.	Command.
Their Sound is gone out	Ch	F major beautiful, virtuous (Mattheson). Punctuated chords proclaim.	Triumphal news.
Unto the Ends of the World		Rising scales.	
Why do the Nations?	B	C major militant (Charpentier). Agitated semiquavers. Random patterns and repeated figures imply chaos.	Vehement rhetorical question and complaint.
Let us break their Bonds	Ch	C major. Staccato syllabic falling wide intervals.	Invitation, incitement to action.
And cast away		Falling slower staccato arpeggio (quasi hornpipe), then runs away.	
He that dwelleth	T	Transition to E major.	Sarcastic prediction.
Thou shalt break them	T	A minor serious (Rousseau). Big leaps and stabs. Insistent high semiquaver figure reiterated.	Threat.
Hallelujah	Ch	D major for trumpets. Choral harmonised shout. Dialogue with instruments reinforces message.	Exclamatory praising, triumphal celebration and prediction.
For the Lord God		Unison authority.	
And He shall reign		Striding intervals promote feeling of confidence.	

PART THREE

I know	S	E major grand, tender (Rousseau). Rising interval asserts then calms for end of phrase.	Heavenly confident affirmation of belief.
Worms and sleep		Undulating dotted figure.	
For now is Christ risen		Firm steady rising crotchets support the facts.	
Since by Man	Ch	A minor is serious (Rousseau) then moves to C major then G minor to A minor. Slow unaccompanied chorus desolate effect, repeated.	Comparisons used to confirm predicted outcome.
By Man came also		Answers hopeful, lively and bright.	
Behold, I tell you	B	D major prepares for trumpet. Mysterious chords then surprise stabs in strings lead to resolution.	Exclamation, narrative prediction.

2.1 Decorum – Tone of Voice

		Key affect and mode of expression	**The speaker and tone of voice**
The Trumpet shall sound For this corruptible	B	Dotted trumpet for waking the dead. B minor/major. More conciliatory, just continuo.	Prediction, announcement.
Then shall be brought	A Secco recit	Transition to B♭ major. Victory.	Narrative prediction.
O Death	A-T	E♭ major pathetic, serious (Mattheson). Andante bass gives purposeful effect.	Exclamation of joy and triumph.
But Thanks be to God	Ch	E♭ major clamorous (Charpentier). Lively, fun short comments in choral argument.	A light command, statement.
If God be for us	S	G minor sad (Rousseau), serious, magnificent (Charpentier). Serene melody. Calm.	Argument to convince.
Worthy is the Lamb Amen	Ch	D major triumphant. Starts grand then change of tempo moves argument forward. Amen starts calmly then builds in fugue to climactic end.	Statement, reasoning, conclusion.

The 'Speaking' Style

Punctuation

As Quintilian claims that clarity is the first virtue of eloquence, the performer (either speaker or musician) needs to self-punctuate to make sense of the material (Q, II iii 8).

In speaking or reading, gradations of articulation between syllables, words, phrases, sentences and paragraphs divide the text into shorter units which are then linked to make a whole thought. In order for the structure of the whole to be understood, gaps or articulations should be graded according to their importance in the structure. For example, in music a smaller gap would be taken after a passing cadence than at the end of a paragraph such as a double bar. Not all gaps require new breaths to be taken. These structural pauses have to be incorporated into the musical performance in spite of the fact that most music (apart from *secco* recitative) is normally governed by a tactus, a regular beat into which the phrases have to fit.

Unlike text, where the reader can pause for any length of time, music dictates the length of each note. When singing text or playing music which is regulated by a beat, value may have to be taken out of the note before the space in which breath is taken, to accommodate the relentless march of time, especially when parts overlap as in counterpoint. If the voices are singing in the same rhythm (in homophony, the rhetorical figure *noema*), all should agree on how much time should either be taken away from, or added to the written note in order to breathe together. Longer notes with fewer syllables afford more time for breaths than quicker notes where the syllables are packed together.

2.1 Decorum – Tone of Voice

Ex. 2.1.1 'All we, like Sheep'

When text is set to music, gaps between words or phrases can be measured by written rests, or punctuation can be used to supply gaps between words. For example the text 'All we, like Sheep' is set using equal crotchets for the three syllables 'we', 'like' and 'Sheep'. The comma implies that the note on 'we' should be the shortest, and the next two words 'like Sheep' are naturally slightly detached by the use of their consonants. The character of this phrase then provides a contrast with the smoother 'have gone astray'.

The King James Bible has no commas in the above text, and punctuation varies throughout Handel's manuscript and conducting score. The 1743 word-book based on Jennens' original text, which was published for the first London performance, demonstrates more detailed and useful punctuation than any of the manuscript material: Handel's composition score, his conducting score copied by his assistant or the Foundling Hospital part-books, which have no punctuation at all. Perhaps because music

2.1 Decorum – Tone of Voice

has punctuation written into it in the form of note lengths and cadences, punctuation of the text was considered unnecessary in a musical score created in the eighteenth century.

Decorum for a group of performers means not only singing or playing to express the sense and the appropriate 'passion', but knowing your role within the group and adjusting your style accordingly (more about this in Dynamics 2.3).

As can be seen above, rhetorical ways of speaking which use emotional tones of voice to enhance the text can be transferred to music by imitating the spoken manner and tone quality. Apart from the obvious rising question and falling answer, ascending figures can be hopeful and optimistic. Sighing, falling intervals are sadder and more pathetic. Short, fast, equally emphasised syllables tend to be comic, and longer, more drawn-out ones, serious. Large, striding intervals are confident, small, close ones hesitant and searching. Rhythm, either regular or irregular, tessitura and dynamics can be used to imitate various ways of speaking.

> The following two examples show how the same rhythmic unit can have very different affects. In general, the dotted crotchet followed by one or more quavers in the vocal parts indicates a long syllable, which is smoothly joined to the next one. The first, long note should be fully sustained, and the following three short ones separated: WAS des-pi-sed and HAL-le-lu-jah. Although the two examples below use the same rhythm pattern, the affects are very different. The text influences the choice of key (warm E♭ major or bright D major), tempo, tessitura (relatively low and high), and orchestration (low solo voice and strings only, or full choir and orchestra).
>
> The start and shape of note will contribute to its affect. One has an upbeat (He WAS ...) which softens and introduces the idea in an insinuating way, the other is more direct and forceful (HAL-lelujah). The dotted crotchet 'was' (a relatively unimportant word in the phrase) should be sustained and lead towards the quavers which express the cruel focus of the idea, 'des-PI-sed'. In contrast the dotted crotchet of HAL-lelujah needs a good front on it, then a slight dip in the sound, especially when the voices and instruments are in dialogue.
>
> Both instrumental ritornellos introduce the text so should already portray the different shape of the dotted crotchet before the vocal entries.

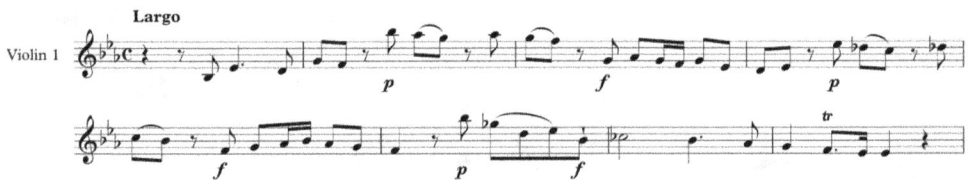

Ex 2.1.2 'He was despised'

Ex. 2.1.3 'Hallelujah'

The size of intervals and their direction up or down have particular expressive effects.

2.1 Decorum – Tone of Voice

Ex. 2.1.4 'Behold and see'

The rising intervals in the voice plead: first they are broken up on a rising fifth followed by a rest, descending for 'and see', then the plea is amplified on the more plangent rising sixth which is sustained to the end of the phrase, and decorated.

Ex. 2.1.5 'Behold and see'

The empty main beats in the violin and bass parts give a sobbing or sighing affect in dialogue with the voice.

2.1 Decorum – Tone of Voice

Ex. 2.1.6 'Behold and see'. 'He was cut off'

This is followed by the repeated violin pleading rising minor sixth already heard in bars five to six (see Ex. 2.1.4). The suspended stab of pain on the cadence is now marked piano.

Dialogue - Delivery

Agon, or conflict, is a necessary ingredient of all art. Without disagreement, there can be no resolution: without *antithesis*, no coming together. *Agon* is the life-blood of the musical ensemble. A voice or voices can be set against the instruments; instruments can argue amongst themselves; choral forces can be made to provoke questions which they answer themselves. Performers should avoid blending into the ensemble in situations where to assert themselves or defend their own corner in the argument would be more appropriate. Agreement at the cadence usually follows the working out of the argument, often preceded by a harmonic crisis such as an interrupted cadence or a sudden silence following a discord.

The standard mode of musical composition for dialogue between voices is counterpoint. Voices converse independently of each other. They answer and argue. They may quarrel, contradicting each other, then agree at cadences. When there are only two voices (and there are never fewer than two in a dialogue), the bass line will be in continuous dialogue with the solo voice or instrumental line. 'Accompaniment' is not a useful concept to apply to Handel's music where the continuo bass is always present as an equal voice, supporting, provoking or interacting with the voices above it in argument. The possible exception to this approach is found in recitative, where the chordal accompaniment supports the meaning of the words, occasionally illustrating them, but does not enter into any dialogue with the solo voice.

The questions and answers in the text can be manipulated by using groups of voices to argue or interrogate. The lower voices demand 'Who is this King of Glory?' and the higher ones answer 'The Lord Strong and Mighty in Battle'. Even one line can be divided to argue with itself (see Exx. 2.2.4, 1.3.12).

The bass can disagree with the violins:

Ex. 2.1.7 'I know that my Redeemer liveth'

Here the violins agree with and support the solo voice (see also Ex. 2.2.6).

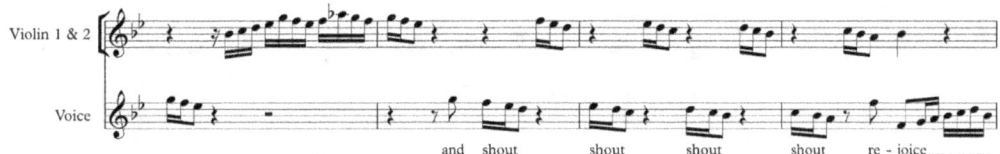

Ex. 2.1.8 'Rejoice'

The parts can chase each other in a rhythmic conversation using a rising tessitura in competitive one-upmanship:

Ex. 2.1.9 Sinfony (Overture)

All parts can agree on the same idea:

Ex. 2.1.10 'Behold the Lamb of God'

2.1 Decorum – Tone of Voice

Ex. 2.1.11 'The Trumpet shall sound'

The whole string section is engaged in dialogue in two parts. Lower strings and voice converse with upper strings in a rising and falling phrase, each one overlapping the other, and contributing to a rising sequence where 'we SHALL be changed'. The three quaver up-beat leads to the emphasis in turn, and the trumpet soars overhead.

Watkins Shaw thought this aria (not without justification) was 'without spontaneity' using 'endless mechanical phrases to the word "changed"' which 'are exceedingly tedious'. He considers that the presence of the trumpet saves this movement from the axe which was so often applied to 'Thou art gone up on high' and that the middle section is seldom performed, perhaps because of its very long and tedious A section which needs to be repeated (1946, p.11). Mozart omitted the B section of this aria from his arrangement.

Having chosen the most appropriate tone of voice, the meaning now needs to be made clear by emphasising the important words, notes or syllables.

2.2 Emphasis

or 'Words to be Taken Notice of'

In the eighteenth century, it was thought that speaking and performing music shared the same aims and techniques. Both use emphasis to make the meaning clear. William Tans'ur (1756) first addresses the meaning of the text through the correct grammatical emphasis, using the strength and length of sound for important words, and then the various tones required to represent the prevailing 'passion'.

> In common Speech, the Word *accent* signifies the *Tone* of the *Voice*, of which the *Grammarians* have sundry Sorts, mark'd by various Dashes over the Vowels; signifying a more *high* or *low*, *longer* or *shorter Tone* of the *Voice*; or a more *pressing Emphasis*, or *Tone*, on such Syllables or Words, as are more to be taken Notice of than any other, in order to *strike* such *Vowels, Words, Syllables,* or *Sentences* more *pressing* to the *Audience*, according as the *Passion* and *Subject* requires, &c – So, in *Musick*, An *Accent*, is a Sort of *wavering* or *quivering* of the *Voice*, or *Instrument*, on certain *Notes*, with a *stronger* or *weaker Tone* than the rest, &c to express the *Passion* thereof; which renders *Musick* (especially *Vocal*) so very agreeable to the Ear, it being chiefly intended to *move* and *affect*; and on this the very *Soul* and *Spirit* of *Musick* depends, by reason it touches and causes Emotions in the Mind, either of *Love, Sorrow, Pity*, or any other *Passion* whatsoever, &c. (p. 29).

A sentence without emphasis is hard to understand. All the correct sounds are there, but extra effort has to be made to understand what is being said. Quintilian places emphasis among the ornaments of oratory, not just to make a thing intelligible, but more intelligible (Q, VIII ii 11). Speaking in the rhetorical style involves a mixture of stating facts and raising 'the passions'. The type, frequency and strength of the emphasis supports the prevailing 'passion' to move and affect the mind. The important words are stressed, the unimportant are unstressed and in rhetoric long syllables are generally stronger than short ones. Music uses an inflected manner which imitates speech, even without text, so long high notes will be even more emphatic than lower shorter ones. Short syllables or notes are weaker than long ones.

The shape and emphasis of a phrase needs to be understood to make its meaning clear. Factors which influence how we emphasise something include repetition, tessitura, the length of the note or phrase, articulation marks, and harmony. Usually an emphasised word and its harmonic support will be louder but any sudden change in dynamic can draw attention to a word. An important word may be extended and decorated musically using a melisma with many notes.

From the moment that music and rhetoric combined their purposes around 1500, composers had reflected the word emphasis in the musical setting using various devices such as dissonant harmony or tessitura. Handel takes this process a step further by varying and surprising us with new, unexpected emphases, even for the same text, for example in 'But who may abide' which is set using two quite different musical effects and 'Hallelujah' in which each syllable is emphasised at various points.

Shaping a phrase by making a crescendo towards the strongest emphasis and a diminuendo away from it will prevent the emphasised place from sticking out suddenly. The constant variety of rise and fall arranged around a strong emphasis will hold the attention of the listener. Where sequences of short repeated motifs build to a climax (see *auxesis*, p. 42), the amount of emphasis needs to be judged and graded so that the tension builds throughout the sequence, arriving at the peak with the appropriate amount of force.

Words are a mixture of consonants and vowels. The vowel sounds are interspersed with consonants which give the words their character and sound. The choice of words, and how they sound together (diction) will influence their emotional appeal. Rhetorical devices such as patterns of repetition and alliteration then attract the listener and hold his attention.

Combinations of sounds can illustrate the emotion embedded in the words: 'darkness' is mysterious and uncertain; 'rejected' needs forceful delivery; 'exalted', equally forceful but triumphant.

In archaic or poetic language some final weak syllables are pronounced but not emphasised. As Handel shows us from his word setting, the following words should have the final syllable –ed pronounced: despised, walked, shined, unstopped, bruised, turned, looked, healed, redeemed (avoid making –ed sound like –id). Do not pronounce the final syllable in the following words: open'd, chang'd, rais'd, pow'r, swallow'd, or the middle one in ev'ry, heav'nly.

Ex. 2.2.1 'The People that walked in Darkness'

The weak syllable –ed, although pronounced, should not be emphasised whether rising or falling. Note the beaming (as Handel wrote it) of walk-ed, showing the pronounced second syllable. The first 'walk-ed', although a group of three rising notes, should become softer on the weak syllable, even though it is the highest note in the phrase.

Ex. 2.2.2 'But who may abide?'

The word ap-PEAR-eth, is set on two equal quavers, but the second should be short. The delivery of the weaker syllable should match the weak, falling resolution in the harmonic progression 6-4/5-3 normally found at cadences where the sixth falls to the fifth and the fourth falls to the third.

The *Epizeuxis*

In rhetoric, the exact repetition of a word or short phrase is used for emphasis, and important words or phrases in the text are nearly always repeated, either to impress them on the memory of the hearers or for additional emphasis. In a musical setting it is not unusual to change the emphasis of an important word when it is repeated, for variety. The musical setting shows the syllables to be stressed placed on longer notes (Ex. 2.2.8).

Tessitura

When a short phrase is repeated it is often changed in some way. If it is transposed higher this implies that it should gather more force, and probably should be played or sung louder. Sometimes a rhythm, interval or expected pattern is changed. This is to catch the ear and provide variety in what otherwise would be a tedious exercise.

Ex. 2.2.3 'For behold'

When the voice repeats 'and gross Darkness the People' higher and with even larger leaps, it is more emphatic. Both 'Darknesses' are set on seventh chords, leading eventually to the very remote chord of F♯ major.

The stressed notes or syllables should be fitted into a shaped phrase which not only leads towards and away from the high stress points but undulates through the various levels of shape and accent, often building towards a high point. Many figures of rhetoric use this device (*auxesis*) which was known as 'the orator's scaling ladder'.

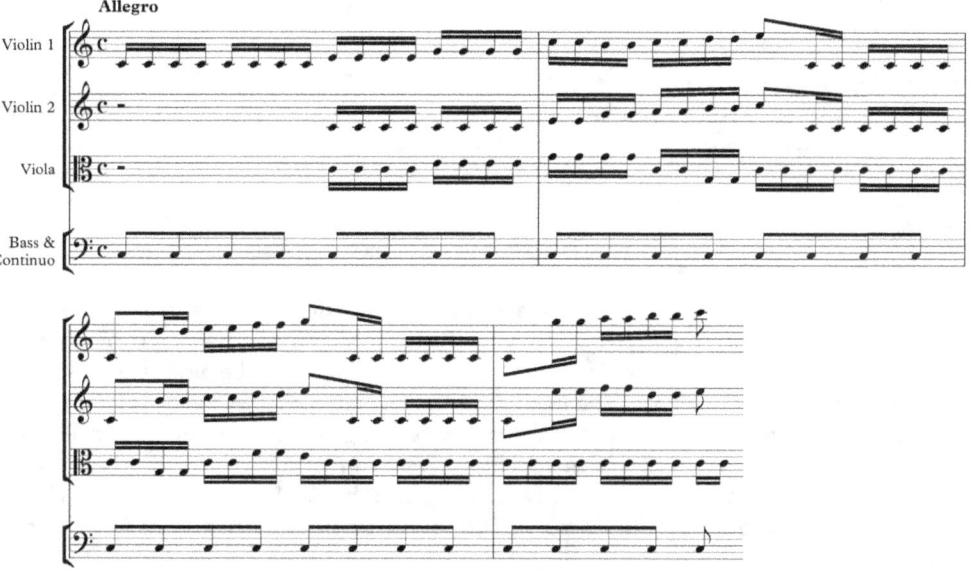

Ex. 2.2.4 'Why do the Nations?'

Whenever one part starts and another joins in, imitation can be expected to confirm the shape and sound of the motif (Exx. 2.2.27, 2.5.46). Closely-spaced entries can reinforce the point. In 'Why do the Nations?' the entries start in unison then branch off in harmony, returning to the unison each time. Each rising phrase between the unisons goes another step higher in a double-voiced *auxesis* (a dialogue between the unison and the rising movement). After the initial explosive entries, the rising sequence should be graded in intensity until the top C is reached.

2.2 Emphasis

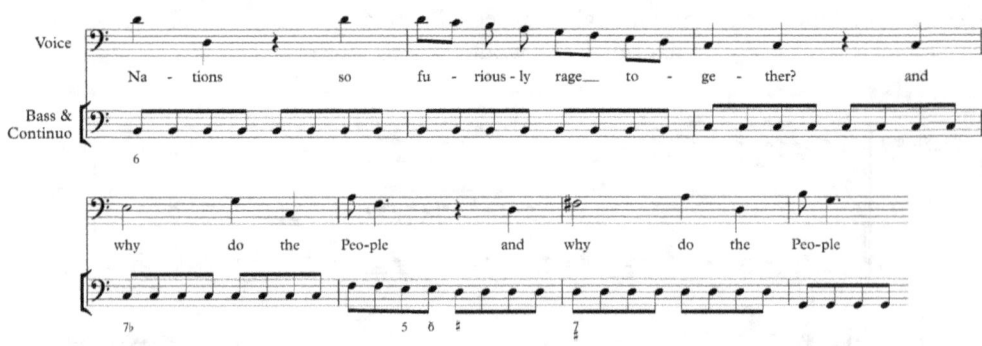

Ex. 2.2.5 'Why do the Nations?'

The demand 'and why do the People?' lurches from C major up to D major for the repetition, with 'why' on a dissonant seventh both times. Each repetition of the demand 'why?' should be reinforced.

Ex. 2.2.6 'If God is for us' (Arnold's underlay)

The violins suggest the pitch which the voice takes up, then in a surprisingly sudden move, repeats a third higher immediately, without the violins commenting in between, implying an impatient demand: 'who can be against us? who can be against us?' which concludes with a full cadence. The next phrase reverts to a calmer complete question: 'If God be for us who can be against us?' the voice rising as in a question but remaining on the same for 'against us?' which should not be so vehement. The first phrase is in dark G minor and the second in the more hopeful B♭ major. Handel wrote 'be for' in his first phrase and 'is for' in the second. The (corrected?) conducting score has 'is for' both times.

Ex. 2.2.7 'All we, like Sheep'

The emphasis here is always on the highest note, however long the phrase is. The shape of the phrase is built up in steps using falling pairs of notes.

102

Length of Note

Handel sometimes sets the same word or phrase in a number of different ways, with the resulting variety in emphasis (see below 'the Everlasting Father, the Prince of Peace' Exx. 2.2.19 – 2.2.22). A phrase set with short notes on every syllable can then be repeated in longer notes for emphasis at the culmination of the argument, or the final cadence (see 2.7 for many examples).

Ex. 2.2.8 'Hallelujah'

The emphasis is changed for the final 'Hallelujah' from 'Halle-LU-jah' to 'Hal-LE-lu-jah'.

Ex. 2.2.9 'Thus saith the Lord'

'And I will shake' uses three equal quavers then, after a gasp, a semiquaver and two quavers a tone higher, making an impatient repetition to emphasise the threat.

Articulation Marks

As a foil to the normal inflected text and its musical setting, equality of word or note stress has a special emphatic effect, AS IT IS IN SPEAKING. It can be indicated in various ways, by using either equal note values or special marks of articulation.

Normally, first beats of the bar can be expected to be stronger than the middle parts. Geminiani called these 'buono' i.e. 'good', normally first beats, and he called the bad or intermediate weak beats 'cattivo'. The emphasis of the text can override this pattern, making bar-lines of less importance, especially in counterpoint. Articulation strokes, often

2.2 Emphasis

called daggers to distinguish them from dots, can also act as a warning not to slur. Handel uses daggers which imply not only a degree of separation but also equal emphasis.

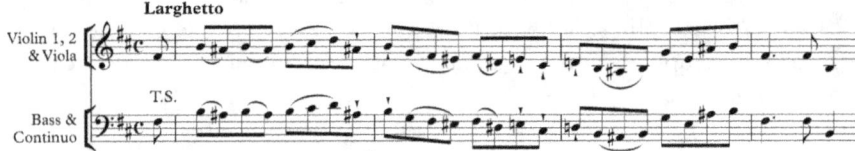

Ex. 2.2.10 'The People that walked in Darkness'

The mixture of daggered notes and slurs highlight the exploratory, hesitant and uncertain feeling. The three-note slurs should diminuendo, whether rising or falling.

Ex. 2.2.11 'Thou shalt break them'

In the opening ritornello of 'Thou shalt break them', the single emphasised first beat of bars two and three in the bass acquires a provocative second chromatic one in bars five and six which adds force as the argument continues.

Ex. 2.2.12 'He trusted in God'

'If He delight' is emphasised with equal note values at the final cadence.

2.2 Emphasis

Ex. 2.2.13 'Let us break'

Daggers are found in the instrumental parts only of 'Let us break our Bonds asunder', marked Allegro e Staccato. It is assumed that the syllabic setting will result in the short delivery of the text. However, it is unlikely that the instruments would want to play this motif legato, even without the daggers. Although equally separated, the overall shape of the phrase still needs emphasis either on the word 'break' which, when combined contrapuntally in all the voices produces wonderful cross rhythms, or on the 'let us' entries which compete with each other in encouragement. The falling nature of the theme implies the latter.

Ex. 2.2.14 'All we, like Sheep'

The emphasis of 'one to his own Way' is intoned on every syllable equally, ironically sticking to the same pitch.

2.2 Emphasis

Ex. 2.2.15 'All we, like Sheep'

The final statement of 'ev'ry one to his own Way' uses short daggered crotchets. A comic effect may be produced by singing and playing very short syllables, or an emphatic one by merely detaching each word slightly. Daggers appear only in the instrumental parts (short syllables are assumed). Before the final adagio the note values are halved again to minims for 'his own Way'. These will be naturally more sustained and serious than the detached version.

Ex. 2.2.16 'Hallelujah'

Here the degree of separation should be less than in the comic 'Sheep' as this is a weightier, more serious passage. The three emphases on the repetition of the same pitch produce a grand effect.

Slurs

Few slurs are found in either Handel's manuscript or the conducting score. If a continuous passage, such as the opening of 'For behold, Darkness shall cover the Earth', or 'And lo, the Angel of the Lord' requires slurs, only the first few groups of notes have them marked. Slurs seldom join more than two or three notes in the instruments or voices, although the opening of 'thou shalt Break them' (Ex. 2.2.11) exceptionally slurs five notes.

When instruments imitate vocal melismas there is a case for not slurring, e.g. 'shout' (Ex. 2.5.39) and 'He trusted in God' (Ex. 2.4.14) on the word 'would' which is slurred over three notes by Handel in all the voices. Keeping separate bow-strokes defines the lines, and the mixture of slurred and separate creates a clear texture. In 'Let us break their Bonds asunder' (Ex. 2.2.17), the words 'and cast away' are set using a tie which is absent from the doubling instrumental parts in Handel's manuscript, but present in the conducting score only the first time it occurs (an error?). There is something to be said for having a reiteration on the second beat from the instruments to provide rhythmic stability for the voices.

Ex. 2.2.17 'Let us break'

'And cast away' can omit the vocal tie in the instrumental doubling.

Slurs in instrumental parts should be regarded as a diminuendo from the first note (for example Exx. 2.2.10, 2.2.11 and 2.2.18).

Ex 2.2.18 'He was despised'

The pathetic pairs of slurred falling quavers in the violins offer a contrast with the similar but more vehement vocal rhythmic motif '-spi-sed, -jec-ted'. The strings should make a point of the difference between the pathetic slurred piano falling pairs and the rising imitation of 'rejected' and 'dejected' which can be more detached and firm (bar four, first beat). In the first violins, bar six, three quavers are slurred and one very clearly daggered quaver indicates where the forte begins.

Written-out decorative features notated in fast note values such as the slide for 'Behold' in 'O Thou that tellest' and the decorative turn in 'If God be for us' should be slurred together (Ex. 2.3.1 Dynamics).

Variety

The various ways of the sheep have shown us how much variety can be found, even in setting the same text. In the revised version of 'He shall feed his Flock' Handel uses the device of starting with the alto voice in the Old Testament, moving to the soprano, introducing a change of pitch, timbre and harmony (moving from F into B♭) for the New Testament text 'Come unto Him all ye that labour', a magical moment of hope.

Ex. 2.2.19 'For unto us a Child is born'

Compare these four versions of 'the Everlasting Father, the Prince of Peace'. In the first there is a gap after 'Father' and 'Prince of Peace' has daggers and equal notes, separated but not comically short. The gap is filled by a suspended violin top D.

Ex. 2.2.20 'For unto us a Child is born'

The second time there is still a gap after 'Father' but the cadence is softened by a long dotted crotchet instead of equal syllables on 'Prince of Peace'. The gap is now filled with figuration from both violin parts.

Ex. 2.2.21 'For unto us a Child is born'

'Father' is now equal, there is still a comma but 'the' is omitted, throwing more emphasis on 'Prince' if the comma is observed.

Ex. 2.2.22 'For unto us a Child is born'

In spite of a comma (derived from the word-book), the final time there is no rest and 'Father' is connected to 'The Prince of Peace' with a syncopated *iamb* (short-long) on 'FA-ther'. If the comma is observed, the gap should probably be less than the written rest in the previous versions (above Exx. 2.2.19, 2.2.20).

2.2 Emphasis

It is very important to observe exactly the small differences such as found in Exx. 2.2.19, 20, 21, and 22. The modern tendency to iron out inconsistencies and 'tidy up' some things which are judged to be carelessness on the part of the composer is misplaced. By making these phrases sound the same, the rhetorical points of variety and comparison are lost.

Compare the smooth vocal connections on one syllable and the corresponding instrumental ones which define the line:

Ex. 2.2.23 'Amen'

Instrumental parts often play separate notes where voices are slurred on a melisma. This gives a sharp outline to the sound which might otherwise be too diffuse. Bass parts are frequently found to be more detached than upper string parts for the same reason. Other examples where slurs should not be added in the instrumental parts where vocal melismas occur include Exx. 1.3.15, 1.5.16, 2.2.2, 2.2.17, 2.2.33, 2.3.15, 2.4.16, 2.5.22, 2.6.15, 2.7.24.

Length of Phrase

A common structure in the rhetorical style found in Baroque music sees two similar short phrases, which take a step up in dynamic, being followed by a long one which starts the same but with the emphasis thrown further forward.

Ex. 2.2.24 'Rejoice' simple version (opening ritornello)

Avoid emphasising the D on the third rising interval, but direct the sound to the next down-beat.

Ex. 2.2.25 'Rejoice' (closing ritornello)

The decorated version in the closing ritornello imitates the opening (above). The same pattern of short-short-long phrases pushes the expected third emphasis further away.

Harmony, Intervals

Music can use harmony to emphasise an idea or word and give the phrase shape and meaning. Tension and relaxation are generated by dissonance and consonance. The choice of chord will dictate which intervals are available, and these, when used melodically, will give emotional direction to the phrase. A rising minor sixth is generally considered to be pleading; a rising fourth or fifth more matter-of-fact; the augmented fourth, either rising or descending is a sign of strong, usually dark emotions. Small, close intervals imply hesitancy; wide striding ones confidence.

2.2 Emphasis

Dissonance is generally loud and tense, and resolution soft and relaxed. Dissonant harmony can show us which are the words or phrases of importance.

Ex. 2.2.26 'He was despised'

A change of chord is a change of feeling. Pairs of sighs (more/less, more/less) point the changing long note in the bass. The first 'more' motif in the first violins is tone-semitone and the second is semitone-tone (both times). The low E♭ pedal feels profound (with D♭ above), but when the bass moves up to the B♭ it feels less severe as the parts converge in a more 'homely' key.

Ex. 2.2.27 Sinfony (Overture)

The highest note in the first violins leads to the strongest harmony at bar three where the bass, in imitation of the violins, rises an augmented fourth giving a discordant diminished seventh at the highest point. In dotted overtures, the first beat will probably be a bit more sustained than the second, leaving a longer gap before the next strong beat. All parts are aligned in the same harmonic purpose (author's articulation marks).

Ex. 2.2.28 'Amen'

In the bass line many held and tied notes lead onto strong 4-2 dissonances so should be fully sustained.

111

2.2 Emphasis

Ex. 2.2.29 'And lo'

The exclamatory word 'lo' is set on a strong dissonance (the arioso version has 'But lo').

Ex. 2.2.30 'And the Glory'

After musical repetitions of 'and all Flesh shall see it', 'to-GE-ther' is set on a seventh which is also the longest note, doubled and decorated in the first violins. The whole phrase is under-pinned by the slowly-intoned text in the lower voices which use the snappy *iamb* for 'SPO-ken it'.

Ex. 2.2.31 'O thou that tellest'

'The Glory of the Lord' descends to a pedal decorated by a repeated dominant seventh arpeggio which signals the end of the aria just before the chorus version.

Ex. 2.2.32 'And suddenly'

This example shows the relative strength of the dissonance **6-4-2** which builds to another, greater dissonance **7-4-2**, even though the violins are falling in tessitura. The relaxation of the harmony where the voice enters implies a diminuendo.

Ex. 2.2.33 'He was despised'

'A Man of Sorrows and acquainted with Grief' is illustrated by 4-2s and 7s. 'Sorrows' is still and calm before the voice lurches onto G♭ to illustrate 'Grief' on a 6-4-2 chord. This move is approached and prepared by the tortured intervals in the first violins. The various forms of their three up-beat quavers in bars one and four imitate the same three up-beats in the voice, bar two for 'a Man of Sorrows'. A consonant rising octave in bar one then falls in extreme intervals using an augmented fourth for 'Grief' in bar four.

2.2 Emphasis

Ex. 2.2.34 'He was despised', B section

The dissonant 4-2 on 'Back' should be gently emphasised in the dotted rhythm although marked 'un poco piano'.

2.3 Dynamics

or Raising and Lowering the Voice

Decorum

> For the voice possesses a marvellous quality, so that from merely three registers, high, low and intermediate, it produces a rich variety in song. [...] The superior orator will therefore vary and modulate his voice; now raising it and now lowering it, he will run through the whole scale of tones (C, *Orator* 59).

The decorous tone of voice will look for and find its own natural dynamic. This could be a neutral, even tone in the middle register suitable for informing, or an emotional tone suitable for anger or pity. Alongside these vocal affects derived from speaking are the written dynamic instructions of decorum for the instruments (nearly always simply piano or forte). These give information to help the player to recognise their role, for example to hold back when a soloist is singing. It is essential that the instrumentalists, by listening, make a note of when they have centre stage, when they should retreat, when it is appropriate to attack strongly or when to shadow the voices. The commonly-used dynamic instructions mezzo forte, mezzo piano, or fortissimo tell the performer very little about either the prevailing affect or their role in the larger sound picture, and can only be used as a comparative measure which depends on these other factors. If no dynamic marking is found at the start of a piece, this usually implies forte if it opens with an instrumental ritornello, but this rule also depends on the prevailing affect. Handel mostly marks piano when appropriate ('Comfort ye', 'For behold'). In 'But who may abide' and 'I know that my Redeemer liveth' the opening ritornello can be full-toned without being aggressive.

Tessitura

Messiah is a continuously changing aural feast of voices and instruments sounding in harmonious agreement or contrasted in argument. Changes of tone and dynamic provide the variety essential for holding the listener's attention. Rhetorically-led dynamics assume 'natural' degrees of volume. Rising music will get louder and descending music softer, as in raising and lowering the voice. Phrases repeated higher will normally be louder than phrases repeated lower.

Where parts move in contrary motion, a large distance between them is usually indicative of a strong dynamic, and where the parts converge, less volume (Ex. 2.5.4). But contrary motion which enlarges the distance between top and bottom parts assumes a diminuendo for dispersing or straying sheep (Ex. 1.5.21).

At the same time, the emphasis of the text should always dictate subtle gradations of tone on strong and weak syllables within the general dynamic level. These basic rhetorical principles should be applied continuously unless a special marking overrides the normal inflections.

2.3 Dynamics

Ex. 2.3.1 'If God be for us'

This phrase descends from middle to lowest range, in a dialogue between the violins and the voice, where the violins decorate the held note of the voice on each downward step. Following the rather static but calm arpeggios, the dotted rhythm in bar eight introduces a note of impatience as the voice ascends alone in a melismatic crescendo which winds its way towards the final triumphant syllable of the word 'justifi-eth'. The dotted notes of the melisma which start in bar eight return to the same level (the weakest note in the bar) and the following three even notes lead upwards in steps to the next bar, giving a dynamic dip in the middle of four rising bars. The micro-dynamic units in each bar build a longer crescendo over the six bars of rising music.

A similar decoration of the vocal line by the violins occurs in 'Rejoice Greatly' on the text 'He shall speak Peace'.

Ex. 2.3.2 ' Rejoice Greatly'

The dotted rhythms are made equal to calm the phrase 'He shall speak Peace' on its repetition. The temptation to continue the dotting should be resisted. The harmonic tension (7) on the first 'Peace' is relaxed during the further two repetitions of the word.

2.3 Dynamics

Ex. 2.3.3 'Since by Man'

The chorus 'Since by Man' starts in the dark key of A minor and low tessitura doubled only by the bass line. The second phrase rises in chromatic movement towards the explosive 'Death' on the repeated phrase, implying a crescendo. At the sudden change to the Allegro in C major, the strings (and oboes if present) join in, making a brilliant contrast to the dark opening. The tessitura is now relatively high. There are no dynamic markings, but the tessitura, orchestration and key change lead the affect from the darkness of death to the triumph of resurrection.

2.3 Dynamics

Repetitions of short motifs can rise and grow in volume or, if used in a cascading downward sequence, get softer.

Ex. 2.3.4 'How beautiful are the Feet' (chorus version)

Printed dynamics are used to inform the players of their roles. In a solo aria, piano indicates that the singer is singing, forte that the singer is resting. In other words, drop back to accompany, play up in the instrumental ritornello to fulfil the demands of decorum. If a forte is marked for an instrumental phrase it can be assumed that the preceding solo passage is piano, whether so marked or not. In Ex. 2.3.5 dynamics of decorum for the instruments are clearly defined by the presence of the solo singer, first following loudly in imitation, then piano punctuation when the singer returns.

Ex. 2.3.5 'Ev'ry Valley'

More dynamics of decorum (although marked 3/8 and sub-divided, Handel's big barring is reproduced here).

Ex. 2.3.6 'But who may abide?'

2.3 Dynamics

Choruses

The dynamics of decorum are not purely black and white, but should be adjusted to match the general affect.

Ex. 2.3.7 'O Thou that tellest'

Handel's forte marking, combined with the descriptive word 'tutti' against the first voice entry, is describing the effect of the chorus following the solo version of the same music.

In the choruses, instruments often double the vocal lines, as above. Whenever this happens, the instruments should keep their level below the voices in order that the words are heard. The 'natural' dynamic in the choruses will be quieter when one voice is singing alone, and louder when all voices sing together. Crescendos are created naturally by more voices entering or singing at once. For example, in 'For unto us a Child is born' only one or two voices sing at any time (a legacy of the Italian duet source), until 'and His Name shall be called', and then all the voices sing together 'Wonderful, Counsellor, The Mighty God, The Everlasting Father, The Prince of Peace'. The independent violin figuration, which has been saved to enrich this moment, is at that point is marked forte. After that the voices drop back to single lines and there are no more dynamics marked in the instrumental parts, which return to a subsidiary role. It is assumed that they will drop back decorously to match the voices.

Most of the choruses end with all voices singing together, so it is not considered necessary to specify dynamics, as the full choral sound will naturally be loud unless the affect of the text denies this, for example the 'Iniquity' cadence at the end of 'All we, like Sheep' (Ex. 2.7.13). Often the most forceful moment, such as a sudden silence preceded by a dissonance, or a culmination of some sort, occurs just before the final cadence, in which case the very final few bars are more of a relaxation than an arrival, especially if the final syllable is a weak one such as 'REIGN-eth' or 'GLO-ry'. The last chord or note should not be the loudest if it coincides with a weak syllable.

2.3 Dynamics

Harmony

This topic has already been visited in the sections on Emphasis (2.2) and Word Painting (1.5), so there is only a little more to be said along similar lines. According to Quantz's table of dynamics relative to dissonance, the chords 7s and 9s are quite loud, the chord 4-2 is loud and 7-4-2 is the loudest (XVII. 14).

Ex. 2.3.8 'Thus saith the Lord'

In 'Thus saith the Lord', a glance at the figures will show the relative strength of the instrumental interjections. The 4-2 chord should be louder than the following chords. Dissonance is nearly always louder than consonance.

Volume should always be considered alongside affect, which is composed of different elements: rhythm, intervals, tempo, key, harmony. Sometimes the highest note is not the strongest harmonically, in which case, harmony normally wins over tessitura.

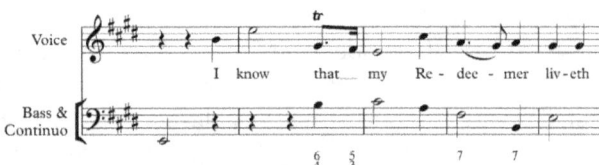

Ex. 2.3.9 'I know that my Redeemer liveth'

The long minims on 'know' and 'my' should not sag, but create direction towards Re-DEE-mer (the most dissonant syllable on a seventh) and then phrase away on 'LI-veth'. Some higher notes in the phrase should be lightened (the C♯).

Ex. 2.3.10 'Since by Man came Death'

The text 'For as in Adam all die' is harmonically intensified when repeated. Although the augmented fourth in the soprano line introduces the first 'Adam', the high point of the phrase, the second 'Adam' is more dissonant than the first, even though the soprano line falls at that point, so should be louder.

Affect

Certain rhetorical affects carry their own dynamics. For example, repeated instrumental semiquavers (when the voice is silent) will probably be loud (see Ex. 1.5.32).

Ex. 2.3.11 'He shall feed His Flock'

A pastoral larghetto in compound time will be gently piano, specified above. The lilting melodic opening falls away in waves. It can be full without being forceful or accented.

Ex. 2.3.12 'But who may abide the Day of His Coming?'

A stronger dynamic here need not be feeble in tone.

2.3 Dynamics

The rhetorical affect should always dictate the chosen dynamic, and may override the general principles given above. For example, 'The Lord gave the Word' is a commanding statement by the male voices alone, without instrumental doubling, which obviously requires a strong delivery. The instruments are held in reserve to reinforce 'Great was the Company of the Preachers' which follows (Ex. 1.5.16). 'But thanks be to God' (Ex. 1.3.23) is lighter in tone, even when all voices sing together.

Ex. 2.3.13 'He was despised'

Instruments are *p* then a rare *pp* for 'A Man of Sorrows'.

Ex. 2.3.14 'He was despised' B section

In a few special cases Handel feels it necessary to write additional dynamic instructions to counteract the natural tendency. For example in the middle section of 'He was despised' where it might be expected to play the dotted rhythms strongly, he marks 'un poco piano' to control the balance of the whole string section against one voice. Possible choices would include a small drop in the dynamic (the 'poco') without covering the voice, or playing really piano with stabbing emphases on the dissonances, which is very effective, and enables the passage to build up to the final 'spitting'.

In general short instrumental interjections in an aria should be softer than longer passages which introduce or round off the vocal sections (Exx. 2.3.15 and 2.3.16). Where the voice enters in 'Rejoice greatly', the violins imitate playfully piano in the gaps.

2.3 Dynamics

Ex. 2.3.15 'O thou that tellest'

Ex. 2.3.16 'And He shall purify'

In 'And He shall purify' the short orchestral interjections, which do not double the voices, are specially marked piano.

Ex. 2.3.17 Pifa

The Pifa is headed mezzo piano but the general dynamic should still rise towards the first beats of bars 2 and 3, falling away to the middle of each bar.

Repeat piano?

In the eighteenth century Quantz recommended altering the dynamic on repeats for variety, though he may not have been referring to complete sections of music, but rather to small repeated motifs (1752, XVII 7.26, XIV 14.15). Vivaldi often marks sections 'si replica piano'.

By adhering to 'natural' dynamic schemes, it should not be necessary to contrive unnatural effects such as piano repeats. Where rhetorical repetition is for emphasis, repeats should be reinforcements, not echoes. If the music is soft, as in the Pifa, the repeat or da capo can be even more so. The serious and dramatic opening of the overture should be intensified on the repeat and the connections in the first time bar can be used to encourage this. In making the repeat piano, a problem arises: where do the dynamics

2.3 Dynamics

revert to normal? It is difficult to overcome the weight of tradition hanging over us, but it is important to have the courage to do things differently if this means more rhetorically.

Ex. 2.3.18 Sinfony (Overture)

The approach to the repeat of the first section of the overture can crescendo through the first-time bar, making the repeat even more dramatic and intense (see also 1.6 Size and Decorum p. 78).

2.4 Tempo

or 'Confusing Our Utterance'

In the eighteenth century, the human pulse was used as a measure of the *tactus*, a regular beat around which notes were arranged. The pulse or *tactus* never went extremely fast or extremely slowly, but hovered around a medium speed, the *ordinario*. Within that pulse, the note values, combined with the rate of harmonic change, dictated how the music was perceived. Naturally, in the same pulse minims and crotchets represented slower music than quavers and semiquavers. The pulse was seldom measured in note values smaller than the crotchet, so if it is found to be necessary to count or conduct in eight then it is likely that the pulse is too slow, and there will be too many accents in the bar. Even at the slowest tempo, the larger beats should still be felt.

A common tendency to go too fast or too slow for effect undermines the continuity Handel designed between slow and fast music built around a common pulse.

Quintilian sums up this fault as follows:

> We must also [as well as not pressing our voice beyond its powers which results in lack of clarity] beware of confusing our utterance by excessive volubility, which results in disregard of punctuation, loss of emotional power, and sometimes in the clipping of words. The opposite fault is excessive slowness of speech, which is a sign of lack of readiness in invention, tends by its sluggishness to render our hearers inattentive (Q, XI iii 52).

To find a suitable tempo, the easiest and most appropriate method is to declaim the text, either with the solo voice or choral group. Strong syllables or words will be set on notes of longer value or on chord changes for emphasis. Important words will also be set on melismas which decorate important syllables. Weak syllables will occur on subdivisions of the beat, should not be prominent or sustained and will usually occur on up-bows.

The tempo is also governed by the rate of harmonic movement. If too much is crammed into too short a space of time it will probably be unintelligible to the listener. Very fast passages will probably have fewer changes of harmony than slower music which has space for more elaborate harmonic changes. Emphasising unimportant, consonant harmonic events, or subdivisions of the beat which coincide with weak syllables of the text will drag the music back and make it sound heavy.

Tempo words should not be regarded as a guide to a fixed measurable pulse. The same music will have a different affect according to the tempo adopted. Even at the same tempo, the choice of articulation, emphasis and phrasing will produce different affects. Measuring a tempo from a recording and transferring it to a different situation is no guarantee of the same result, as a combination of other factors will influence the affect of the music on the listener. The fugue of the overture and the final 'Amen' chorus are both marked Allegro Moderato, but it would be difficult to find a tempo which suited both. However, the minim beat of the overture could be the same as the crotchet beat in 'Amen'.

Tempo words are also used to describe what is happening in the music (e.g. adagio at cadences Exx. 2.7.12, 2.7.14, 2.7.20).

Numbers and Words

In *Messiah*, Handel uses the time signature C (4/4) with and without the supplementary word qualifications Grave, Largo, Larghetto, Andante, Andante larghetto, Andante allegro, Allegro, and 'a tempo ordinario'.

Grave is only used for the associated 'Since by man' and 'For as in Adam', and for the opening of the Sinfony (overture).

Cut C is only used once, for the old-fashioned style alla breve 'And with his stripes' (Ex. 1.5.31).

The trumpet of the last judgement gets a suitably unique 'pomposo ma non allegro' marking.

'Thou art gone up on high' at various times had versions marked andante, allegro, and andante larghetto (for identical music). Arnold's score has Andante for the alto voice version and Allegro for the bass voice.

Handel uses 3/8 for 'But who may abide' but his large four-beat bars are subdivided (reproduced in Arnold's edition Ex. 2.3.6). This implies that the feeling of four 3/8 bar units should be preserved in the phrasing.

Adagio

In *Messiah*, the word adagio is found in two situations:

- At final cadences where the note values of the repeated text are often doubled, and not always then. This means adagio used at a final cadence has a descriptive function which could be considered as a form of written-out ritardando

- Indicating extra time for a short cadenza in solo arias

Ex. 2.4.1 'But who may abide'

Adagio often indicates extra time for the cadenza moment at the end of the 'A' section of an aria. A short cadenza or decorative flourish is expected on the 6-4 chord when it occurs the second or, as in the above example, the final time round. Tempo primo is assumed at the start of the final ritornello, marked forte.

Ex. 2.4.2 'Rejoice greatly'

Adagio gives licence for a cadenza, and again tempo primo is assumed where the forte appears.

Ex. 2.4.3 'If God be for us'

After a silence (which may be of indeterminate length), the soloist is given two bars marked adagio during which there is scope for a short flourish (at the place marked with an arrow). The violins are always silent at these places and the cadenza has to be negotiated with the continuo players. They may cease playing altogether, leaving the voice to elaborate over the 6-4 chord (bar eight of the example) and return with a dominant chord (the low D) just before the resolution on 'us'. The singer can assist the entry of the continuo by a rhythmic ending to the ornament on the words '-ion for us', which will suggest the second beat. Tempo primo is assumed after the cadence, from the violin up-beat.

Burney describes a performance in Dublin by the solo singer Dubourg who had a cadence to decorate, *ad libitum*:

> He wandered about in different keys a great while, and seemed indeed a little bewildered, and uncertain of his original key [...] but, at length, coming to the shake which was to terminate this long close, Handel, to the great delight of the audience, and augmentation of applause, cried out loud enough to be heard in the most remote parts of the theatre: 'You are welcome home, Mr. Dubourg!' ('Sketch of the Life of Handel', foot-note, p. 27)

2.4 Tempo

Ex. 2.4.4 'All we, like Sheep'

The final section of 'All we, like Sheep' is marked adagio, but it is exactly at this point that the note values change into minims and dotted crotchets. In other words the note values are halved, making the music automatically much slower, now only two beats in a bar. The minim *tactus* can remain the same. The word adagio is describing what is happening, not prescribing any affirmative action. The busy chorus has arrived at its conclusion.

Handel never uses adagio in *Messiah* at the head of a movement to indicate the general tempo. As we have seen above, the choruses often have the final cadence written in longer note values which dispenses with the need for any extra word instruction. Sometimes he writes adagio, sometimes he doesn't. The manuscripts are inconsistent on this point, even between themselves, but if the notation is allowed to speak for itself, the effect is the same.

Other examples of this occur in 'of Glory' (Ex. 2.7.16) at the end of 'Lift up your heads O ye gates', at the end of the 'Hallelujah' chorus, and the following extract from the 'Beautiful feet' chorus, where there is no adagio marking.

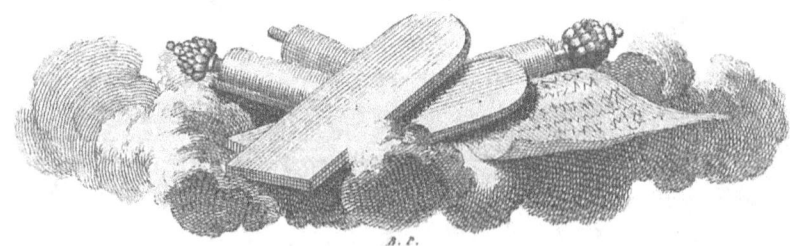

Ex. 2.4.5 'Break forth into Joy'

The final bars of 'Break forth into Joy', the ending of 'How beautiful are the Feet'. This choral version is now rarely performed.

Andante

'Andante' appears alone ('Ev'ry Valley') and also modified by the words allegro, larghetto and moderato. It indicates a purposeful forward movement, in character and affect, but the tempo cannot be measured with an invented metronome marking. It appears in C, 3/4 and 6/8. Andante can be bright and optimistic ('Ev'ry Valley', 'O thou that tellest', 'For unto us' and 'O Death') or lyrical and flowing ('How beautiful are the Feet'), dark ('For behold'), violent ('Thou shalt break them'), or mysterious ('And lo').

Ex. 2.4.6 'O Death'

'O Death', has a typical andante 'walking' bass-line. Look for continuous quaver movement in the bass wherever andante occurs, and make the quavers detached. The early eighteenth-century musical commentator Roger North says they should sound like equal steps. The lines of quavers should have shape towards and away from the harmonic high points, but stay separated.

Largo

Largo at this time is a middle tempo, should not be divided into less than crotchet beats and should flow without feeling hurried or pressed. All the Largo movements are serious in content ('Behold the Lamb of God', 'He was despised', 'Surely', 'Behold and see', 'Worthy is the Lamb').

2.4 Tempo

A quartet composed in 1784 by John Marsh describes a slow movement as 'Largo 8 in a bar' with '8 in a bar' underlined in his MS. It becomes clear from another occasion, when the players were criticised for playing a quartet marked largo too fast, that the meaning of the term might be changing, and only then was largo thought of as a slower tempo than it had been (John Marsh, *Journals*, Vol. 1, p. 774).

Larghetto should have a little more movement than largo. It flows ('But who may abide', 'How beautiful are the Feet', 'I know that my Redeemer liveth', 'If God be for us'), but is slower in 3/8 than 12/8 (e.g. 'He shall feed His Flock' Ex. 2.3.11 more flowing than 'But who may abide' Ex. 2.3.12).

Part Two opens with a sequence of movements which can be related in tempo from 'Behold the Lamb of God' up until the end of 'He trusted in God'. The tempo markings for this group of related movements read: largo, largo, largo e staccato, alla breve moderato, allegro moderato, larghetto, allegro. This might seem to indicate varying tempos, but if we look at the notation, which uses a variety of rhythmic patterns, the tempo markings become descriptions of the character and affect of internal rhythms rather than purely indications of speed.

A common crotchet beat can be continued through the three largo movements below which open Part Two, even though the affects are quite different. Using tempos which vary too much will destroy the unity and dramatic inevitability of the sequence. The same pulse can continue through 'And with his Stripes' and 'All we, like Sheep'.

Ex. 2.4.7 'Behold the Lamb of God'

Ex. 2.4.8 'He was despised'

Ex. 2.4.9 'Surely'.

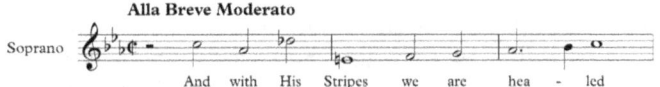

Ex. 2.4.10 'And with His Stripes'

The music then becomes alla breve, with the same crotchet pulse now equal to a semibreve.

Tempo Relationships

There are several places where it is important to create relationships between consecutive numbers. In the overture, a standard tempo relationship between the two sections should form a link without slowing up at the double bar. The crotchet of the grave can become the minim of the fugue without disruption of the *tactus*. It may be easier to set the tempo by testing it out on the fugue before applying it to the opening grave. The allegro moderato marking of the fugue recurs in 'Amen', where a similar tempo would seem to fit the crotchet pulse rather than the minim.

> The connection between the end of 'Refiner's Fire' and the opening of 'And he shall purify'. A successful transition depends on not slowing down for the final cadence bar but keeping the pulse going through the rest for the start of the bass quavers. The half bar becomes the new crotchet beat.

Ex. 2.4.11 'And He shall purify'

The transition into 'But who may abide' uses the rhetorical figure *anadiplosis* where the last sound of a section is repeated as the first sound of the next section or phrase, albeit with a radical change of mood. Too large a gap and this feature will be lost (see also Ex. 1.3.21).

Ex. 2.4.12 'But who may abide'

Other connections are obvious: the recitative 'And suddenly' where the angel praises God should lead straight into 'Glory to God' without missing a beat. In anticipation of this, the opening of the string recitative should therefore start at the same tempo as the chorus (both are marked allegro), a bit faster than 'And lo' which is marked andante. This will give the effect of the scene gathering pace as it moves towards 'Glory to God'.

Ex. 2.4.13 'All they that see Him'

The end of 'All they that see Him' (above) should be linked in tempo to the start of 'He trusted in God' (below). The continuing vehement effect depends on not slowing up after 'saying' and holding the tension through the empty bar (often cut in half by nervous conductors).

Ex. 2.4.14 'He trusted in God'

Ex. 2.4.15 'Since by Man'

'Since by Man' and 'For as in Adam' are marked grave and the following sections 'By Man came also the Resurrection' and 'even so in Christ' are marked allegro. The doubling of the tempo will account for most of the change of affect (crotchet equals minim). If the graves are too slow the effect of the gasp for the first syllables 'since' and 'for' will be lost, especially in bar four which lacks a down-beat. It should sound like a syncopation, not the second beat of a four beat bar. The first allegro should finish without slowing up to capture the effect of the following silence, changing the mood suddenly back to grave for 'For as in Adam'.

2.4 Tempo

Ex. 2.4.16 'And the Glory of the Lord'

Adagio describes the slow cadence which should surprise after the repetitions which lead to the silence (see Ex. 2.7.2).

Ex. 2.4.17 'Worthy is the Lamb'

'Worthy is the Lamb' moves from largo to andante for 'to receive Power' where the tempo should move on slightly and immediately on the syllabic text which makes it sound more urgent than the grand drawn-out 'Worthy' start. This is a good example of either fewer or more notes creating the affect without a radical change in the *tactus*. The process is repeated, taking the tempo back for the second 'Worthy'.

2.4 Tempo

Ex. 2.4.18 'Blessing and Honour'

'Blessing and honour', marked larghetto, will be similar in tempo to the andante, with more forward movement, but still holding the rather grand effect.

The approach to 'Amen' (Ex. 2.7.22) is written in long note values, so the slowing up need not be exaggerated. The graceful lines of 'Amen' should then be a relaxation, building up naturally to the final cadence as the voices join. The silence is more striking if it is sudden and approached without slowing up.

Pauses

The pause or fermata sign can mean various things:

- The end of the A section of a da capo aria, in which case the note marked with a pause is often played shorter than the written length, especially first time round
- A cadenza point
- The last note (which can be played shorter than written)

Ex. 2.4.19 'Ev'ry Valley'

Handel wrote a pause sign at the end of the first ritornello, which indicates the end of the da capo. The pause sign may be omitted in editions where the ritornello is written out at the end of the aria. The pause sign in these cases is at the end but only means 'this is the end', and does not require a long note.

135

2.4 Tempo

Ex. 2.4.20 'But Thou didst not leave'

'But Thou didst not leave' ending shown by pauses. The bass section should stop as the violins play the lower A, i.e. shorter than written and with very little slowing up.

Ex. 2.4.21 'He was despised'

'He was despised', transition into the middle section. The note marked with a pause will be shorter first time when the music continues in the same pulse.

Ex. 2.4.22 'Comfort ye'

A pause can indicate a cadenza point in some editions.

Recitative

In contrast to the way a short text is extended, repeated and decorated in the arias and choruses, recitative uses no elaboration of musical motifs. Repetition is occasionally used, as in speech, for special effect or to show gradations of emotion which lead to a climax. Recitative is used to move the narrative forward quickly, and provide an idea or describe an event which is then elaborated in the following aria without delaying tactics which might enable reflection or contemplation.

The few short passages of *secco* recitative in *Messiah* (that is, accompanied just by the continuo cello and keyboard) should be delivered as if spoken, in the tempo of speech,

2.4 Tempo

but with a certain amount of rhythmic freedom. If there is more than one phrase or sentence, the tone should be changed for the second phrase.

Recitative Example One

Ex. 2.4.23 'And the Angel'.

The chord changes indicate important words.

'And the Angel said unto them"

> (Change of tone from narrative to angel's words which end in a confident and conclusive tone)

'Fear not: for be-HOLD, I bring you good TI-dings of great JOY, which shall be to all PEOPLE'.

> (A short wait then change of tone back to narrative new idea led by rising chromatic bass line)

'For unto you is born this DAY in the City of DA-vid, a SAV-iour which is CHRIST'

> (The strongest word supported by a crescendo to the dissonance, followed by a gap before)

'the Lord'

> Ends on a bright F♯ major chord.

Recitative Example Two

For 'For then shall be brought to pass the Saying that is written'

> (narrative voice then imagine quotation marks and become more declamatory)

'Death is swallowed up in Victory'.

Recitative Example Three

'Unto which of the Angels said He at any Time',

> (question or statement)

'Thou art my Son, this Day have I begotten Thee'?

> (strong questioning statement to confirm the fact of Christ made flesh).

Most of the recitative in *Messiah* is accompanied by the full string section, either with persistent rhythmic motifs or sustained chords. Recitative often emerges from the previous music where the strings are already playing (for example the end of 'Why do the Nations' in the short version). Sometimes they join in at the end of a *secco* passage: 'And lo, the Angel of the Lord' comes directly out of 'And there were Shepherds', and 'And 'suddenly' should follow directly from 'which is Christ the Lord'. There should be a sudden change in feeling from the free spoken discursive to the excited rhythmic music.

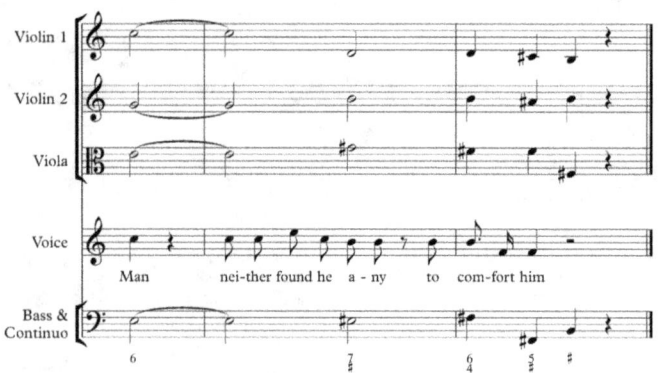

Ex. 2.4.24 'Thy Rebuke'

Where the strings are sustaining notes under the voice, they should cut off their sound before cadences for clarity (here on the word 'any'). Generally cadences should be played short and the dominant chord elided with the singer's last word.

Accompanied recitative, that is where the voice is accompanied by all the strings, not just the cello, always needs to be sung in reasonably strict tempo. In other words, when the vocal soloist sees the violinists lifting up their instruments to start playing, they should try to sing in time!

Handel directed performances from the keyboard rather than conducting, so the tempo relationships between closely connected movements would need to be related in some way for the performers to accomplish continuity (see 1.2 Structural Connections). Handel would have been relying on the performers' instincts and experience concerning tempo, filling the tempo ordinario *tactus*, with either a few or many notes, determining whether the music sounded slow or fast.

2.5 Rhythm

or 'Trochees, What are Trochees?'

Cicero wrote that there are two things which charm the ear: sound and rhythm. The sound is dependent on the understanding, but it is rhythm which produces pleasure (C, *Orator*, 162, 163). Quintilian includes rhythm in his summary of artistic structure, which consists of order, connection and rhythm (Q, IX iv 22).

Affect of the Length of Notes

Quintilian wrote that every schoolboy knows that language is made up of long and short syllables where two shorts equal one long. Sounds have length and weight, or quantity and quality (Q, IX iv 46). Long sounds are serious and short ones lighter in character, as in ways of speaking. The shorter the syllables or notes are, the more comic they sound. For example, as seen above, the articulation marks on 'His own way' in 'All we, like Sheep' imply shorter, and so more comic syllables than the grander 'King of Kings' (See Exx. 2.2.15, 2.2.16). Quintilian describes the grand effect made by placing long syllables at the end of sentences, calling to mind the text set in long notes which end many of Handel's choruses (Q, IX iv 93).

The affect of the length of notes is related to tempo, so if short notes are surrounded by too much space, the wrong, spiky or even happy affect is created, when a sad or angry one is intended. The degree of separation and intensity should be adjusted to the tempo. As can be seen in the adagio cadences above (Exx. 2.4.5, 2.4.16) and in the next example, setting a repeated part of the text in longer note values gives it extra emphasis.

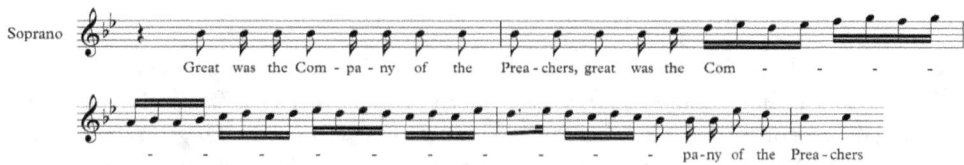

Ex. 2.5.1 'The Lord gave the Word'

Short syllables on 'Preachers' become long at the end of the phrase for an emphatic conclusion to the phrase.

Variety of Phrase Length

Groups of long and short syllables or notes in patterns have their own affects which are related to tempo. If the beat is too slow or too fast, the pattern or rhythmic group will lose its character. Rhythmic motifs are often repeated with small differences for comparison and surprise. The Greek rhetorician Longinus describes prose with regular, predictable rhythms as being devoid of passion because, 'Foreseeing the Places where they must necessarily rest, they have Gestures answering every to Turn, can even beat the Time, and tell beforehand as exactly as in a Dance where the Pause will be' (p. 73). If poetry is compared to dance with its predictable rhythms and regular phrase lengths, counterpoint could be compared to oratory because it uses a variety of phrase lengths, called haphazard by the rhetorician Dionysius of Halicarnassus ('On literary composition', p. 213). These unequal phrases can interact and surprise, thereby holding the attention of the listener.

2.5 Rhythm

Dotted Notes

Dotted rhythms are principally an instrumental device used in French music (overture and dance) where the violin-dominated style dictated that the bow should be lifted on the dotted note to make a jerky affect. Dotted notes in common time are generally lively, but if too slow they will sound laboured, and if too short, flippant. The amount of dotting combined with the attack determines the affect. If the tempo is too slow, unsuitable over-dotting will be required, which will produce an unwanted aggressive affect. It is crucial for the dotted overture to sound magnificent and dramatic but at the same time maintain energy. Although Handel writes grave for the overture, it should not be heavy and lugubrious. The opening chorus of Part Two, marked Largo in 4/4 (Ex. 2.4.7) also uses the grand dotted overture style, but 'Lift up your Heads' (Ex. 2.5.6) is lighter in character.

Rhythmic Alteration

Whenever *Messiah* is rehearsed it will not be long before someone cries 'Is it double-dotted?' In the past, this question was used to demonstrate the player's (usually scanty) knowledge of 'authentic' performance practice. As more players become acquainted with Baroque style, especially French overture style, the question will become increasingly superfluous. As seen above, affect depends on the relative lengths of the dotted note and the short note which follows it. Mathematical formulae will not help establish this.

The tempo, combined with the right amount of attack on the dotted note, and the lifting of the bows before the main beats, will establish the affect of the overture. The slower it goes, the more over-dotted it must become. However, it should never be played exactly as written at any tempo. The grave affect should be grand, noble and serious without being heavy and turgid. In general second beats will be weaker than first beats (Ex. 2.2.27). Lilting dotted rhythms in compound or common time can be tripletised in the proportion 2:1 ('I know that my Redeemer liveth'), but the trumpet waking the dead needs to sound more arresting, as written.

'Behold the Lamb of God' could be considered to be a French overture in style and so be all dotted, i.e. by shortening the single quavers to semiquavers (Ex. 2.4.7). However, it is possible and reasonable to play the rhythms exactly as written, making a suitably grave affect which highlights and gives extra weight to the word 'Behold'. If everything is over-dotted in this movement, it loses some of its gravity. The tempo has its part to play in all this, and it should be borne in mind that a 'speaking' tempo will carry the text and music to its best effect.

'Lift up your Heads' often takes up too much time in rehearsal while people argue about the dotted notes and what should be changed. Before altering anything, try it exactly as written. In 'I know that my Redeemer liveth' and 'The Trumpet shall sound', the note before the dotted quaver could be shortened or left as a quaver (Exx. 2.1.7, 2.5.4).

Other situations which could benefit from alteration are:

- Bar 1 of 'Thus saith the Lord' (Ex. 2.5.2)

- Bars 1-2 of 'Surely' (Ex. 2.5.5)

The manuscript parts of the Foundling Hospital (1757) show intermittent use of the (more accurate) semiquaver rest and semiquaver in all these situations before the dotted note, even after a rest where it is normally printed as a quaver. The inconsistency may be accounted for by an assumption that players would naturally shorten the note before the dot except, as has been seen above, in 'The Trumpet shall sound' where the exact rhythms may be preserved. It is impossible to give any strict ruling about this other than that it is necessary to consider the effect created by various degrees of alteration.

2.5 Rhythm

Ex. 2.5.2 'Thus saith the Lord'

Lively and dramatic dotted notes in the instruments introduce the text 'Thus saith the Lord'. A loud rest is implied by the lack of down beat, creating an impatient affect. The dotted rhythms shouldn't sound too static, pompous or grand, and the singer should interrupt the strings' crescendo towards the first explosive 'Thus'.

Ex. 2.5.3 'The Trumpet shall sound' (Arnold)

In the above example, Arnold's late eighteenth-century edition continues the same dotted rhythms in bars 3-5 (as does Mozart's arrangement, which is double-dotted), altering Handel's rhythm just where the rising arpeggio on repeated notes should turn into a melodic feature. By maintaining the dots, Arnold spoils the interplay between the dotted notes on one pitch, and the equal rhythms which rise and fall.

Ex. 2.5.4 'The Trumpet shall sound'

2.5 Rhythm

Arnold corrects these notes in the closing ritornello (Ex. 2.5.4, bar 7), so it is possibly an engraver's error in the first statement.

Dotted rhythms are commonly used to announce something or someone of significance. The trumpet is announcing the last judgement and waking the dead. The solo bass voice only uses this device for one ornamental bar shadowing the instrumental version. The exact dotted rhythms make a good foil for the bars with even quavers in smooth melodic lines.

The rhythm of the up-beat and first two bars of this number (as shown in Ex. 2.5.3) was traditionally used as a flourish (by two trumpets) to announce the arrival of the judges at Assizes Courts throughout Britain. A manuscript belonging to the eminent trumpeter Crispian Steele-Perkins and used at Guildford Assizes called 'Upon the Arrival of the Judge' records these exact rhythms, even stopping on a long note at the point where Handel introduces the smooth quavers (the third whole bar). Steele-Perkins maintains that Handel's audiences would have recognised the fanfare when heard in *Messiah*, here used by Handel to announce the ultimate judgement, but perhaps the trumpets had appropriated the flourish from Handel.

Ex. 2.5.5 'Surely'

> In 'Surely', the word staccato implies that the dotted notes should be short, but not laboured. The three note dotted up-beats should lead towards the long crotchets which should be sustained in all parts to produce the full intensity of the tragic affect in F minor.

Vocal Dots

Handel's contemporary Johann Mattheson names dotted rhythms and arpeggios as being unsuitable for the voice (II.5.118).

> In vocal lines, dotted notes which are detached (as in the instrumental types) are rare. Exceptions include 'Lift - up - your heads' and 'and - the go - vernment - shall be - upon - His shoulders'.

2.5 Rhythm

Ex. 2.5.6 'Lift up your Heads'

Ex. 2.5.7 'For unto us'

2.5 Rhythm

Ex. 2.5.8 'Lift up your Heads'

The dotted note gives an impatient feel to the emphasis in the syllabic question 'who IS – this King of Glory?' which is a foil to the smooth answer in *antithesis*: 'The Lord of Hosts', with 'Lord' dotted but on one smooth syllable.

Other dotted rhythms occur on the words: 'WONderful, COUNsellor', 'DeLIver Him', and 'SUrely', all of which form part of a whole word which, although the emphasis is on the first syllable, should not be chopped up by stopping the sound on the dot. Here, where the strings double or imitate the voices, the bows should stay on the string.

2.5 Rhythm

Ex. 2.5.9 'Surely'

If 'Surely' is too slow, the middle syllable will assume too much prominence. Speak the text to find a naturally emphatic tempo. The opening of this chorus creates a dramatic shock as F minor follows 'He was despised' which finishes in beautiful E♭ major.

In 'Surely', the instrumental dotted notes stay on the same pitch and should be detached and demanding, whereas the voices move on different pitches using longer note values and are smoother. This passage often falls apart in performance because the voices tend to be late after the rests and drag when they reach the drawn-out 'born our Griefs and carried our Sorrows' and the instruments tend to rush on the dotted notes creating tension between the slow and faster moving elements. After the repetition of 'Surely', instrumental dots are maintained as the voices declaim homophonically over the top. A sublime combination.

2.5 Rhythm

Dotted Affects

Ex. 2.5.10 'But who may abide?'

Dotted rhythms in compound time *are* suited to the voice and are more languid and benevolent, evoking a pastoral atmosphere. The descending fauxbourdon in bar six (a line of parallel first inversions, bass figured 6) contributes to the pastoral effect. The third note of the rhythmic group should always be lightened. If sung or played completely legato this will spoil the graceful affect of the dotted rhythm and make it heavy. Instruments should reproduce the emphasis of the text, where the third quaver always occurs on a weak syllable: 'But WHO may a-BIDE the DAY of His COming'.

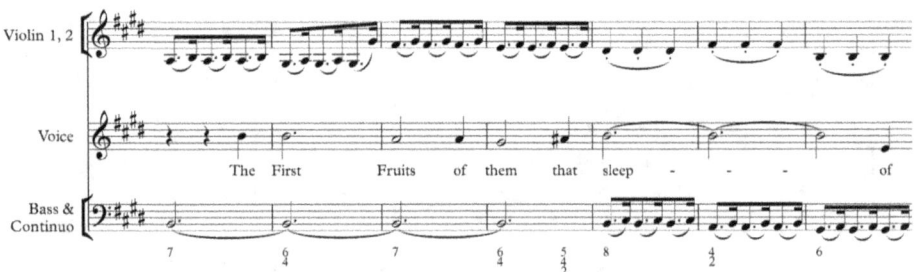

Ex. 2.5.11 'I know that my Redeemer liveth' (Arnold's underlay)

The slurred, languid, dotted rhythm of 'the First Fruits of them that sleep' is gentle and should lull us into sleep.

Ex. 2.5.12 'He was despised' B section

Soft but tense dotted notes in the instruments form the background to the pathetic middle section of 'He was despised'. There must be a gap on every dot for the anguished affect.

Syncopations

Syncopations or ties generally lead to dissonant harmonies and should be sustained, anticipating the next chord. Avoid an ugly lurch or bulge in the middle of the note.

Ex. 2.5.13 'Ev'ry Valley'

At the beginning of the ritornello the second violins should bounce off their first down-beat and then sustain the E for long enough to clash momentarily against the first violins' F♯ before both parts rise in parallel thirds.

Ex. 2.5.14 'But Thou didst not leave'

In this extract the tied D in the violins impatiently follows the interrupted cadence halfway through the bar, anticipating the dissonant seventh, the final moment of tension before the more relaxed ending.

Ex. 2.5.15 'Behold the Lamb of God'

This example is similar to the previous one, where one part has a displaced down-beat sustained onto a dissonance (the C in the second violins). Here the second violins are a fourth higher than the firsts, thus drawing attention to the important note.

2.5 Rhythm

In the next two extracts from the overture, the violas and first violins move up in anticipated steps and are chased by the bass line. The line only starts descending after the main dissonance has been reached at the top of the phrase (first violin tied C), preceded by a gap in the bass line which draws attention to the climax of the phrase.

Ex. 2.5.16 Sinfony (Overture)

In the example below, the violas rebound off their first beats in rising fourths, the second time more, even though the phrase is descending, as they bounce off the dissonant 7 chord. The emphasis should be on the first beats of these bars. Do not try to create jazz by accenting the tied note or the harmonic rhythm will be destroyed.

Ex. 2.5.17 Sinfony (Overture)

2.5 Rhythm

Ex. 2.5.18 'Surely'

Four bars of dissonances illustrate 'our Transgressions'. The dotted minims and all vocal dotted and tied notes must be sustained for the full affect, or moments of vital dissonance will be lost. Breath may be taken by all voices and instruments after '-GRES-sions', long-short but set on equal note values with a dissonance on the strong syllable. The syllable directly before the breath shouldn't sound snatched.

Ex. 2.5.19 'Behold the Lamb'

The anticipated tied down-beat 'of' stands out and maintains the tension through the gap in the figure *epizeuxis* which uses close repetition to reinforce. The word 'of' is first heard in the soprano line as a weak syllable, then a strong one when repeated: 'The Sin of the World, OF the World'.

149

2.5 Rhythm

Repeated Semiquavers

Repeated semiquavers usually represent anger, which Handel uses as a purely instrumental affect (see 1.5 Word Painting, p. 71). If the tempo is too fast, the individual notes become impossible to articulate separately and the effect becomes fuzzy and, instead of fizzing and sparking, sounds like a tremolo (not used in this period). A slightly slower tempo where every note can be heard is more gritty and exciting.

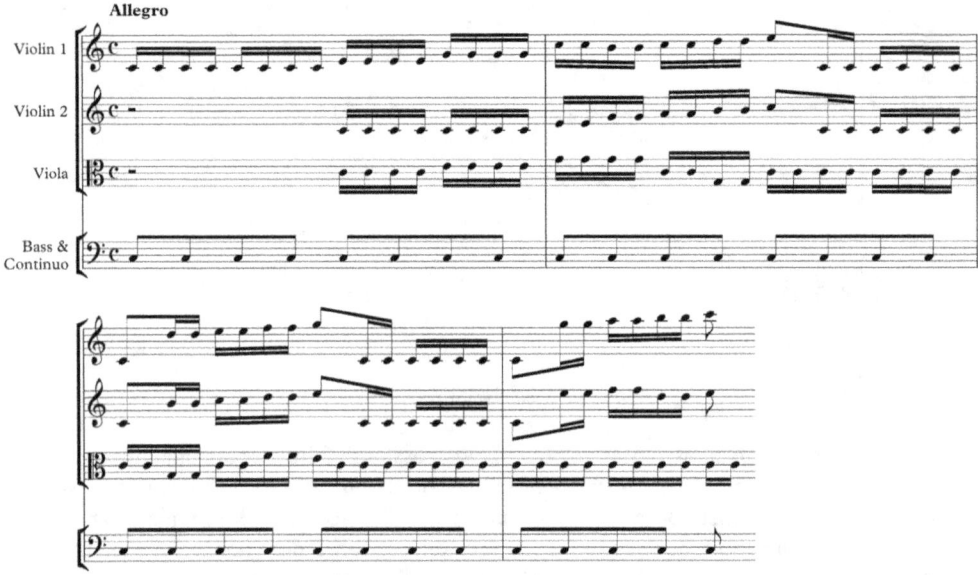

Ex. 2.5.20 'Why do the Nations'

Compare these two examples (Ex. 2.5.20 and 2.5.21). The semiquaver passage marked prestissimo (Ex. 2.5.21) should be faster and lighter than the first example ('Why do the Nations?') for a different affect. The exciting fast notes illustrating 'the Refiner's Fire' should sizzle and flare, but bear in mind that they should move seamlessly in and out of the gentle 'But who may abide' without slowing up (quaver equals crotchet). The allegro semiquaver speed in 'Why do the Nations' should be slower and more aggressive than the prestissimo.

Ex. 2.5.21 'But who may abide' transition to 'He is like a Refiner's Fire'.

Mixed Rhythms

In vocal works, 'sublime' affects can be achieved by mixing dotted instrumental music with smooth vocal lines, as in 'Surely' (Ex. 2.5.9). Quantz described the combination of an andante 'walking' bass-line with contrasted (usually smooth) lines over the top as 'sublime' (XII.24). This combination of two opposing rhythmic strands can be used in various ways with a solo voice, or chorus.

Ex. 2.5.22 'And He shall purify'

The 'sublime' affect, with falling sustained lines against two levels of rhythm. Each line should maintain its own character for the effect to work. The emphatic syllabic text, here reinforced by the bass line, acts as a foil to the longer lines.

Ex. 2.5.23 'Why do the Nations'

The crazy jagged patterns of the angry 'Why do the Nations'. The strings insistently hold on to semiquavers of D while the voice moves around in triplets. There is chaos!

Iamb and *Trochee*

In an anecdotal exchange recalled by the librettist Thomas Morell, Handel, on reading the last air in *Alexander Balus*, cried out 'D...n your Iambics'. To which was replied 'Don't put

2.5 Rhythm

yourself in a passion, they are easily Trochees'. 'Trochees, what are Trochees?' 'Why, the very reverse of Iambics, by leaving out a syllable in every line, as instead of 'Convey me to some peaceful shore', 'Lead me to some peaceful shore'. The first uses an up-beat syllable, con-VEY, the second starts directly on a strong beat, LEAD me (quoted in R. Smith 1995, p. 29).

This example shows clearly how *iamb* and *trochee* can have quite different affects. The *trochee* is easy and trips along in a relaxed way, and the *iamb* is more emphatic. Cicero writes that the *iamb* is the equivalent of a *trochee*, both being composed of a short and a long syllable (C, *Orator*, 217). How the two elements are placed determines their effect. Quintilian says that when a short syllable is followed by a long one, the affect is of vigorous ascent, while a long followed by a short produces a gentler impression and suggests descent (Q, IX iv 92). He describes how the *iamb* is used for its attack in violent and abusive language (Q, IX iv 141). All slow movements in compound time use the *trochee* as a basic rhythmic unit.

The *trochee* is used in gentle descending phrases.

Ex. 2.5.24 'He shall feed His Flock'

Compare these two versions of the voice entry. A 'normal' up-beat appears first.

Ex. 2.5.25 'Thou art gone up on high'

When this phrase returns, the entry gains energy by starting impatiently on the second beat, which needs more effort and is emphasised by its early appearance.

Ex. 2.5.26 'Thou art gone up on High'

2.5 Rhythm

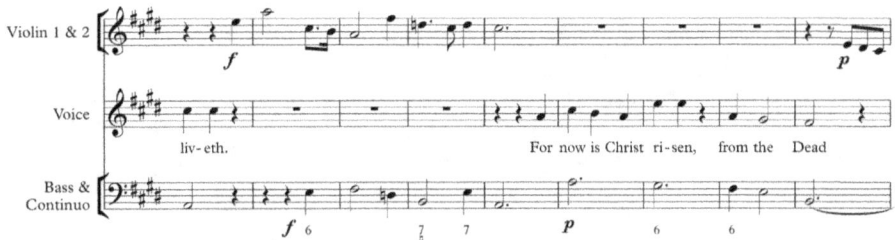

Ex. 2.5.27 'I know that my Redeemer liveth'

'From the Dead', by being preceded by a rest becomes more emphatic, and although the emphasis is on 'the', an unimportant word, this makes the phrase, short-long, more authoritative than it would be long-short which would sound more casual: 'FROM the Dead', instead of 'from THE Dead'.

Anapaest

In general, long note values on main beats are more stressed than short ones on intermediate beats. In music the *anapaest* rhythmic unit consists of two shorts and a long, with the emphasis on the first short. In other words, the long third syllable or note becomes the weakest. Literally from the Greek 'struck back' or rebound, the *anapaest* is a lively, fast-moving, snappy rhythmic unit, usually placed on the front of a strong beat for emphasis. As can be seen from these examples, it has a whole range of uses according to tempo and word emphasis.

Ex. 2.5.28 'Ev'ry Valley'

The word 'exalted' gets various treatments using the *anapaest*. It is important that the last syllable is always weak and often needs to be shorter than the written note value.

Ex. 2.5.29 'Ev'ry Valley'

'Ex-AL-ted' is used in a melodic flourish which starts low in a long rising melisma which uses the *anapaest* on the main beat to build in rising steps to the highest note, in the rhetorical figure *auxesis*. The effect of the snappy final short syllable is lost if it is emphasised.

2.5 Rhythm

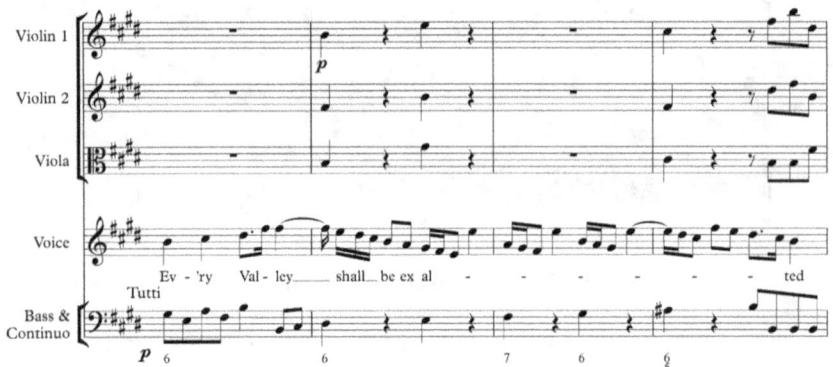

Ex. 2.5.30 'Ev'ry Valley'

Another use of the *anapaest* for the word 'exalted'. It brings an energetic decoration into the phrase. The third repetition is tied, and should be more sustained than the other two, driving the word forward to its conclusion. The rising bass builds towards the strong A♯, resolving weakly onto the B octave quavers after the voice peaks.

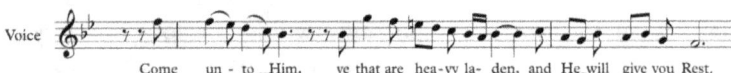

Ex. 2.5.31 'Come unto Him, ye that are heavy laden' (Arnold's underlay)

The first syllable of 'LA-den' should be emphasised, not the long note that follows which should float away on the weak syllable '-den'.

Ex. 2.5.32 'He was despised' B section.

The emphasis in this phrase should be on 'Back' (strong 4-2 chord) leading to 'Smiters'. The second syllable of 'Smiters' can be short but still vehement.

Ex. 2.5.33 'And the Glory'

'Flesh' 'see' and 'together' are equally emphasised by repeating the same *anapaestic* rhythm and staying at the same pitch. Although the notes are the same, 'Flesh' has three notes for one syllable, 'see' only two, making the second group, which has more syllables, more active.

Ex. 2.5.34 'The Trumpet shall sound', B section

The repetition of the *anapaest* emphasises the alliterative 'Mortal must'.

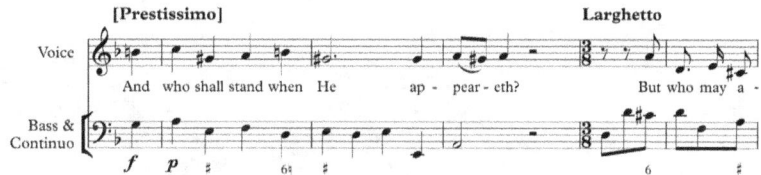

Ex. 2.5.35 'But who may abide?'

The transition back into 'But who may abide'. The provocative silence will be ruined if the final syllable of the *anapaest* is too long, or the singer slows up. The *antithesis* between the vehement 'Refiner's Fire' and the gentle 'But who may abide' will be lost.

2.5 Rhythm

Ex. 2.5.36 'But who may abide'

Another example of 'appeareth' on an *anapaest*. Both versions should emphasise ap-PEAR-eth, making –eth short. After the paused note (normally decorated), 'appeareth' should not be delayed, but give the strings back the tempo, assisted by the bass-line, in order to link into the next section in a related tempo.

Ex. 2.5.37 'But who may abide?'

Complementary *anapaests* rise on 'like' and fall on 'Fire'. The third note should always be short and phrased away.

2.5 Rhythm

Ex. 2.5.38 'O thou that tellest'

'Arise' and 'Behold'. A lively command. Two *anapaests* with different note values, one rising, one falling; one acting as a snappy up-beat, the other repeated as an emphatic down-beat. The voices only have the faster, rising one. The violins have an extra turn after 'your God'. 'Risen' should arrive promptly onto the second quaver. The second syllable of 'Judah' needs to be very short and weak to make time for a breath before 'Behold' which should stand out in a new tone of voice.

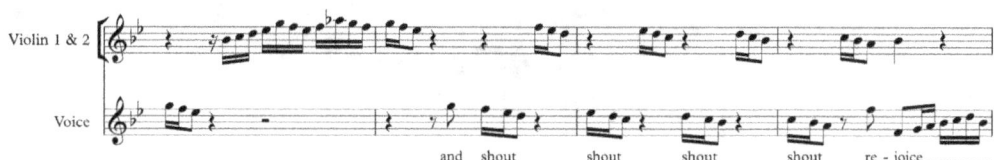

Ex. 2.5.39 'Rejoice greatly'

2.5 Rhythm

Many 'Shouts' are encouraged by the violins; these are probably best not slurred, giving a good front on the rhythmic motif.

Ex. 2.5.40 'Rejoice greatly'

The 'Shout' *anapaest* is later used in a softened form with added two-note up-beat for the different text.

Ex. 2.5.41 'His Yoke is easy'

'Easy', 'Burthen', and 'light' are all illustrated rhythmically.

Ex. 2.5.42 'His Yoke is easy'

The light springy rhythm sometimes illustrates two different words simultaneously. This device, using many short repeated phrases, prepares for a coming together of the text in the future.

Ex. 2.5.43 'He trusted in God'

The emphasis should be 'de-LIV-er Him' not 'deliver HIM' even though 'Him' uses a longer note value.

Ex. 2.5.44 'Lift up your Heads'

The *anapaest* emphasises 'King' and 'Glory'.

Ex. 2.5.45 'Let us break their Bonds'

The *anapaest* illustrates snapping of bonds 'a-SUN-der'.

Dactyl

The *dactyl*, the reverse of the *anapaest*, is the long-short-short unit and although more relaxed in feeling, retains a sprung character. The long syllable or note should not be sustained in an allegro movement. The Greek rhetorician Longinus says dactyls are noble and contribute to the affect of grandeur.

Ex. 2.5.46 Sinfony (Overture)

The fugue subject uses a falling *dactyl* which decorates the melodic line. Note the slight differences in the intervals of the fugue subject in the first and second violins (the standard tonal answer).

Ex. 2.5.47 'Rejoice'

The sprung character of the *dactyl* illustrates 'Rejoice'.

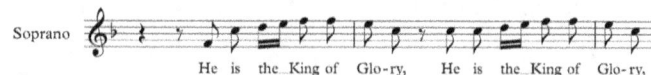

Ex. 2.5.48 'Lift up your Heads'

Word setting using the *dactyl* for affirmation: 'He IS the King of Glory'. 'Is' should be emphasised without being sustained.

2.5 Rhythm

Ex. 2.5.49 'Let all the Angels'

'Let all the Angels' uses two levels of *dactylic* rhythm on the word 'Angels' simultaneously for rich affect (crotchet/two quavers and quaver/two semiquavers).

Ex. 2.5.50 'Hallelujah'

An obsessive use of the joyful *dactyl* in the instruments continues through and fills the gaps in the voices, until all fall silent together.

2.5 Rhythm

Ex. 2.5.51 'The Lord gave the Word'

Two consecutive *dactyls*, one leading to the second. The second beat ('Great was the') forms an up-beat group to 'COM-pany of the Preachers'. We know 'COM-pany' is stronger than 'Preachers' because this is the word chosen to be decorated by a melisma when it is repeated.

Ex. 2.5.52 'Blessing and Honour, Glory and Pow'r be unto Him'

In 'Blessing and Honour, Glory and Pow'r be unto Him', the fugue subject shows the *dactyl* used first as an up-beat then as a down-beat in a balanced mirror image phrase which, by deliberately intoning on the same pitch level, leads first to 'Honour' and then towards 'Pow'r' which then falls away.

161

2.6 Silence

or 'Interrupting the tale'

Silence can be used in a number of different ways, either to make sense of the text through various levels of articulation (see 'The Speaking Style', p. 92) or for a special purpose which strives for affect when the speaker or singer breaks off unexpectedly, sighs or gasps as if overcome with emotion.

Aposiopesis

In rhetoric, silence is often used to create a shock or interrupt an argument. The *Rhetorica ad Herennium* says this figure occurs when what the speaker has begun to say is left unfinished (RH, IV xxx). Quintilian writes that it indicates some passion or anger (Q, IX ii 54). It is generally used to express a vehement emotion. Peacham describes it as

> a forme of speech by which the Orator through some affection, as either of feare, anger, sorrow, bashfulness or such like, breaketh off his speech before it be all ended [...] The use of this forme of speech serveth to say the vehemency of our unmoderate affections, proceeding to some excesse or outrage.

Puttenham describes 'the figure of silence, or of interruption'. He tells of a learned acquaintance of his who 'will upon the sodaine for the flying of a bird overthwart the way, or some other such sleight cause, interrupt his tale and never returne to it againe'. In other words, a sudden silence can interrupt the argument, bringing the discussion to an end before its conclusion.

The rhetorical figure *aposiopesis* is in music a sudden general silence in all voices, and is often used in conjunction with an abrupt cutting off of sound, as opposed to the *apocope* which fades out gradually (see Exx. 1.5.27, 1.5.28). There are no such figures in Jennens' choice of texts, but Handel's musical setting makes liberal use of the *aposiopesis* at the conclusion of many choruses, nearly always combined with a final *noema* in homophonic form, where all voices sing the last phrase of the text together. The surprise is created by the silence being unexpected, so any holding back or slowing up will always undermine its affect. The musical affect of this figure is strengthened by frequently being preceded by a provocative strong dissonance, like a shaken fist, which leaves the listener's expectations hanging through the silence, waiting for the answer or resolution. The silence will hold the sound quality by which it is approached, and forms a bridge connecting to the next sound heard. The music may then either carry on the same thought or change the tone radically, in which case the energy with which the last note is left can be used to prepare for a sudden change of affect or dynamic.

Ex. 2.6.1 Sinfony (Overture)

Sudden silences near the end of contrapuntal movements before the final cadence are often preceded by a 'crisis' discord or a surprising harmony, as in the overture. If the

note before the silence is sustained for its full length, the final phrase may be picked up in time with the same strong tone, without slowing up very much before the final chord. The second part of a French overture may always be repeated, in which case this figure of silence may be delivered with less vehemence the first time, and continue without slowing up to the end of the section. Too much spreading out of the final cadence on the second ending will prevent a smooth transition into 'Comfort ye'. The end of the overture shouldn't sound like the end of the whole work.

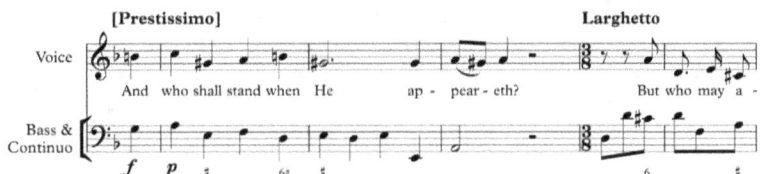

Ex. 2.6.2 'But who may abide'

The solo voice ends the middle section of 'But who may abide' in a vehement rhythmic finish in the character of the 'Refiner's Fire' music, which lashes the word 'appeareth', like a challenge, creating a pregnant silence before returning to the mild Larghetto. As has been pointed out in the discussion of the *anapaest* (-pear-eth), the singer should avoid any tendency to slow up which will destroy the vehemence of the final word and undermine the effect of the *antithesis* between sections. It has been suggested that a major chord on the last bar will provide extra contrast with the return of D minor and also resonate in the silence.

Ex. 2.6.3 'But who may abide'

Contrast this example with Ex. **2.6.2**. Unlike the former passage, the next transition finishes gently in the manner of 'who may abide' before the sudden change of affect for the following 'Refiner's Fire' Prestissimo. The text 'and who shall stand when He appeareth?' appears in both types of music in this number, enabling two settings, the calm and the fiery.

2.6 Silence

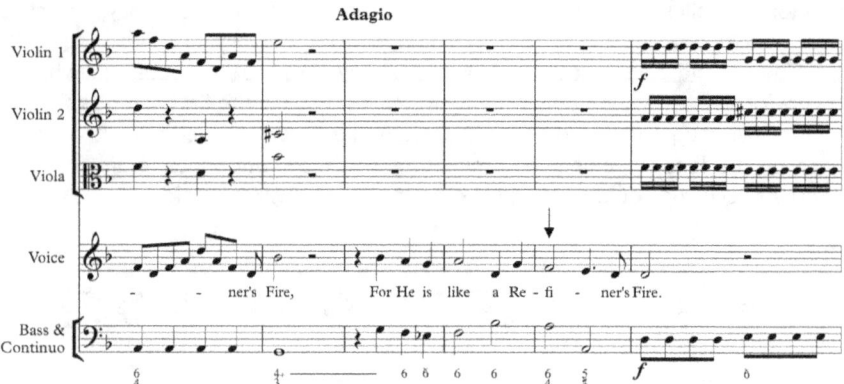

Ex. 2.6.4 'But who may abide'

The culmination of the aria arriving on a rising, provocative interval for 'Fire' is followed by a pregnant silence. The figured bass notation implies that the chord may be sounded again on the first beat or simply held on the organ. After this the singer can continue more or less in time for the last phrase, perhaps changing the voice tone to express the figure *anadiplosis* (the last tone of the phrase before the silence 'Fire' is the same as the first of the next, 'For'). The final 'Refiner's Fire', marked adagio, should be decorated on the 6-4 chord, but any decoration on the word 'Fire' before the silence would destroy its vehement affect.

Ex. 2.6.5 'He was despised'

The middle section of 'He was despised' comes to an abrupt and discordant end on 'He hid not his Face from Shame......' before the final amplification 'from Shame and Spitting' which should be flung at the audience. The word 'Shame' should be held strongly until the strings have arrived at their (short but strong) discord. The silence can be of an indeterminate length as the music becomes quasi recitative for the last few words. The strings should wait until the final syllable is uttered before they play the cadence, reinforcing the singer's vehemence with short, conclusive chords. Handel's conducting score has equal quavers for 'from Shame and Spitting'.

The climax of a chorus is frequently 'adorned' with a sudden figure of silence after the contrapuntal working out, 'interrupting the tale'. The final phrase of the text uses amplification to create a grand cadence. This point is sometimes marked adagio, but more often notated in long note values which do not require dragging out for extra effect (choral examples of this figure can be found in 2.7).

'Sospiro' in Pathetic Affects

Apocope is a rhetorical figure which cuts off; it can be used to conclude a phrase which disappears and runs out of breath through sadness or weakness, in imitation of dying, dispersing or disappearing. Unlike the more violent *aposiopesis*, the sound disappears gradually into silence. The sheep disperse into silence, going astray in contrary motion (Ex. 2.1.1 diminuendo assumed, bars 4-6).

Ex. 2.6.6 'The People that walked'

The violins rise up and then disappear over the held pedal of 'Death'. The music comes to life (in D major) just at the moment the lonely unison F♯ has been reached.

Silence can be used as a moment of change to a new feeling.

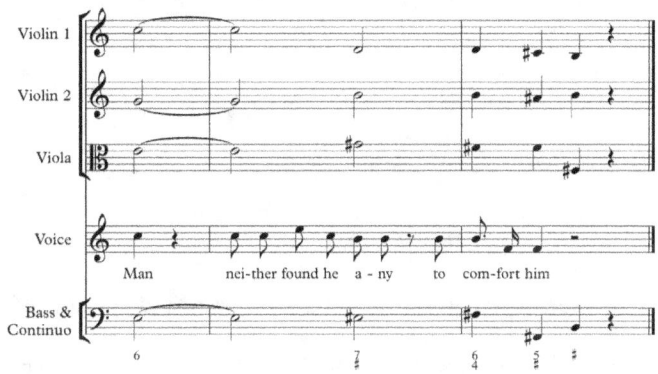

Ex. 2.6.7 'Thy Rebuke'

The desolate ending 'neither found He any to comfort Him' drifts into silence before the more hopeful rising pleading intervals of 'Behold and see'.

2.6 Silence

Ex. 2.6.8 'Behold and see'

Quintilian describes hesitation and words broken by silences as being most effective for appealing to the emotions of the listener (Q, IX ii 71).

Here, intermittent silences are used to give a hesitant, pathetic affect.

Ex. 2.6.9 'Behold and see'

The whole of 'Behold and see' is designed to evoke pity and sorrow. After sighing in their upper range, the violins disappear downwards. The voice fades on the word 'Sorrow', which is also in the lowest register. Both the violins and voice descend to the bottom of their range to express sorrow using the figure *catabasis* (Bartel, pp. 214-5).

2.6 Silence

Ex. 2.6.10 'Behold and see'

After the final phrase 'like unto His sorrow' has faded out it is followed by a strongly pleading rising sixth. A pathetic sobbing tie onto a seventh in the first violins then resolves onto a weak major chord. The brief silence should be held before the interruption of 'He was cut off'.

Ex. 2.6.11 'He was despised'.

The intermittent *sospiro* silences illustrate the words (beginning of the first bar and third beat of the second).

2.6 Silence

Ex. 2.6.12 'Glory to God'

The violins vanish downwards into silence. Diminuendo is assumed, arriving at an unaccented short note before 'and Peace on Earth'.

The effectiveness of the above examples of silence depends on how they are approached. Some silences are preceded by a strong dissonance, and some by a particularly strong rhythmic motif, in which case a determined approach is needed, keeping up the tempo. If the silence is preceded by a fading out as in 'Sorrow' or before 'Peace on Earth', avoid any excessive dragging out which will detract from the affect which is built into the musical notation. Have the courage to rely on the notes to make the affect for you. Experiment with doing as little pulling up as possible, or even rushing into the silence for its full impact. It may be that this feels impossible to achieve with large forces, but the weight of tradition can be overcome by not bowing to the pressure of ingrained habits. When performing in a resonant acoustic, the direct approach to the silence will have an even stronger affect. These dramatic silences have far more impact when performed in tempo, with the vehemence which the figure deserves.

2.6 Silence

After the first day of the Handel Commemoration performances in Westminster Abbey, 1784 (a selection of anthems and choruses), Charles Burney writes

> Nothing, however, discovered the admirable discipline of the band, and unwearied and determined attention of the audience, so much as the *pauses*, which are so frequent in HANDEL'S Music: for these were so unanimously calculated, and measured, that no platoon, or single cannon, was ever fired with more exact precision or unity of effect, than that with which the whole phalanx of this multitudinous band resumed its work, after all the sudden, and usually, unlimited cessations of sound, commonly called *pauses*, which, in general, catch loquacity in the fact; but now, at all these unexpected moments, the silence was found as awful and entire, as if none but the tombs of departed mortals had been present ('Commemoration of Handel', p. 41).

Rhythmic Silence – the 'Loud Rest'

Ex. 2.6.13 'Thus saith the Lord'

The silence at the start of 'Thus saith the Lord' throws the phrase forward to the first downbeat, coinciding with the entry of the voice which interrupts the rising arpeggio.

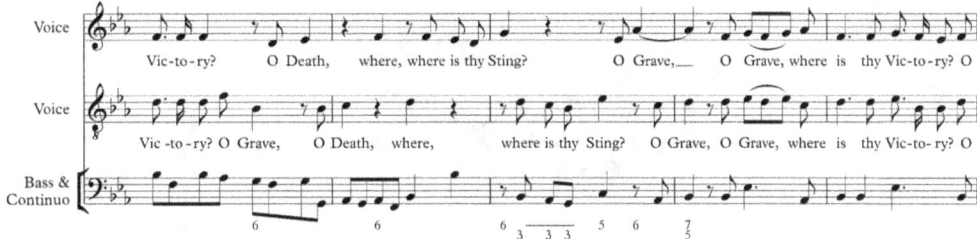

Ex. 2.6.14 'O Death, where is thy Sting?'

After a long and continuous dialogue between the two voices, they finally coincide on the same word 'Grave' (fourth bar, first beat) where they stop together on a dissonance (in surprise?), in a small gasping *aposiopesis* before being united in next phrase 'O Grave where is thy Victory?'

2.6 Silence

Ex. 2.6.15 'His Yoke is easy'

A similar situation in 'His Yoke is easy' where, after a long passage of counterpoint, all voices and instruments stop momentarily together before the cadence (second beat of bar 2). The repeated idea, 'His Burthen' is completed with 'His Burthen is light' after the silence.

2.6 Silence

Ex. 2.6.16 'He was despised'

In 'He was despised', every quaver rest in the opening ritornello is silent in all parts. The sobbing affect of the text caused by the short rest (*sospiro*) depends on the singer singing a short syllable on –ed, making the silence as rhythmic as possible. There is a continuing *antithesis* between the two strongly-enunciated separate quavers in the solo voice, supported by the bass, and the two pairs of pathetic slurred ones in the strings which have silence in between.

Silences of Articulation

Whereas the *aposiopesis* looks for a shocking or other strong affect, rests or punctuation are for clarifying meaning. They are of two types: notated and not notated, or as Morley (1599) describes 'told or not to be told' (p. 118). Just as when reading aloud we make spaces between syllables, words, phrases and sentences, so in music we connect notes which belong together and separate those which need space before or after them. Handel marks certain connections and separations. Slurs connect sounds in the vocal parts and daggers appear over notes where either equal emphasis and/or separation need to occur.

Sometimes the natural space for breath is notated by Handel (see The 'Speaking' Style p. 92).

2.6 Silence

Ex. 2.6.17 'Worthy is the Lamb'

The whole chorus and orchestra breathe after 'slain' and 'Blood'.

Ex. 2.6.18 'Hallelujah'

The device of leaving a gap which is then filled on repetition is used in the 'Hallelujah' chorus. In this passage there are two silences which should be savoured, before the trumpets, timpani and strings fill the third one giving the effect of two short phrases followed by a long phrase. This builds extra tension and richness in any repeated passage. In the final few bars of this chorus, all the gaps between Hallelujahs are filled by the instruments (Ex. 2.5.50).

2.7 The Choruses

or 'A Glow of Harmony'

John Mainwaring, Handel's first biographer, describes Handel's choruses as abounding in 'sublime strokes' and declared that 'in his choruses he is without a rival'. The three concluding choruses ('Worthy is the Lamb', 'Blessing and Honour', and 'Amen') 'each of which surpasses the preceding, till in the winding up of the Amen, the ear is fill'd with such a glow of harmony, as leaves the mind in a kind of heavenly extasy'. Mainwaring then expands on the 'grandeur of conception' which predominates in the choruses (pp. 187, 190).

As a composer of Italian opera, where chorus opportunities hardly existed, Handel found in the English oratorio form a new, more prominent and extensive role for the chorus. It is these moments which tended to have the strongest affect on audiences in the eighteenth century, just as they do now and to hear a choir in full harmonic mode is a moving experience. Harmony has the power to both 'raise and quell' the passions. A poem published in *The Gentleman's Magazine*, May 1740 by an unknown poet declared 'But Handel's harmony affects the soul, to sooth by sweetness, or by force controul' (Deutsch pp. 500-501).

If everyone singing together has a powerful harmonic affect, multi-voiced music gives the composer many opportunities to introduce a variety of textures. A lone voice can initiate a call and receive a response from the other voices, like a gospel choir; voices can sing in pairs, answering each other; voices can enter in fugal style with phrases of different lengths. Most of the *Messiah* choruses are in four parts, but 'Lift up your Heads' has two soprano parts to facilitate the double chorus effect. The choruses which borrow music from the Italian chamber duets (composed July 1741) reflect that dual aspect, but Handel turns the thinner texture to his advantage with the interpolation of sections for the full chorus which stand out amid the surrounding material. The newly-invented music occurs in 'And He shall purify', 'For unto us', 'His Yoke is easy', and 'All we, like Sheep'.

Homophony, where all voices sing the text simultaneously in the same rhythm, is called *noema* in musical rhetoric. This figure was defined by Burmeister in his *Musica Poetica* (1606), the first musical catalogue of rhetorical devices. He calls it a 'harmonic affection or period that consists of voices combined in equal note values. When introduced at the right time, it sweetly affects and wondrously soothes the ears, or indeed the heart' (p. 165).

The compositional device of having all the voices singing the text together in harmony is usually reserved for an important idea which requires emphasis, and follows a working out of smaller fragments of the text using polyphony. In many choruses it is placed at the culmination of an argument to emphasise and clinch the idea in the minds of the listeners. The device can also be used for the purposes of exclamation, or salutation such as 'Kyrie Eleison' when sung by the whole choir at the opening of a movement. Bach's Mass in B minor opens with three cumulative cries of 'Kyrie Eleison' before an extended fugal setting of the same text. Burmeister describes the affect of *noema* as being revealed in the context of the whole piece, principally by being surrounded by counterpoint. Homophony is thus revealed as a structural device, a grove of trees in the forest of polyphony (p. 165).

Modern choirs have the advantage of being able to use a vocal score. A singer can glance down the page and see immediately the passages where the same words are sung by all voices simultaneously. Another advantage of using a vocal score for chorus members is that it will show points where the responsibility lies with one part or another, for fugal entries, for example. Identifying your job and rising to any specific challenges is good rhetorical decorum.

2.7 The Choruses

In the eighteenth-century choirs sang from separate parts. The Foundling Hospital part-books show little or no punctuation and only a few text cues before the choruses start. The 'principale' voices (soloists) also sang all the choruses, as can be seen in their separate part-books which contain both solos and choruses.

Handel uses *noema* in several ways. Sometimes the effect is reserved for the culmination of the working out of a text, sometimes it is used at the opening of a chorus, and sometimes as a short response to a single voice.

'And the Glory'

Ex. 2.7.1 'And the Glory' (Arnold's rhythm for 'Glory')

The first case of *noema* we encounter in *Messiah* is 'And the Glory of the Lord'. Handel adds a repetition to Jennens' single 'Glory', to emphasise the most important word, transforming a simple statement 'And the Glory of the Lord' into the emphatic figure *epizeuxis* 'And the Glory, *the Glory* of the Lord'. The first 'Glory' is set on a slow dotted rhythm which holds the phrase back, and the second on faster quavers which move the phrase forward to 'Lord'. The altos suggest the first phrase to the whole choir, who respond enthusiastically together, repeating the phrase exactly. Single voices in turn then finish the sentence 'shall be revealed'. Throughout the chorus, it is the initial text 'And the Glory, the Glory of the Lord' which is reserved for the *noema*, until the powerful ending (For the Mouth of the Lord) 'hath spoken it'.

2.7 The Choruses

Ex. 2.7.2 'And the Glory'

The sudden silence at the end of 'And the Glory' (*aposiopesis*) occurs at the end of a pedal in the upper parts slowly intoning 'For the Mouth of the Lord', while a diminution of the same words moves underneath it. This silence should be the culmination of the repetitions which use the rhetorical figure *epizeuxis* to intensify the repeated text. The last two bars, marked adagio, proclaim 'hath spoken it' in a grand gesture for the final cadence.

2.7 The Choruses

'And He shall Purify'

Ex. 2.7.3 'And He shall purify'

This chorus starts with the short statement 'And He shall purify'. We are left to wonder what it is that will be purified. This is followed by a long decorated version which is passed around the voices until finally we hear 'And he shall purify the Sons of Levi'. The *noema* is delayed until the following text 'that they (the Sons of Levi) may offer unto the Lord an offering in Righteousness, in Righteousness', offering a purpose for the purifying. Note Handel's emphatic repetition of 'in Righteousness', set in firm, equally weighted syllables with just a few moving quavers providing rhythmic stability. The music intensifies with the violin rising quavers introducing the *noema*, and then they continue to elaborate over the top of it. The mood becomes tangibly more dramatic and significant at this point, modulating into C minor. After the cadence in C minor the opening text returns to the relaxed mood. This is one of the numbers where Handel 'borrowed' music from a previous source. The text 'that they may offer' is newly composed, and this passage stands out in its intensity.

2.7 The Choruses

Ex. 2.7.4 'And He shall purify'

After a further contrapuntal passage using the opening text, the final long *noema* again highlights 'The Sons of Levi that they may offer unto the Lord an Offering in Righteousness, in Righteousness'. Again, the word 'Righteousness' receives extra emphasis. The violins decorate intensively as before and, after arriving at their top D bring this number to a restful close, ending a sequence of texts from the prophet Malachi (the last book of the Old Testament) before the next scene introduces the Christmas narrative predicted in Isaiah.

2.7 The Choruses

'O thou that tellest good Tidings to Zion'

Ex. 2.7.5 'O thou that tellest good Tidings to Zion'

The music and text of 'O thou that tellest good Tidings to Zion', has already appeared in a solo version, so the choral version emphasises and embellishes everything already heard by using more voices. Once the voices have entered in turn with the initial exclamation, the whole chorus has an extended *noema* with 'Say unto the Cities of Judah, Behold your God'. 'Behold' is then reiterated and followed, still using *noema*, by: 'the Glory of the Lord is risen upon thee'. For the very last phrase the altos break away with 'the Glory of the Lord' in a call and response to introduce the final unified thought 'is risen upon thee'. As before, the elaborate orchestral figuration weaves against the block-work of the *noemas*, stopping at points to reinforce the words 'Arise, Arise' and 'Behold, Behold' in the vocal gaps. All sing 'Say unto the Cities of Judah' together in the same equal syllabic rhythm. A long syllable 'be-HOLD your God' is followed by a commanding and emphatic shout 'Behold' (a good example of *copia* see 1.3, p. 19). The whole passage is then repeated for extra impact.

2.7 The Choruses

'For unto us a Child is born'

This movement also uses recycled music, but the newly composed section contains perhaps the most powerful *noema* in the whole work: 'Wonderful, Counsellor, The Mighty God, The Everlasting Father, The Prince of Peace'.

Ex. 2.7.6 'For unto us a Child is born'

In the opening of this chorus, the phrase 'For unto us a Child is born' is followed by short phrases, 'unto us ... a Son is given ...' eked out against a long melismatic 'born' in each voice, the orchestra punctuating in the background. Suddenly the violins take off in a brilliant rising passage which continues in glittering movement over the *noemas* of the 'Wonderful, Counsellor' passage. The conclusive 'Prince of Peace' is, in the first conclusion only, set in slower, equal crotchets for emphasis and to conclude the sequence. The following three re-iterations of the passage have a more relaxed dotted cadence for 'Prince of Peace'.

2.7 The Choruses

Charles Burney described his impression of those words and Handel's placing of them:

> 'Wonderful! Counsellor! The mighty God! The everlasting Father! The Prince of Peace!' which he so long and so judiciously postponed, the idea and effect are so truly sublime, that, assisted by the grandeur and energy of this band, I never felt the power of Choral Music and full harmony, in enforcing the expression of words, so strongly before ('Commemoration of Handel', p. 76).

The ecstatic shouts of the chorus in the 'Wonderful' passage come no fewer than four times before the closing orchestral ritornello rounds off the movement by bringing us back to earth from the glittering heavenly heights. This chorus finishes the sequence of text taken from the prophet Isaiah. The 'action' now moves into the New Testament with the story of the nativity, introduced by the shepherds' pastorale.

'Glory to God'

'Glory to God' commences with a rousing *noema*, sung by the previously mentioned 'Multitude of the Heavenly Host' and emphasised by the effect of distant trumpets. 'Glory to God' is immediately repeated and extended: 'Glory to God in the Highest, and Peace on Earth'. The first two statements of 'Peace on Earth' are on calm unison octaves, the third is warmly harmonised. Counterpoint is adopted for the second thought 'Goodwill towards Men' which completes the movement (see 1.3 Comparison, Exx. 1.3.9, 1.3.10).

'His Yoke is easy, His Burthen is light'

Ex. 2.7.7 'His Yoke is easy, His Burthen is light'

The text of this chorus doesn't invite any grand affect, rather seeking to persuade us of the ease and lightness of the 'Burthen', using lightly decorated counterpoint. *Noema* is not employed until the final statement, which concludes Part One. This is a light persuasive chorus except for a dark passage of rich harmony from the Italian duet source which seems to pre-figure Part Two. The silence before the final cadence, which adds the emphatic word 'AND his Burthen is light', should also be 'easy' and 'light', rounding off Part One in a mini-peroration. The temptation to make a heavy protracted ending with too much emphasis on the word 'is' in such a light chorus should be resisted.

2.7 The Choruses

'Behold the Lamb of God'

Part Two opens with voices in counterpoint 'Behold the Lamb of God'. *Noema* is only used for the final statement of the text 'that taketh away the Sin of the World'.

'Surely'

Ex. 2.7.8 'Surely'

This chorus is a reaction to the aria 'He was despised', and is a provocative and passionate exclamation set in *noema*: 'Surely, SURELY he hath born our Griefs, and carried our Sorrows!' The repeated 'Surely' reinforces the first word in an *epizeuxis*.

2.7 The Choruses

Ex. 2.7.9 'Surely'

> As in 'Glory to God', the second part of the text 'He was wounded for our Transgressions, He was bruised for our Iniquities' is set homophonically with 'bruised' repeated for emphasis, before breaking into counterpoint for 'the Chastisement of our Peace was upon Him'.

The pattern of *noema* use is now becoming familiar: short parts of the text use its solid structure in all voices, and the following or preceding text is set in counterpoint, the order depending on the importance and rhetorical function, which could be a strong exclamation such as 'Glory to God', 'Wonderful', or 'Surely'. The text is often set unified in all voices for emphasis at the final cadence, sometimes followed by a short instrumental ritornello to round off the movement.

'And with His Stripes we are healed'

This purely contrapuntal chorus uses the old-fashioned Renaissance alla breve notation to sooth the wounds in a smooth rising line. The text nearly always repeats the last three words 'And with His Stripes we are healed, we are healed' in a soothing 'there, there' comforting gesture. The whole is doubled by the instruments. Burney describes the chorus as

> written upon a fine subject, with such clearness and regularity as was never surpassed by the greatest Choral composers of the sixteenth century. This fugue [...] may fairly be compared with movements of the same kind in Palestrina, Tallis, and Bird, which, in variety, it very much surpasses ('Commemoration of Handel', p. 79).

2.7 The Choruses

'All we, like Sheep'

Ex. 2.7.10 'All we, like Sheep'

The poetic biblical word order is contrived to place 'Sheep' at the end of the first short phrase for emphasis before 'have gone astray'. The two ideas are separated in Handel's musical treatment. The first phrase is broken up into short syllables. 'All we, like Sheep' being (naturally) in agreement, this text is always set with all voices together, and the 'have gone astray' is broken up in individual voices, until the culmination which Handel marks with daggers to emphasise the *noema*.

Ex. 2.7.11 'All we, like Sheep'

The emphatic culmination of 'ev'ry one to his own Way'.

Ex. 2.7.12 'All we, like Sheep'

The humour in the opening of this chorus is suddenly brought to a serious end with the extended cadence 'his own Way' followed by the multiple entries 'and the Lord hath laid on Him'. The final thought, 'The Iniquity of us all', is emphasised by being set in *noema*.

2.7 The Choruses

Ex. 2.7.13 'All we, like Sheep'

After the levity of being sheep the seriousness of our iniquity is painful to contemplate in the final cadence. Burney comments 'This fragment is full of sorrow and contrition' ('Commemoration of Handel', p. 80).

'He trusted in God'

Ex. 2.7.14 'He trusted in God'

'He trusted in God' is principally written in counterpoint, with the final conditional 'if', set in *noema*. The counterpoint is brought to an abrupt end with a vehement taunt 'let Him deliver Him' on a strong 4-2 dissonance followed by the cadence 'if He delight in Him' marked (descriptively) Adagio in slow note values, which should still be strongly delivered and push on to the final chord. The syllables of 'de-LI-ver Him' should be weighted for their full affect, with 'Him' strong but short. The final chord should be fully sustained in order to create as much contrast as possible with the next soft chromatic *pathopoeiac* 'Thy Rebuke hath broken His Heart'.

'Lift up your heads O ye Gates'

Ex. 2.7.15 'Lift up your heads O ye Gates'

Instruments and then voices play the text all together. Dialogue, with pairs and groups of voices, poses questions and replies. 'Who is this King of Glory?' is repeated three times on the same pitch, inviting a more vehement demand with each repetition. The full *noemic* moment is saved for the answer to 'Who is this King of Glory?' ... 'The Lord of Hosts, HE is the King of Glory', the conclusive answer to the question. The *noema* is emphasised in the responses, rising in tessitura on each 'the Lord of Hosts' using sopranos to lead the call and response.

Burney describes how, at the Handel Commemoration performance 1784, the semi-chorus phrase was sung by

> Three of the principal singers [...] then the whole Chorus from each side of the Orchestra, joined by all the instruments, burst out, 'He is the king of glory'. This had a most admirable effect, and brought tears into the eyes of several of the

performers. Indeed, if we may judge from the plenitude of satisfaction which appeared in the countenances of all present, this effect was not superficial, nor confined to the Orchestra ('Commemoration of Handel', p. 112).

Ex. 2.7.16 'Lift up your Heads'

'He is the King of Glory' is repeated many times, chased by the strings who have the last word, in brilliant imitation of 'Glory' before a short dramatic silence. Note another *anadiplosis* as the violins finish on the same pitch that they play after the silence, an opportunity for Handel to change the tone for everyone on the final repetition from the short and snappy 'of Glory' to a suave 'of Glory' for the final phrase. As usual, the cadence which follows the silence is an extended and unified version 'of Glory'. This grand triumphal finish ends the scene.

'Let all the Angels of God worship Him'

Ex. 2.7.17 'Let all the Angels of God worship Him'

'Let all the Angels of God worship Him' starts with one statement by the unified voices before many angels are decorated with melismas. Then counterpoint is used for the rest of the piece, finally emphasising 'worship Him' for the final cadence.

Burney describes this chorus as follows:

> This spirited fugue, seemingly on two subjects, is, perhaps, the most artificial that has been composed in modern times. HANDEL, in order to exercise his abilities in every species of difficulty which the most learned and elaborate Canonists and Fughists of the fifteenth and sixteenth centuries were ambitious of vanquishing, has composed this movement in what ancient theorists called *minor Prolation*; in which the reply to a subject given, though in similar intervals, is made in notes of different value: as when the theme is led off in semibreves and answered in minims, or the contrary.

A footnote continues

> As it is only professors who can estimate the difficulty of finding a subject which will serve as an accompaniment to itself in notes of augmentation or diminution, it is to them that the examination of this Chorus is recommended, who will see that while one part is performing the theme in crotchets and quavers, another is constantly repeating it in quavers and semi-quavers: an exercise for ingenuity often practised about two hundred years ago, on a few slow notes, or in fragments of canto fermo; but never before, I believe, in so many parts, with such perfect airy freedom, or little appearance of restraint and difficulty ('Commemoration of Handel', p. 82).

'The Lord gave the Word'

'The Lord gave the Word' is declaimed by the voice of the Lord represented by male voices in unison, unaccompanied, before the whole choir responds with 'Great was the Company of the Preachers'. The reiteration of 'Great was the Company' dissolves into decorated counterpoint at the word 'Company', and the whole process is repeated, starting with the male voices again and an immediately decorated 'Company', which continues until the final 'of the Preachers', a short *noema* (Ex. 1.5.16).

Burney writes:

> The majesty and dignity of the few solemn notes with which this Chorus is begun, without instruments, received great augmentation now, from being delivered by such a number of base and tenor voices in unison; and the contrast of sensation occasioned by the harmony and activity of the several parts, afterwards, had a very striking effect ('Commemoration of Handel', p. 82).

'Their Sound is gone out'

'Their Sound is gone out' starts in counterpoint and only the final grand phrase 'the Ends of the World' is set with all voices together.

'Let us break their Bonds asunder'

'Let us break their Bonds asunder' is entirely contrapuntal, the voices broken up, encouraging themselves to break their bonds. 'And cast away their Yokes from us' is similarly contrapuntal, set using bouncy rhythmic motifs borrowed from the hornpipe to illustrate the desire to break free (Ex. 2.2.17).

2.7 The Choruses

'Hallelujah'

Ex. 2.7.18 The end of 'Hallelujah'. Note, no adagio marking.

The 'Hallelujah' chorus uses the most extended passages of *noema* of the whole work and perhaps this is part of its power to thrill. The shout of joy of the whole choir is extended through endless repetitions of the word Hallelujah in harmony, set in varied rhythms and using different emphases. The voices (without sopranos) stay together in unison for 'For the Lord God omnipotent reigneth' before eventually the two ideas are set against one another, the quick, harmonised Hallelujahs against the slow-moving unison 'For the Lord God'. The final five Hallelujahs use *noema*, four on the same pitches, and should increase in intensity towards the silence, the very last one extended in slow notes for amplification. This is a big finish, the peroration of Part Two.

Burney describes the performance of this chorus in the 1784 Handel Commemoration as

> the triumph of HANDEL, of the COMMEMORATION, and of the musical art. The opening is clear, chearful, and bold. And the words, 'For the Lord God omnipotent reigneth', set to a fragment of canto fermo, which all the parts sing, as such, in unisons and octaves, has an effect truly ecclesiastical. It is afterwards made the subject of fugue and ground-work for the Allelujah. Then, as a short episode in plain counter-point, we have 'The kingdom of this world' – which begun *piano*, was solemn and affecting. But the last and principal subject proposed, and led off by the base – 'And he shall reign for ever and ever', is the most pleasing and fertile that has ever been invented since the art of fugue was first cultivated. It is marked, and constantly to be distinguished through all the parts, accompaniments, countersubjects and contrivances, with which it is charged. And, finally, the words – 'King of Kings, and Lord of Lords, always set to a single sound, which seems to stand at bay, while the other parts attack it in every possible manner, in 'Allelujahs – for ever and ever', is a most happy and marvellous concatination of harmony, melody, and great effects ('Commemoration of Handel', p. 83).

Later he describes how

> At the first performance of the Messiah [in the Handel Commemoration], his Majesty expressed a desire to the earl of Sandwich of hearing the most truly sublime of all Choruses: 'Allelujah! For the Lord God omnipotent reigneth' a second time; and this gracious wish was conveyed to the Orchestra, by the waving of his lordship's wand. At this second performance of that matchless Oratorio, his Majesty was pleased to make the signal himself, with a gentle motion of his right hand in which was the printed book of words, not only for the repetition of this, but of the final Chorus, in the last part, to the great satisfaction of all his happy subjects present ('Commemoration of Handel', p. 112).

'Since by Man came Death'

Ex. 2.7.19 'Since by Man came Death'

In 'Since by Man came Death', the voices all move together, except for the decorated cadence on 'Death', sounding effectively like an ancient *a capella* choir. The two statements use a double *antithesis* to alternate slow and dark with fast and triumphant. The key concepts of *Messiah's* message are made clear: Death leads to Resurrection and Adam leads to Christ (see also Ex. 1.3.17).

2.7 The Choruses

Ezech. XXXVII: 1.
תמונת לתחית המתים.   TYPUS RESURRECTIONIS MORTUORUM.
A Type of the resurrection of the Dead.   Image de la résurrection des morts.
Abbildung der auferstehung der Todten.   Gezicht van de opstandinge der dooden.

2.7 The Choruses

'But Thanks'

Ex. 2.7.20 'But Thanks'

'But Thanks' starts with the voices together and soon breaks into a contrapuntal game where 'Thanks' pop up all over the voices, but are finally unified in 'who giveth us the Victory through our Lord Jesus Christ'. The second 'Thanks' added to the text creates an *epizeuxis* to work with in all the voices, extending and emphasising the effect of the word. Use the commas to heighten the affect. The alternation of counterpoint and homophonic voices together serves to emphasize the text, sometimes momentarily, before breaking into parts again. 'But Thanks' ends with another sudden breaking off into silence followed by a slowly notated cadence. The word before the silence, 'Victory', invites a strong rhythmic delivery to portray the triumph and joy of death being overcome. This moment is the culmination of the text which started with one voice and continuo, then two voices and then the whole choir and instruments.

2.7 The Choruses

'Worthy is the Lamb that was slain'

Ex. 2.7.21 'Worthy is the Lamb that was slain'

The final chorus 'Worthy is the Lamb that was slain' is the chorus which Mainwaring describes as filling the ear with 'the glow of harmony as leaves the mind in a kind of heavenly extasy' (p. 191). Burney remarked upon the 'very ingenious and pleasing accompaniment for the violins, totally different from the voice-parts' ('Commemoration of Handel', p. 88). This multipart chorus uses *noema* from the start up until 'Blessing', moving on in tempo and harmony from the slow 'Worthy' thought into 'to receive Power', a process which is then repeated, holding back for 'Worthy' and moving forward again. The moment of transition at the end of this passage can sound uncertain if the two passages are not sufficiently connected. The momentary silence needs a sure forward movement into the following fugue. Enjoy the three versions of the word 'Blessing', one finishing on a cadence in longer note values, and the next one ('Blessing and Honour') emphasised by the first note being longer than subsequent up-beat entries. The next section 'Blessing and Honour' sets out in fugal style for the final thought, reinforced by being sung by the two male voices in unison, coming to rest in a *noema* 'for ever and ever' before the extended 'Amen'.

2.7 The Choruses

Ex. 2.7.22 'Blessing and Honour'

This cadence is only transitional and should not sound like the end of the work.

'Amen'

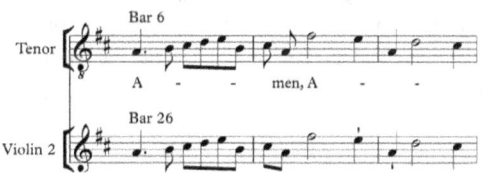

Ex. 2.7.23 'Amen'

The start of the 'Amen' chorus uses a smooth rising motif which then becomes falling and more detached (marked with daggers in the instruments). Starting with the lowest voice, the entries build a natural crescendo, each joining voice being clearly heard, one rising element against the other, falling one. The affect is at the same time 'glowing' and calming, bringing to a close past conflicts. The following violin duet interlude uses the same material, and acts as a holding-back device before the full choral sound is heard again. The sound of the two violin sections should sound rich and heavenly in their unusual close high tessitura without bass. In the last bar the first violins fall away but the second violins should lead towards the grand re-entry of the whole chorus and all the instruments, including trumpets and timpani, for the grand ending.

2.7 The Choruses

Ex. 2.7.24 'Amen'

> The elaborate, closely worked Amen chorus delays any further *noema* until the very final cadence, arrived at after a complete bar of silence approached by a strong dissonance. The final silence of the work is the culmination of three hours' worth of music. The audience should now feel the end is very close (even if they have not heard the work before) and be held spell-bound by a dissonant 4-2 chord. The chord should be sustained for its full written value, and the length of the whole bar of silence can be judged according to the acoustic of the building. The very final 'Amen' needn't be too drawn out. Allow the music to have its own affect.

The devices of counterpoint and *noema* are combined to highlight the text in their different ways. Counterpoint breaks up the text into small pieces, usually leaving the listener suspended and waiting for the complete thought to be revealed. It is then that *noema* brings together all that has been previously hinted at. It secures, clinches and rounds off the argument. It can also serve as a structural pillar, at the opening, the middle or the end of a movement, between which counterpoint can weave. The ideas are thus delivered effectively in a variety of ways, first in pieces, and then as a whole, powerful thought. The singers of the choir should be as conscious as possible of the potency of the *noema* passages, so that they may deliver them with appropriate energy and gusto.

Charles Burney writes of Handel's music

> that all the judicious and un-prejudiced Musicians of every country, upon hearing or perusing his noble, majestic, and frequently sublime FULL ANTHEMS, and ORATORIO CHORUSES, must allow, with readiness and rapture, that they are utterly unacquainted with any thing equal to them, among the works of the greatest masters that have existed since the invention of counterpoint ('Sketch of the life of Handel', p. 41).

PART THREE – THE AUDIENCE

The Audience

> Much depends on the character of the audience and the generally received opinion [...] for there can be little doubt as to the attitude of the audience, if that attitude is already determined prior to the delivery of the speech (Q, III vii 23).

> Few indeed are those orators who can sweep the judge with them, lead him to adopt that attitude of mind which they desire, and compel him to weep with them or share their anger (Q, VI ii 3).

> Just as lovers are incapable of forming a reasoned judgement on the beauty of the object of their affections, because passion forestalls the sense of sight, so the judge, when overcome by his emotions, abandons all attempt to enquire into the truth of the arguments, is swept along by the tide of passion, and yields himself unquestioning to the torrent [...] for it is in its power over the emotions that the life and soul of oratory is to be found (Q, VI ii 6-7).

> The listener's judgement is often swept away by his preference for a particular speaker, or by the applause of an enthusiastic audience. [...] For we are ashamed to disagree with them, and an unconscious modesty prevents us from ranking our own opinion above theirs, though all the time the taste of the majority is vicious, and the *claque* may praise even what does not really deserve approval. [...] On the other hand, it will sometimes also happen that an audience whose taste is bad will fail to award the praise which is due to the most admirable utterances. [...] What he says will often seem comparatively ineffective where it actually occurs, since we do not realise his motive and it will be necessary to re-read the speech after we have acquainted ourselves with all that it contains (Q, X i 17-21).

> [judges and members of the tribunal] should carry within them to court some mental emotion that is in harmony with what the advocate's interest will suggest. For, as the saying goes, it is easier to spur the willing horse than to start the lazy one (C, *de Oratore* II xliv 185).

> The supreme orator is recognised by the people [...] What need to wait for the verdict of some critic? It is plain that what the multitude approves must win the approval of experts (C, *Brutus* 186, 188).

Messiah's reception in Dublin had been rapturous. Edward Synge, Bishop of Elphin, who attended the first performance, wrote that the words 'are all Sublime, or affecting in the greatest degree'. A report in Faulkner's *Dublin Journal*, 17 April 1742 described Handel's music as 'The Sublime, the Grand, and the Tender, adapted to the most elevated, majestick and moving Words, conspired to transport and charm the ravished Heart and Ear' (Deutsch, p. 546). Mainwaring writes of the Irish appreciation of Handel 'a kind of tacit reproach on all those on the other side of the water, who had enlisted in the opposition against him' (pp. 133, 136-7).

Back in London the following spring, oratorio performances were recommenced at Covent Garden. Handel's relations with his audience on religious issues and various quarrels involving Italian performers may have led to the indifferent reception of *Messiah* (Mainwaring, p. 135). The advertisement in the *London Daily Advertiser*, 19 March 1743, had announced the performance of

> A NEW SACRED ORATORIO. With a *Concerto* on the *Organ*. And a Solo on the Violin by Mr. *Dubourg*' at the Theatre Royal in Covent Garden (Deutsch, p. 562).

The Audience

It is likely that the title *Messiah* was avoided in order not to offend those who considered the performance of religious music in a theatre inappropriate. A letter written under the pseudonym 'Philalethes' was published in the *Universal Spectator*:

> An *Oratorio* either is an *Act of Religion*, or it is not; if it is, I ask if the *Playhouse* is a fit *Temple* to perform it in, or a Company of *Players* fit *Ministers of God's Word*, for in that Case such they are made [...] if it is not perform'd as an *Act of Religion*, but for *Diversion* and *Amusement* only (and indeed I believe few or none go to an *Oratorio* out of *Devotion*), what a *Prophanation* of God's Name and Word is this, to make so light Use of them? (Deutsch, pp. 563-4).

Other voices (possibly Jennens himself) spoke out in support of Handel:

> These hallow'd Lays to Musick give new Grace
> To Virtue Awe, and sanctify the Place;
> To Harmony, like his, Celestial Pow'r is giv'n,
> T' exalt the Soul from Earth, and make, of Hell, a Heav'n (Deutsch, pp. 565-6).

Apart from the religious controversies, there were other views of Handel's music. He was often criticized for favouring the instrumental element over the vocal, and a letter, possibly a draft never posted, from Jennens to an unknown friend (30 August 1745) admitted *Messiah* was a fine entertainment, but

> I have with great difficulty made him correct some of the grossest faults in the composition, but he retain'd his Overture obstinately, in which there are some passages far unworthy of Handel, but much more unworthy of the Messiah (Deutsch, p. 622).

The regular performances at The Foundling Hospital, in aid of that charity and commencing with the opening of the chapel there, eventually established *Messiah*'s popularity with 'a very numerous and splendid audience' (*London Daily Advertiser*, 17 May 1751, Deutsch, p. 709). *Messiah*'s popularity became even more widespread when the oratorio ticket price, which had been the same as for the opera, was reduced to playhouse terms, enabling many less well-off lovers of Handel's music to attend. Samuel Arnold's performances at the Haymarket theatre drew such a huge crowd that the ticket sellers had to flee their posts and the crowd rushed unimpeded into the boxes. The blaze of light and dazzling array of instruments and voices caused an astonished fish-woman to cry out 'which is the Messiah?' When Dr. Arnold was pointed out to her at the harpsichord she was convinced he was indeed the Messiah, which both amused the house greatly and gave his friends a new title with which to compliment him (Busby, vol. 1, p. 103).

By the time Handel's biographer put pen to paper in 1760 it is clear into which category of master Handel falls:

> the masters may be distinguished into two classes, as their principal merit consists in *invention* or *taste* [...] those who have an *inventive* genius will depart from the common rules, and please us the more by such deviations. These must of course be considered as bold strokes, or daring flights of fancy. Such passages are not founded on rules, but are themselves the foundation of new rules [...] Hence we may discern the reason why great invention and perfect taste are seldom, or never united (Mainwaring, pp. 161-3).

Mainwaring describes the bold strokes of the inventive genius as being sometimes coarse or extravagant, but the audience is obliged to suffer these faults in order to benefit from the other, sublime moments. The quotation on the title page of his *Memoirs of the Life of the Late George Frederick Handel* quotes in Greek from Longinus *On the Sublime*, paragraph 33, where the possibility of a faultless and consummate writer is considered: 'In great writing as in great wealth must needs be something overlooked'. Longinus observes that any genius is often far from correct, but it is impossible for 'a low and grov'ling Genius to be guilty of Error, since he never endangers himself by soaring on high' and 'in passing Judgment upon the Works of an Author, we always muster his Imperfections, so that the

Remembrance of his Faults sticks indelibly fast in the Mind, whereas that of his Excellencies is quickly worn out' (pp. 59-60). Mainwaring suggests that Longinus' description of the flawed genius, applied in that work to Demosthenes, could equally well have been written with Handel in mind (p. 193).

The Sublime

or 'Heavenly Extasy'

John Mainwaring writes how the final suite of choruses 'leaves the mind in a kind of heavenly extasy'. In another passage he describes Handel's 'sublimity in many of the effects he has work'd up by the combination of instruments and voices, that they seem to be rather the effect of inspiration, than of knowledge in music' (p. 175).

The quality of 'sublimity' was a preoccupation for many commentators in the fine arts in eighteenth-century England. Two contemporary works analyse in detail the factors which collude to create a sublime effect. An English translation of a small book of literary criticism then thought to be by the first century Greek writer Longinus, but probably by an earlier author, called *On the Sublime*, defines the qualities of the sublime. Longinus, although writing about literary composition, draws parallels between the arts, for example describing how silence might be represented in painting. This small volume, available in English for the first time in 1652, stimulated the search for sublimity in painting, poetry and music. A new translation by William Smith with commentary and notes quoted throughout this book was published in 1740.

The other influential book, published in 1757, was Edmund Burke's *A Philosophical Enquiry into the Origin of our Ideas of the Sublime and Beautiful*. The idea of the sublime is not unlike the *enargeia* (vividness) which is described in the rhetoric texts. It goes beyond the merely beautiful, and transports the viewer or listener into Mainwaring's 'Extasy'. This heightening of awareness, and the feeling of being overtaken by emotion was sought in music, painting, sculpture and landscape design. Later in the century, travellers to Italy and the remoter parts of the British Isles were describing rugged natural landscapes as 'sublime', in that they brought man closer to nature and therefore to God.

Longinus defines the sublime style as emotionally intense and elevated, as opposed to merely pleasing and soothing. He cites the Greek rhetorician Hermogenes in support of this definition, who suggests solemnity and vehemence as the necessary qualities to express the sublime, the opposites of charm and delicacy. It is this forcible character which is necessary not just to persuade, as in an argument, or to move 'the passions' in a general sense, but to transport the listeners out of themselves, to inspire wonder and amazement, rather than merely be satisfactorily convinced. The power of the sublime is directed at getting the better of every listener by using an irresistible power, which Handel was perceived to have accomplished, especially in his choruses (pp. 2-3).

How did this power work on the listener? Longinus defines the elements of the sublime:

> Bold metaphors and those too in good plenty, are very seasonable in a noble Composition, where they are always mitigated and soften'd by the vehement Pathetic and generous Sublime dispersed through the whole. For as it is the nature of the Pathetic and Sublime to run rapidly along, and carry all before them, so they require the figures they are worked up in to be strong and forcible, and do not so much as give leisure to a Hearer to cavil at their Number, because they immediately strike his Imagination, and inflame him with all the Warmth and Fire of the Speaker (p. 56).

Longinus considers that any work worthy of the description sublime should be able to win the

> Esteem and Applause of succeeding Ages.[...] Visions [...] contribute very much [...] to the Weight, Magnificence, and Force of Compositions [...] When the Imagination is so warm'd and affected, that you seem to behold yourself the very things you are describing, and to display them to the life before the Eyes of an Audience (p. 30).

Quintilian had described this 'displaying before the eyes' as central to the idea of *enargeia*, a vivid mode of performance which can be applied to match Handel's sublime music (Q VI ii 29; Q VIII iii 62; Q IX i 45).

Various literary and rhetorical devices are employed to capture sublimity. The employment of figures of rhetoric is central to achieving the sublime, and Longinus suggests a few specific figures which elevate the style, 'For these when judiciously used conduce not a little to Greatness [...] Figures naturally impart assistance to, and on the other side receive it again in a wonderful manner from sublime Sentiments.' If we are suspicious about the use of figures to beguile and persuade, he thinks that 'a due mixture of the Sublime and Pathetic very much encreases the force, and removes the Suspicion that commonly attends on the use of Figures. For veil'd as it were and wrap'd up in such Beauty and Grandeur, they seem to disappear and securely defy discovery.' He quotes Demosthenes who says the orator's figures are concealed in his own lustre: 'For as the Stars are quite dim'd and obscur'd, when the Sun breaks out in all his blazing Rays, so the Artifices of Rhetoric are entirely overshadowed by the superior Splendor of sublime Thoughts.' In general Longinus thinks figures 'render Compositions more pathetic and affecting. For the Pathetic partakes as much of the Sublime, as writing exactly in Rule and Character can do of the Agreeable' (p. 53).

Longinus names Interrogation as a device (also considered a figure) which lends itself to the sublime style. 'Is not discourse enlivened, strengthened and thrown more forcibly along by this sort of Figure?' 'The Energy and Rapidity that appears in every Question and Answer, and the quick Replies to his own Demands, as if they were the Objections of another Person, not only renders his Oration more sublime and lofty, but more plausible and probable. [...] and thus this Figure of Question and Answer is of wonderful efficacy in prevailing upon the Hearer, and imposing on him a Belief, that those things which are studied and laboured, are uttered without Premeditation, in the Heat and Fluency of Discourse' (pp. 39-40).

Longinus suggests a collection of figures 'well adapted to Emotion, and serviceable in adorning, and rendering what we say in all respects more grand and affecting', which include *polyptonon*, as well as 'collections, changes and gradations' such as *asyndeton* (see pp. 41-2 for examples).

Another figure, *hyperbaton*, employs the departure from normal word order for special affect. John Smith (in *The Mysterie of Rhetorique Unvail'd*, 1657) describes its use 'such as the cause and comeliness of speech requires' and for 'elegancy and variety'. Smith also thinks the change in word order is used more 'to excuse the license or the error of authors, then to shew that we may do the like'. For example 'We have all gone astray, like sheep' or 'Like sheep, we have all gone astray' is turned around in Isaiah to make 'All we, like Sheep, have gone astray'. The commas in the word-book either side of 'like Sheep' are not present in Isaiah, and in the autograph Handel uses the first, the second being superfluous because of the gap in the music before 'have gone astray'.

Another figure mentioned by Longinus to assist the power of conviction is *apostrophe* or adjuration. This is a breaking off to address some person or personified thing, either present or absent. John Smith describes it as a diversion of speech made to God, angels, 'men in their several ranks, whether absent or present, dead or alive [...] to the heavenly bodies and Meteors, to the earth and things in it, to the Sea and things in it, to beasts, birds and fishes, to inanimate things'. One of Smith's 'scriptural examples' of this figure is the Messianic 'Thou shalt break them with a rod of iron'. Henry Peacham describes the use of it: 'This forme of speech serveth to a pleasant variation, by removing from one person to another, and it is verie apt to vehement objections, & grievous complaints, and sometimes to praise'. His caution for usage is 'First, that the aversion be not too abrupt and violent. Secondly, that the matter be not of lesse importance, or lesse vehement which is spoken to the second person, then that which was spoken of the third: for it is always counted a fault to speake more behind the backe then before the face, I meane in the speech of an adversary'.

Longinus uses a musical comparison to recommend another figure for evoking the sublime:

> That a Periphrasis (or Circumlocution) is a Cause for Sublimity, no body, I think, can deny. For as in Musick an important Word is rendred more sweet by the Divisions which are run harmoniously upon it, so a Periphrasis sweetens a Discourse carried on in propriety of Language, and contributes very much to the Ornament of it, especially if there be no Jarring or Discord in it, but every part be judiciously and musically tempered (pp. 51-52).

Longinus could be describing the decorated melismatic setting of important words. Smith describes this figure as 'a long circumstance, or a speaking of many words, when few may suffice'. He gives scriptural examples which include Ecclesiastes 12. 5: 'Man goeth to his long home, (i.e. dies)'. Peacham warns that the circumlocution should not be too long in case it makes the speech 'both tedious and barren'. It is to 'garnish the Oration with varietie of wordes and never encreaseth matter'.

Hyperbole may be called into service to assist the sublime. Longinus warns that 'overshooting the Mark often spoils an Hyperbole, and whatever is over-stretched loses its Tone, and immediately relaxes, nay, sometimes produces an Effect contrary to that for which it was intended' [...] 'Those Hyperboles in short are the best [...] and this never fails to be the Sate of those which in the heat of a Passion flow out in the midst of some grand Circumstance'. He says 'Hyperboles equally serve to two Purposes, they enlarge, and they lessen. Stretching any thing beyond its natural Size is the property of both. And the Diasyrm (the other species of the Hyperbole) increases the Lowness of any thing, or renders Trifles more trifling' (pp. 67-68). Katrin Ettenhuber has argued that, far from bringing doubt about the credibility of the speaker or truth of the matter, the use of *hyperbole* is appropriate where God is concerned as it brings us into the realm of, and helps us comprehend, the impossible (Adamson *et al.*, pp. 197-213. For *Messiah* text examples see p. 34).

Burke's *Enquiry* describes how powerful forces in nature produce astonishment. He thinks the sublime

> is productive of the strongest emotion which the mind is capable of feeling. [...] The mind is so completely filled with its object, that it cannot entertain any other, nor by consequence reason on that object which employs it [...] it hurries us on by an irresistible force (p. 53).

He puts astonishment at the top of the effects of the sublime, closely followed by admiration, reverence and respect. Burke describes various elements of the sublime: words he says have three effects:

> The first is, the sound; the second, the picture, or representation of the thing signified by the sound; the third is, the affection of the soul produced by one or both of the foregoing (p. 53).

Add Handel's music to the already powerful biblical text and we have enhanced sublimity.

Magnificence is another source of the sublime. Burke defines magnificence as 'a great profusion of things which are splendid or valuable in themselves' (p. 71). Monumental vastness is another quality which he considers 'a powerful cause of the sublime'. It might be for this reason that Handel's choruses were so described. The Handel commemorations in 1784 would certainly have provoked this feeling in the audience if only from the vastness of the resources employed in the performance, combined with the Westminster Abbey setting.

Longinus gives the structure of the whole work the final place in his sources of sublimity (1.2 Structure and Performance). It should be remembered that he, or the author whoever he was, was possibly writing this in the first century A.D. while Smith's translation was made in 1740:

> Harmonious Compositions has [sic] not only a natural tendency to please and to persuade, but inspire us to a wonderful degree with generous Ardor and Passion. Fine Notes in Music have a surprising effect on the Passions of an Audience. Do they not fill the Breast with inspired Warmth, and lift up the Heart into heavenly Transport? The very Limbs receive Motion from the Notes, and the Hearer, tho' he has no skill at all in Music, is sensible however that all its Turns make a strong Impression on his Body and Mind. The Sounds of any musical Instrument are in themselves insignificant, yet by the Changes of the Air, the Agreement of the Chords, and Symphony of the Parts, they give extraordinary Pleasure, as we daily experience, to the Minds of an Audience (p. 69).

He continues with the virtues of the human voice and speech, which become a fitting description of Handel's sublime music:

> What an Opinion therefore may we justly form of fine Composition, the Effect of that Harmony which Nature has implanted in the Voice of Man? It is made up of Words which by no means die upon the Ear. And then, does it not inspire us with fine Ideas of Sentiments and Things, of Beauty and of Order, Qualities of the same date and Existence with our Souls? Does it not by an elegant Structure and marshalling of Sounds convey the Passions of the Speaker into the Breast of his Audience? Then, does it not seize their Attention, and by framing an Edifice of Words to suit the Sublimity of Thoughts, delight and transport, and raise those Ideas of Dignity and Grandeur which it shares itself, and was designed by the Ascendant it gains upon the Mind, to excite in others (p. 69).

A Peroration

The foregoing work has aimed to set out what is rhetorical about Handel's *Messiah*, and how to start going about bringing these ideas to life in performance. It is not the only way of performing this great work, and not everyone will agree with many of the suggestions, but I do believe that rhetorical means need to be understood and employed to deliver a composition written in that style in the most effective way. Even if this approach is adopted, every performance will still retain its unique status as the performers bring their personal style and choices to bear on the music.

Watkins Shaw thought *Messiah* had become a national institution, but at the same time he puts his finger on the reason for too many ill-conceived performances, that *Messiah* 'has saved innumerable bodies from musical insolvency'. Burney describes how Handel's church music 'has been kept alive, and has supported life in thousands, by its performance for charitable purposes [...] this great work has been heard in all parts of the kingdom with increasing reverence and delight; it has fed the hungry, clothed the naked, fostered the orphan and enriched succeeding managers of Oratorios, more than any single musical production in this or any country (Preface p. vi; 'Sketch of the Life of Handel', p. 27).

However well-known and however often performed, there should be no excuse for complacency in performance just because *Messiah* is almost guaranteed to draw a full house. Fulfilling the expectations of the audience should always be a challenge, and the task should not be approached as an easy, routine day's work. The frequency with which *Messiah* is performed may encourage unfortunate comparisons with last year's performance (usually based on the choice of soloists) or comparison with a favourite recording listened to at home, but imagine that there is one person in the audience (and there may well be more) who has never heard it before, and the effect it will have on them. To replace the tired or pre-digested performance with the freshly minted one, our efforts should be redoubled to discover and relish every possible detail, to convince ourselves and our audience of the work's greatness, and of its universal appeal which has endured since its first performance, showing that it will survive whatever performing circumstances conspire to throw at it, now or in the future.

Bibliography

Adamson, Sylvia, Gavin Alexander and Katrin Ettenhuber	*Renaissance Figures of Speech*. Cambridge, Cambridge University Press (2007)
Bartel, Dietrich	*Musica Poetica. Musical-Rhetorical Figures in German Baroque Music*. Lincoln, University of Nebraska Press (1997)
Bourne, Ella	'The Messianic Prophecy in Vergil's Fourth Eclogue'. *The Classical Journal*, 11/ 7 (Apr. 1916), pp. 390-400
Brennan, J.X.	*The 'Epitome Troporum ac Schematum' of Joannes Susenbrotus, text, translation, and commentary*. Unpub. diss. Urbana (1953)
Burmeister, Joachim	*Musica Poetica* (Rostock, 1606). Trans. Benito V. Rivera. Newhaven, Yale University Press (1993)
Burney, Charles	*An Account of the Performances in Westminster-Abbey and the Pantheon, May 26th, 27th, 29th; and June the 3rd, and 5th, 1784. In Commemoration of Handel*. London Payne and Son (1785)
Burrows, Donald	*Handel: Messiah*. Cambridge, Cambridge University Press (1991)
Burrows, Donald and Rosemary Dunhill	*Music and Theatre in Handel's World. The family papers of James Harris 1732-1780*. Oxford, Oxford University Press (2002)
Busby, Thomas	*Concert Room and Orchestra Anecdotes of Music and Musicians Ancient and Modern*. London (1825)
Charlesworth, Michael, ed.	*The English Garden: Literary Sources and Documents*, vol. 1, 1550-1730, Helm Information, Robertsbridge (1993)
Cicero, Marcus Tullius	*Orator*. Trans. by H.M. Hubbell. Harvard, Harvard University Press (1939)
	De Inventione. Trans. by H.M. Hubbell. Harvard, Harvard University Press (1949)
	De Oratore. Trans. by E.W. Sutton. Harvard, Harvard University Press (1942)
Cornificius [Cicero]	*Rhetorica ad Herennium*. Trans. by Harry Caplan. Harvard, Harvard University Press (1954)
Dean, Winton	*Handel's Dramatic Oratorios and Masques*. Oxford, Clarendon Press (1959)
Deutsch, Otto Erich	*Handel. A documentary biography*. New York, Da Capo (1955)
Duffin, Ross W.	*How Equal Temperament Ruined Harmony (and Why You Should Care)*. Norton, New York (2007)
Dionysius of Halicarnassus	*Critical Essays II*. Trans. Stephen Usher. Cambridge, Mass., Harvard University Press (1985)

Erasmus, Desiderius	*De Ultraque Verborum ac Rerum Copia*. Trans. as *On Copia of Words and Ideas* by D.B. King and M.D. Rix. Milwaukee, Marquette University Press (2007)
Fuld, James T.	'The First Complete Printing of Handel's *Messiah*'. *Music & Letters*, 55/4 (Oct. 1974), pp. 454-7
	'Songs from *Messiah* Published during Handel's Lifetime'. *Notes*, Second Series, 45/2 (Dec. 1988), pp. 253-7
Geminiani, Francesco	*The Art of Playing the Violin* London (1751). Fac. Ed. D. Boyden, London (1952)
Gianturco, Carolyn	'*Cantate Spirituali e Morali* with a description of the Papal Sacred Cantata Tradition for Christmas 1676-1740'. *Music & Letters*, 73/1 (1992), pp. 1-31
Hogarth, William	*The Analysis of Beauty*, ed. J. Burke. Oxford, Clarendon (1955)
Hoskyns, John	see Osborn, Louise Brown
Kidder, Richard	*A Demonstration of the Messias. In which the truth of the Christian religion is proved, especially against the Jews.* London, Aylmer (1684)
Kirnberger, Johann Philipp	*Die Kunst des reinen Satzes in der Musik.* Berlin (1776-9)
Lanham, Richard A.	*A Handlist of Rhetorical Terms.* Second edition. Berkeley, University of California Press (1991)
Larsen, Jens Peter	*Handel's Messiah. Origins, Composition, Sources.* New York, Norton (1972)
Longinus	see Smith, William
Luckett, Richard	*Handel's Messiah. A Celebration.* New York, Harcourt Brace (1992)
Mainwaring, John	*Memoirs of the Life of the late George Frederic Handel.* London (1760)
Marsh, John	*The John Marsh Journals: The Life and Times of a Gentleman Composer (1752-1828) Vol. 1.* Revised Edition, ed. Brian Robins, Pendragon Press (2011)
Mattheson, Johann	*Der Vollkommene Capellmeister.* Hamburg (1739). Trans. E.C. Harriss (1969). Ann Arbor, UMI (1981)
Midgley, Graham	*University Life in Eighteenth-Century Oxford.* New Haven, Yale University Press (1996)
Morley, Thomas	*A Plain and Easy Introduction to Practical Music.* London (1597). Ed. R. Alec Harman, London (1952)
North, Roger	See Wilson, J.
Osborn, Louise Brown	*The Life, Letters, and Writings of John Hoskyns 1566-1638.* New Haven, Yale University Press (1973)
Parke, W. T.	*Musical Memoirs comprising an account of the general state of music in England from the first Commemoration of Handel in the year 1781 to the year 1830. Copiously interspersed with anecdotes, musical, histrionic, &c.* Vol. 1, London, Colburn & Bentley (1830)

Peacham, Henry	*The Garden of Eloquence*. London, Jackson (1593)
Pritchard, Brian W.	*The Musical Festival and the Choral Society in England in the Eighteenth and Nineteenth Centuries: a Social History*. Unpub. diss. Birmingham (1968)
Puttenham, George	*The Art of English Poesy*, ed. by Frank Wingham and Wayne A. Rebhorn. Ithaca, Corbell University Press (2007)
Quantz, Johann Joachim	*Versuch einer Anweisung die Flöte traversiere zu spielen*, Berlin (1752). Trans. Reilly as *On Playing the Flute*. London, Faber (1966)
Quarles, Francis	*Quarles' Emblems, Divine and Moral: Together with Hieroglyphics of the Life of Man*. London, Hogg ([1790?])
Quintilian, Marcus Fabius	*Institutio Oratoria*. Trans. H.E. Butler. Harvard, Harvard University Press (1920)
Shaw, Watkins	*Handel's Messiah. The Story of a Masterpiece*. London, Hinrichsen (1946)
	A Textual and Historical Companion to Handel's Messiah. London, Novello (1965)
Smith, John	*The Mysterie of Rhetorique Unvail'd*. London, Cotes (1657)
Smith, Ruth	'The Achievements of Charles Jennens (1700-1773)'. *Music & Letters*, 70 (1989), p. 161-90
	Handel's Oratorios and Eighteenth-century Thought. Cambridge, Cambridge University Press (1995)
	Charles Jennens. The Man Behind Handel's Messiah. London, Handel House Trust, The Gerald Coke Foundation (2012)
Smith, William	*Dionysius Longinus on the sublime: translated from the Greek, with notes and observations, and some account of the life, writings, and character of the author*. Dublin (1740)
Steblin, Rita	*A History of Key Characteristics in the Eighteenth and the Early Nineteenth Centuries*. Rochester (1981)
Susenbrotus, Joannes	see Brennan, J.X.
Tans'ur, William	*A New Musical Grammar, and Dictionary: or a general introduction to the whole art of musick. In four books. The Third Edition, with large additions*. London, James Hodges (1756)
	The Christian Warrior Properly Armed: or, the Deist Unmask'd. Being a Faithful Defence of the Holy Trinity. For the use of all Christian Families. Cambridge (1776)
Tarling, Judy	*The Weapons of Rhetoric, a Guide for Musicians and Audiences*. St. Albans, Corda Music Publications (2004)
Wilson, J. (ed.)	*Roger North on Music*. London (1959)
—	'An Account of the Third Yorkshire Music Festival held on the 23d, 24th, 25th, and 26th of September, 1828 in York Minster'. York, *Yorkshire Gazette* (1828)

Messiah Editions and Performance Materials:

Bartlett, Clifford, ed., *G. F. Handel Messiah*. Full score. Oxford, Oxford University Press (1998)

Handel Messiah. The Composer's Autograph Manuscript. British Library R.M.20.f.2 in facsimile. Introduction by Donald Burrows. London, The British Library (2009)

Handel's Conducting Score of Messiah. Reproduced in facsimile from the copy in the Library of St. Michael's College, Tenbury Wells, now in the Bodleian Library, Oxford MS. Tenbury 346-7. Introd. Watkins Shaw. Scolar Press for The Royal Musical Association (1974)

Handel, G. F., *Messiah. A sacred oratorio in score. Dr. Arnold's edition with all the additional alterations composed in the year 1741*

Handel, G. F., *Messiah* arr. W.A. Mozart, 1789 (K.572). Bärenreiter Verlag, Neue Mozart-Ausgabe

Vocal and instrumental part books held by The Foundling Hospital

Word-books for performances (Eighteenth Century Collections Online Print Editions):
The Theatre Royal, Covent Garden (?1750); The Academy of Ancient Musick (1758); The Castle-Society at Haberdashers-Hall (1760); Church-Langton, Leicestershire (?1760); Worcester (1761); Dublin (1763); Edinburgh (1772); Theatre Royal, Covent Garden (1775); *Commemoration of Handel* (1784); Worcester (1788); *A selection from the sacred works of Handel, also of the Messiah*, Colchester (1790); Chester Music Festival (1791); York (1791)

Internet Sources

www.dunedin-consort.org.uk/files/media/file/messiah_extended_notes.pdf, (accessed 30/3/2014)

http:/humanities/byu.edu/rhetoric/silva.htm

Index to Movements

Page numbers of musical examples underlined. Facsimile of autograph MS in bold.
Complete text
    Part One 9-10
    Part Two 12-13
    Part Three 14

All they that see Him 35, 73, 132
All we, like Sheep 32, 38, 41, 66, 68, 83, 102, 105, 106, 119, 128, 130, 139, 174, 184, 185, 186, 201
Amen 23, 76, 110, 111, 125, 131, 135, 174, 195, 196
And He shall purify 78, 123, 131, 151, 174, 177, 178
And lo, the Angel x, 44, 61, 76, 112, 132, 137
And suddenly 44, 62, 76, 113, 137
And the Angel said 44, 76, 137
And the Glory 32, 36, 112, 134, 155, 175, 176
And with His Stripes 72, **83**, 130, 131, 183
Behold! A Virgin 53
Behold and see 21, 32, 33, 53, 95, 96, 129, 165, 166, 167
Behold the Lamb of God 13, 33, 71, 97, 129, 130, 140, 147, 149, 182
Blessing and Honour 135, 161, 174, 195
But thanks 32, 48, 122, 193
But Thou didst not leave 31, 76, 136, 147
But who may abide 3, 30, 40, 45, 54, 67, 69, 76, 99, 100, 115, 118, 121, 126, 130, 132, 146, 150, 155, 156, 163, 164
Comfort ye 24, 35, 46, 47, 48, 50, 71, 115, 163
Ev'ry Valley 34, 39, 50, 59, 77, **85**, 118, 129, 135, 147, 153, 154
For behold 37, 47, 48, 69, 77, 101, 107, 129
For unto us 20, 22, 41, 42, 43, 44, 50, 77, 108, 109, 129, 142, 143, 144, 174, 180
Glory to God 3, 20, 26, 27, **28**, 46, 61, 62, 76, 78, 132, 168, 181, 183
Hallelujah 20, 33, 34, 45, 47, 48, 51, 54, 58, 60, 76, **82**, 94, 99, 103, 106, 128, 139, 160, 172, 190, 191
He shall feed His Flock 30, 46, 47, 66, 76, 108, 121, 130, 152
He that dwelleth 36
He trusted in God 50, 104, 107, 130, 132, 133, 158, 186
He was cut off 9, 30, 31, 50, 74, 76, 96, 167
He was despised 3, 22, 32, 50, 94, 107, 111, 113, 114, 122, 129, 130, 136, 145, 154, 146, 164, 167, 171, 182
His Yoke is easy 3, 32, 43, 46, 47, 158, 170, 174, 181
How beautiful are the Feet ix, 45, 48, 53, 75, 118, 128, 129, 130
I know that my Redeemer 2, 22, 30, 41, 59, 76, 96, 115, 120, 130, 140, 146, 153,
If God be for us x, 33, 50, 56, 76, **84**, 102, 107, 116, 127, 130
Let all the Angels 38, 64, 160, 188
Let us break 105, 107, 159, 189
Lift up your Heads x, 30, 36, 47, 50, 55, 64, 128, 140, 142, 143, 144, 158, 159, 174, 187, 188

O Death 30, 37, 43, 45, 49, 50, 56, 77, 129, 169
O thou that tellest 42, 46, 53, 61, 77, 107, 112, 119, 123, 157, 179
Overture see Sinfony
Pifa 65, 123
Rejoice greatly 76, 77, 107, 110, 116, 127, 157, 158, 159
Since by man 31, 39, 43, 47, 49, 50, 51, 77, 117, 121, 126, 133, 191,
Surely He hath borne our Griefs 33, 46, 54, 129, 130, 140, 142, 145, 149, 151, 182, 183
Sinfony (overture) 10, 79, 97, 111, 124, 125, 126, 148, 159, 162
The Lord gave the Word 31, 32, 35, 139, 161, 189
The People that walked in Darkness 32, 39, 70, 77, 100, 104, 165
The Trumpet shall sound 2, 36, 43, 51, 61, 76, 78, 98, 140, 141, 155
Their Sound is gone out 34, 50, 78, 189
Then shall be brought to pass 35, 137
Then shall the Eyes 30, 34, 43, 46, 76
There were Shepherds 76
Thou art gone up on high 31, 47, 51, 61, 76, 152
Thou shalt break them 18, 30, 32, 36, 46, 74, 104, 129
Thus saith the Lord 39, 42, 46, 62, 103, 120, 140, 141, 169
Thy Rebuke 3, 30, 35, 71, 138, 165, 187
Unto which of the Angels 55, 137
Why do the Nations 3, 46, 47, 55, 60, 72, 73, **84**, 101, 102, 137, 150, 151
Worthy is the Lamb 3, 30, 43, 44, 45, 56, 68, 76, 129, 134, 172, 174, 194

General Index

A capella, 191
Academy of Ancient Music, 7
Accusatio, 30
Acoustic, 79, 81, 168, 196
Actio (gesture), 87
Adamson, 34
Adnominatio, 45
Aenigma, 2
Aetiologia, 31
Agon, 96
Alexander Balus, 151
Allegory, 17, 28
Alliteration, 50, 100
Amplification, 28, 37, 38, 42, 84, 164, 165, 190
    See also Augmentation
Anadiplosis, 45, 132, 164, 188
Anamnesis, 31
Anapaest, see Rhythm
Anaphora, 36, 46, 47, 50
Anastrophe, 41
Antanagoge, 31
Anthypophora, 36
Antimetabole, 68
Antistasis, 47
Antistrophe, 47
Antithesis, 26, 39, 40, 41, 59, 74, 96, 144, 155, 163, 171, 191
Antonomasia, 47
Aphorism, 32
Apocope, 162, 165
Aporia, 55
Aposiopesis, 55, 162, 165, 169, 171
Arnold, Samuel, x, 126, 141, 142, 198
Arrangement see Dispositio
Articulation, 87, 92, 111, 125, 139, 142, 162, 171-173
Articulation marks, 71, 99, 103-110, 171, 184, 195
Asyndeton, 41, 42, 201
Audience, 125, 139, 166, 174, 196, 197-199, 200, 202, 203, 204
Augmentation, 38, 189
Auxesis, 38, 42, 43, 64, 99, 101, 153

Bach, J.S., 59
Bartel, Dietrich, 40, 47, 52
Bartleman, James, 79
Bartlett, Clifford, x, 78
Basso continuo, x, 53, 62, 69, 71, 72, 73, 77, 96, 110, 111, 120, 127, 136, 151, 154, 156, 164
Bassoon, 78, 79
Beaufort, Duke of, 5
Bedford, Arthur, 18
Bible, vii, 1, 2, 5, 18, 19, 30, 93, 183
    Messiah text sources, 9-14
Bishop Butler, 5
Bishop Donatus of Fiesole, 4
Book of Common Prayer, 1, 2
Borrowed music see Italian duet cantatas
Bourne, E., 4
Bristol, see Performances

Burke, Edmund, 200, 202
Burmeister, Joachim, 43, 47, 174
Burney, Charles, 10, 18, 38, 65, 70, 77, 80, 127, 169, 181, 183, 186, 187, 189, 190, 194, 196, 204
Burrows, Donald, ix, x, 2
Busby, Thomas, 198
Butt, John, 76
Buxtehude, Dietrich, 20
Byrd, William, 183

Cadence, 37, 45, 54, 59, 70, 71, 74, 92, 96, 100, 103, 104, 109, 119, 125-128, 131, 134, 135, 138, 139, 147, 162-165, 170, 176, 180, 181, 183, 185, 186, 188, 191, 193, 194, 196
Cadenza, x, 126, 127, 135, 136
Capitalisation, ix
Caroline of Ansbach, 5
Catabasis, 166
Cataplexis, 32
Categoria, 30
Characterismus, 32
Charpentier, 88-92
Chester, 82
Choir size, 76
Chorographia, 32
Choruses, 174-196
Chromatic movement, 69, 74, 90, 104, 117
Chrysander, x
Cicero, ix, 8, 11, 15, 19, 30, 32, 36, 38, 87, 88, 115, 139, 152, 197
Circumlocutio, 201, 202
Clarity, 92, 99, 125, 138, 183
Classical education, viii, 5, 19
Classical rhetoric, vii, ix, 17, 87
Climax, 38, 42, 43, 99, 136, 147, 165
Commiseratio, 35
Command, 8, 53, 89, 90, 91, 92, 121, 157, 179
Commoratio, 47
Compar, 43
Comparison, viii, 17, 26-27, 91, 108, 110, 139, 150, 201
Concertos, 11, 197
Concession, 31
Conducting score, ix, x, 85, 102, 107, 164
Conduplicatio, 47
Confessio, 32
Conquestio, 32
Contentio, 40
Continuo see Basso continuo
Contrary motion, 115
Contrast, 17, 26, 40, 55, 77, 115, 117, 151, 163, 187, 189
Copia, 19-24, 26, 45
Corelli, 66
Counterpoint, 17, 18, 92, 96, 139, 170, 178, 181, 182, 183, 186, 188, 189, 190, 193, 196
    See also Polyphony
Covent Garden, see Theatre Royal
Crosdill, Mr., 11

Dactyl, see Rhythm
Dante, 4, 14, 80
Darkness, 37, 58, 69, 70, 100
Decoration (music) see Ornament
Decoration (rhetoric) see Elocutio; Figures of rhetoric
Decorum, ix, 59, 76-81, 87-98, 94, 115, 118, 119, 175
Deism, 1, 5
Demosthenes, 199, 201
Deutsch, Otto Erich, vii, 3, 78, 174, 197, 198
Diacope, 48
Dialogismus, 33, 55
Dialogue, viii, 33, 91, 96, 116, 169, 187
Diasrym, 202
Diastole, 53
Dibdin, Charles, 80
Diction, 20, 99
Diderot, 4
Diminution, 189
Display, 20
Dispositio, 8
Dissonance, x, 22, 35, 40, 74, 90, 96, 102, 110 – 114, 119 – 122, 147-149, 162, 164, 167-169, 186, 196
  See also Harmony
Dotted notes, 24, 53, 58, 71, 72, 73, 89, 90, 91, 92, 111, 114, 116, 122, 140-142, 144-146, 149, 151, 175
Double bass, 78
Doubling, 77, 78, 112, 117, 119, 121, 123, 144, 183
Drone, 65, 66, 89
Dublin, see Performances
Dublin Journal, vii, 197
Dubourg (singer), 127
Dubourg (violinist), 197
Duffin, Ross, 88
Dynamics, ix, 22, 27, 62, 69, 70, 77, 78, 87, 110, 114-123, 126, 127

Ecphonis, 52, 56
Edinburgh, see Performances
Editions, x, 79, 141
Ekphrasis, 34
Elocutio, 17
Emotion, 58, 94, 99, 115, 125, 136, 141, 146, 150, 162, 166, 182, 200, 201
Emphasis, 20, 24, 68, 82, 99-114, 115, 122, 123, 125, 139, 144, 145, 148, 151, 153, 154, 156, 158, 159, 171, 175, 177-179, 183-185, 190, 193
Enargeia, viii, 32, 34, 36, 200
English oratorio, 174
Epenthesis, 53
Epizeuxis, 26, 44, 48-49, 53, 100, 149, 175, 176, 182, 193
Erasmus of Rotterdam, 19, 20, 45
Erotema, 54-55
Erotesis, 54-55
Ettenhuber, Katrin, 202
Exclamatio, 52
Exclamations, ix, 8, 52-54, 89, 90, 91, 92, 112, 174, 182, 183
  See also ecphonis; exclamatio
Exordium, 10, 72
Exuscitatio, 33

Fauxbourdon, 146
Figured bass see Basso continuo
Figures of rhetoric, ix, 17-56, 201
  Accusatio, 30
  Adnominatio, 45
  Aetiologia, 31
  Anapidlosis, 45, 132, 164, 188

[Figures of rhetoric, cont.]
  Anamnesis, 31
  Anaphora, 36, 46-47, 50
  Anastrophe, 41
  Antanagoge, 31
  Anthypophora, 36
  Antimetabole, 68
  Antistasis, 47
  Antistrophe, 47
  Antithesis, 26, 39, 40, 41, 59, 96, 144, 155, 163, 171, 191
  Antonomasia, 47
  Aphorism, 32
  Apocope, 162, 165
  Aporia, 55
  Aposiopesis, 55, 162, 165, 169, 171
  Asyndeton, 41, 42, 201
  Auxesis, 38, 42, 43, 64, 99, 101, 153
  Catabasis, 166
  Cataplexis, 32
  Categoria, 30
  Characterismus, 32
  Chorographia, 32
  Circumlocutio, 201, 202
  Commiseratio, 35
  Commoratio, 47
  Compar, 43
  Concession, 31
  Conduplicatio, 47
  Confessio, 32
  Conquestio, 32
  Contentio, 40
  Diacope, 48
  Dialogismus, 33, 55
  Diastole, 53
  Diasrym, 202
  Ecphonis, 52, 56
  Ekphrasis, 34
  Epenthesis, 53
  Epizeuxis, 26, 44, 48-49, 53, 100, 149, 175, 176, 182, 193
  Erotema, 54-55
  Erotesis, 54-55
  Exclamatio, 52
  Exuscitatio, 33
  Gradatio, 43
  Homoeoprophoron, 50
  Homoioteleuton, 50
  Hyperbaton, 201
  Hyperbole, 34, 38, 202
  Hypophora, 54, 56
  Hypotyposis, 13, 34
  Incrementum, 38, 43
  Indignatio, 34
  Isocolon, 31, 43, 44, 49
  Mempsis, 34
  Metaphor, 17, 28, 200
  Mycterismus, 35
  Noema, 92, 162, 175-196
  Oraculum, 35
  Paralogia, 32
  Parison, 43
  Paromologia, 32
  Paronomasia, 50, 56
  Pathopoeia, 32, 35, 187
  Periphrasis, 36, 202
  Ploce, 51
  Polyptonon, 51, 201

214

[Figures of rhetoric, cont.]
  Polysyndeton, 42, 44, 43, 44
  Prosopopeia, 32, 36
  Pysma, 54-55
  Sarcasmus, 34
  Subjectio, 54
  Syncope, 50
  Synecdoche, 47
  Synonimia, 44
  Tapinosis, 35
  Thaumasmus, 53
  Topographia, 37
  Topothesia, 37
Forkel, Johann, 40
Foundling Hospital, x, 7, 11, 23, 78, 81, 93, 140, 175, 198
French style, 65, 140
Fugue, 183, 189, 190, 194
Fuld, J.J., x

Galpin Society Journal, 5
Geminiani, Francesco, 103
Gentleman's Magazine, The, 174
Gradatio, 43
Guildford Assizes, 142

Halifax, 80
Handel Commemoration Festival (1784) see Burney
Harmony, viii, 9, 18, 27, 33, 40, 58, 59, 61, 69, 70, 72, 87, 96, 99, 100, 110, 111, 113, 116, 120, 121, 125, 138, 148, 162, 174, 181, 189, 190, 194, 198, 203
  See also Dissonance
Haymarket Theatre, 198
Hereford, see Performances
Hermogenes, 200
Hogarth, William, 22
Homoeoprophoron, 50
Homoioteleuton, 50
Homophony, ix, 54, 92, 145, 162, 174, 183, 193
  See also Figures of rhetoric, Noema
Hornpipe, 189
Horns, 77-79
Hoskyns, John, 19, 37, 43, 56
Huddersfield Choral Society, 80
Hume, David, 5
Humour, 66, 106, 185, 186
Hyperbaton, 201
Hyperbole, 34, 38, 202
Hypophora, 54, 56
Hypotyposis, 13, 34

Iamb, see Rhythm
Incrementum, 38, 43
Indignatio, 34
Interval in performance, 11
Intervals, ix, 18, 20, 21, 24, 35, 40, 44, 53, 58, 69, 72, 89, 91, 94, 95, 101, 110 - 113, 120, 121, 148, 164, 165, 167, 189
Inventio, viii, 1, 8, 198
Isocolon, 31, 43, 44, 49
Italian
  Duet cantatas, 1, 2, 119, 174, 180, 181
  Opera, 174
  Singers, 197
  Traditional music, 65

Jennens, Charles, xi, 1, 2, 3, 5, 6, 30, 54, 93, 175, 198
Jephtha, 15
Judas Maccabeus, 15

Key, ix, 10, 40, 87, 108, 120, 163, 177
Key affect, 88-92, 102, 111, 117, 137, 142, 145
Kidder, Richard, 6
King, The 12, 14
King James Bible see Bible
King's Theatre, 7
Kircher, Athanasius, 47
Kirnberger, Johann Philipp, 58

Lanham, R.A., 28
Length
  of note or syllable, 20, 63, 89, 90, 92, 99, 100, 103, 106, 125, 139, 152-154, 156, 179, 184, 186, 187, 189, 194
  of phrase 110, 139, 158, 173, 184
London, see Performances
London Daily Advertiser, 197, 198
London Daily Post, 3, 88
Long notes, see Length of note
Longinus, viii, x, 8, 17, 41, 42, 139, 159, 198, 199, 200-203
Luckett, Richard, xi, 7, 81

McGegan, Nicholas, Eleanor Selfridge Field and John Roberts, x
Mainwaring, John, 174, 194, 197, 198, 199, 200
Manchester, 80
Mattheson, Johann, 45, 52-53, 58, 88-92, 142
Melisma, 107, 116, 125, 153, 161, 180, 188, 202
Memory, 40, 44, 100
Mempsis, 34
Metaphor, 17, 28, 200
Monteverdi, Claudio, 72
Morell, Thomas, 151
Morley, Thomas, 171
Mozart, W.A., 27, 79, 98, 141
Mycterismus, 35

Narrative, 8, 89, 90, 91, 92, 136, 137
Newton, Sir Isaac, 5
Noema, 92, 162, 175-196
Non-juror, 1, 5
North, Roger, 129
Northern choral tradition, 80
Novello, x, xi

Omission, 50
Oraculum, 35
Ornament
  music, 65, 95, 99, 116, 136, 154, 156, 161, 164, 177-179, 188, 189, 191
  rhetoric, see Figures of rhetoric
Osborn, L.B., 19

Palestrina, 183
Paralogia, 32
Parison, 43
Parke the elder, 11
Parke, Miss, 11
Paromologia, 32
Paronomasia, 50, 56
Part-books, 76, 93
Pastoral, 54-55, 65-68, 89, 121, 146, 181
Pathopoeia, 32, 35, 187
Pause, 54, 92, 135-136, 139, 156, 169
Peacham, Henry the elder, vii, x, 2, 18, 19, 30-32, 34-36, 40, 42, 44, 45, 47, 48, 51-53, 55-56, 162, 201, 202

Performances
    Bristol, 80
    Dublin, xi, 7, 76, 82, 127, 197
    Edinburgh, 16
    Hereford, 80
    London, ix, xi, 7, 11, 78, 93
Periphrasis, 36, 202
Peroratio, 9, 15, 181, 190, 205
Philalethes, 198
Piffaro, 65
Ploce, 51
Polyphony, ix, 174
    See also Counterpoint
Polyptonon, 51, 201
Polysyndeton, 42, 44, 43, 44
Pope, Alexander, 5
Pritchard, Brian W., 79, 80
Pronunciatio (delivery), 87
Prophecy, 36, 89, 90, 91
Prosopopeia, 32, 36
Prout, x, 79
Prynne, M., 5
Punctuation, ix, x, 48, 49, 92, 93, 125, 193, 201
Purcell, Henry, 79
Puttenham, George, x, 17, 19, 31, 32, 34, 35, 36, 40, 42, 43, 44, 45, 46, 47, 50, 55, 162, 175
Pysma, 54-55

Quantz, J.J., 120
Quarles, Charles, 4
Questions, ix, 13, 54-56, 88, 89, 91, 94, 96, 137, 187, 201
Quintilian, viii, ix, 8, 11, 15, 17, 19, 20, 28, 34, 36, 40, 44, 52, 54, 87, 88, 92, 99, 125, 139, 152, 162, 166, 197, 201

Rameau, J.-P., 89
Randell and Abel, x
Recitative, 164
    Accompanied, 8, 78, 132, 138
    Secco, 8, 53, 77, 78, 92, 96, 136-138
René Rapin, 5
Rehearsals, 3
Repeated notes, 71, 150
Repetition, viii, 18, 20, 21, 26, 44-51, 79, 85, 99, 100, 102, 103, 106, 112, 115, 116, 118, 121, 123, 124, 126, 132, 134, 136, 139, 149, 154, 157, 163, 172, 173, 175-177, 179, 183, 187, 188, 190, 191, 194
Rhetorica ad Herennium, ix, 8, 15, 19, 26, 39, 42, 44, 50, 52, 87, 88, 162
Rhythm, ix, 35, 40, 44, 58, 72, 78, 87, 88, 90, 91, 94, 101, 120, 130, 137, 139-161, 146, 169, 190
    Anapaest, 153-159, 163
    Dactyl, 159-161
    Hornpipe, 189
    Iamb, 109, 112, 151-152
    Trochee, 139, 151-152
Rhythmic alteration, 23, 140, 141
Ritornello, 9-14, 45, 94, 110, 115, 118, 126, 135, 142, 147, 181, 183
Rome, 65
Rousseau, J., 88-92

St. Augustine, 4
St. Cecilia Festival, 79
St. Paul's School, 19
Samson, 15
Sarcasmus, 34
Scheibe, Johann, 52
Schütz, Heinrich, 20

Semi-chorus, 77, 187
Serpent, 79
Shaftesbury, Third Earl of, 5
Shakespeare, vii
Shaw, George Bernard, 81
Shaw, Watkins, vii, x, 7, 78, 79, 98, 205
Short notes, see Length of note
Siciliana, 66
Silence, viii, ix, 9, 27, 53, 54, 62, 73, 79, 96, 119, 127, 133, 134, 155, 162-173, 176, 181, 188, 193, 194, 196, 200
    See also Articulation; Figures of rhetoric, Apocope; Aposiopesis
Slurs, ix, 66, 104, 107, 110, 158
Smith, J.C. senior, ix, x, 78
Smith, J.C. junior, 81
Smith, John, vii, viii, x, 17, 18, 19, 30, 31, 33, 34, 35, 36, 39, 42, 44, 46, 51, 55, 201, 202
Smith, Ruth, xi, 2, 18, 88, 152
Smith, William, x, 200
    See also Longinus
Solo singers, xi, 76, 88, 96, 205
Sospiro, 95, 165, 167, 171
Sources, ix, 18, 19
Speaking style, 92, 99, 115, 136, 140
Spectator, The, 5
Statius, 4
Steblin, Rita, 88
Steele-Perkins, Crispian, 142
Stretto, 43
Structure, 8, 9, 202, 203
Subjectio, 54
Sublime, vii, viii, 17, 75, 78, 145, 151, 174, 181, 191, 197, 200-203
Surprise, 139, 162, 169, 203
Syncopation, 109, 147-149
Syncope, 50
Synecdoche, 47
Synge, Edward, Bishop of Elphin, 197
Synonimia, 44
Susenbrotus, 8, 43

Talbot, James, 5
Tallis, Thomas, 183
Tans'ur, William, 5, 99
Tapinosis, 35
Tempo, ix, 87, 88, 120, 125–138, 139, 140, 153, 156, 168, 194
    Adagio, 125, 127, 128, 134, 164, 165, 176, 186
    Allegro, 126, 130, 132, 133, 150, 159
    Allegro moderato, 130, 131
    Andante, 126, 129, 134, 135, 151
    Andante allegro, 126, 129
    Andante larghetto, 126, 129
    Andante moderato, 129
    Grave, 126, 131, 133, 140
    Larghetto, 126, 130, 135, 163
    Largo, 126, 129-130, 134
    Pomposo ma non allegro, 126
    Prestissimo, 150
Tempo ordinario, 126, 138
Tessitura, 21, 27, 58, 60, 69, 88, 97, 99, 100, 113, 115, 117, 120, 166, 187, 195
Text complete, 9-14
Thaumasmus, 53
Theatre Royal, Covent Garden, 7, 197
Theatre Royal, Drury Lane, 11, 12
Theorbo, 4
Thomas Coram Foundation see Foundling Hospital

Three Choirs Festival, 80
Time signatures, 126, 130, 131, 146, 183
    See also Tempo
Title page, 3, 4
Tobin, John, x
Tomkins, Thomas, 1
Tone of voice, 87-98, 157
Topographia, 37
Topothesia, 37
Tremolo, 150
Trochee, see Rhythm
Tropes, 17, 19, 28, 30
Trumpets, 27, 60, 76, 78, 90, 91, 98, 126, 140, 142, 195
Tuning, 88

Unison, 27, 58, 70, 72, 74, 89, 91, 101, 165, 189, 190, 194

Variety, 17, 20, 22, 76, 78, 88, 100, 101, 103, 108, 110, 115, 123, 130, 139, 183, 202
Vehemence, 42, 53, 91, 102, 107, 132, 154, 155, 162-164, 168, 186, 187, 200, 201
Virgil, 3, 4, 5
Vocal score, 174

Walsh, John, x
Watkins Shaw see Shaw, Watkins
Westminster Abbey, 79, 80, 202
    See also, Performances, London; Burney, Charles
Whyte, Laurence, vii
Wood, Henry, 79
Woodwind, 78, 79
Word book, ix, x, 3, 4, 8, 9, 16, 93
Word order, 184
Word painting, viii, ix, 17, 30, 58-73
Word play, 17, 28, 44
Yorkshire Gazette, 79

www.ingramcontent.com/pod-product-compliance
Lightning Source LLC
Chambersburg PA
CBHW080858010526
44118CB00015B/2195